"A PRIMER ON OVERCOM[...]
DISORDERS ANOREXIA [...]
BALANCED BOOK ON HOW TO ANALYZE AND
TREAT EATING DISORDERS MEDICALLY AND
PSYCHOLOGICALLY." —*Orange County Register*

Anorexia and bulimia are life-threatening conditions
that must be treated aggressively and thoroughly.
Fortunately, in many cases they are curable. With
compassion and firmness, *It's Not Your Fault* defines
these disorders, puts them into their proper historical
and cultural context, explores their causes, and answers
questions you may have, including:

- Does dieting lead to eating disorders?
- Do eating disorders cause depression?
- Are eating disorders caused by parents?
- Aren't all families of people with eating disorders alike?
- Is an eating disorder a sign that some other psychiatric
  illness exists?

Finally, Dr. Marx outlines the revolutionary biopsychiatric
approach to treating eating disorders. With sympathy
and wisdom, *It's Not Your Fault* shows readers the path
to recovery and offers hope for the millions of Americans
whose lives have been affected by anorexia or bulimia.

RUSSELL MARX, M.D., graduated from the University of
Chicago, where he received a National Science Foundation
research award, and holds his M.D. from the University of
Pittsburgh School of Medicine. He completed his fellowship
in child psychiatry at the Stanford Children's Hospital, where
he was taught by Dr. Bruno Bettelheim. Dr. Marx has served
on the faculty of Cornell University Medical College and as
director of the Eating Disorder Program at the Regent Hospital
of New York City. He currently teaches at the University of
California at San Diego and practices psychiatry in the San
Diego area, where he lives.

It's Not
Your Fault

*Overcoming Anorexia and Bulimia
Through Biopsychiatry*

Russell Marx, M.D.

A PLUME BOOK

PLUME
Published by the Penguin Group
Penguin Books USA Inc., 375 Hudson Street, New York, New York 10014, U.S.A.
Penguin Books Ltd, 27 Wrights Lane, London W8 5TZ, England
Penguin Books Australia Ltd, Ringwood, Victoria, Australia
Penguin Books Canada Ltd, 10 Alcorn Avenue, Toronto, Ontario, Canada M4V 3B2
Penguin Books (N.Z.) Ltd, 182-190 Wairau Road, Auckland 10, New Zealand

Penguin Books Ltd, Registered Offices: Harmondsworth, Middlesex, England

Published by Plume, an imprint of New American Library, a division of Penguin Books
USA Inc. Published by arrangement with Villard Books, a division of Random House, Inc.

First Plume Printing, June, 1992
10 9 8 7 6 5 4 3 2 1

PUBLISHER'S NOTE

The ideas, procedures, and suggestions contained in this book are not intended as a substitute for consulting with your physician. All matters regarding your child's health
require medical supervision.

 REGISTERED TRADEMARK—MARCA REGISTRADA

LIBRARY OF CONGRESS CATALOGING-IN-PUBLICATION DATA
Marx, Russell.
    It's not your fault : overcoming anorexia and bulimia through
biopsychiatry / Russell Marx.
        p.   cm.
    Includes bibliographical references and index.
    ISBN 0-452-26809-5
    1. Anorexia nervosa—Treatment.   2. Bulimia—Treatment.
3. Biological psychiatry.   I. Title.
RC552.A5M37   1991b
616.85'260651—dc20   91-43844
                                                  CIP

Printed in the United States of America
Book design by Mia Vander Els

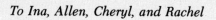
To Ina, Allen, Cheryl, and Rachel

Acknowledgments

I am especially grateful to my patients for all they have taught me. I am also grateful to teachers and colleagues at the Stanford University Medical Center for the wisdom they have shared with me.

For their contributions to this book, my sincerest thanks to Alison Acker; Marc Bailin; Emily Bestler; Lawrence Chilnick; Tom Fiffer; Mark Gold, M.D.; Dan Montopoli; Hans Steiner, M.D.; and especially to Ron Schaumburg.

Contents

CONTENTS

Introduction

I remember the day I first met Susan. I was completing my fellowship in child psychiatry at Stanford Children's Hospital, working with teenagers who had physical as well as emotional problems. Susan had been transferred to us from a community hospital because her doctors felt they were unable to handle someone in her situation.

Her diagnosis: anorexia nervosa.

As I entered the room I saw her—thin, frail, looking as if the slightest breeze would blow her away. Susan looked in my direction, but her empty, glassy eyes seemed to stare right through me, through the walls, and out into a distant . . . somewhere.

We talked for a while. Nothing serious at first, just get-acquainted chatter. Susan answered my questions in a few flat words. Only when the subject turned to her eating habits did she begin to come to life. Strangely, as we talked about her starvation, she didn't express fear or even concern. Instead her lips formed a slight smile as she spoke with pride about her thinness. I remember looking at her wasted body, her gaunt face, and hearing her say, in a voice that seemed not her own: "No one has *ever* been as thin as I am."

After a while I had to leave because she was growing tired. I thought, "This girl has everything going for her. She has a concerned family, a nice home. She's an excellent student. She has friends. *Why does she want to starve herself to death?*"

Shortly after meeting Susan I talked with one of my teachers, the noted psychologist Bruno Bettelheim. I told him how hard I found it to explain her behavior in any way that made sense to me. Dr. Bettelheim said that I needed to set aside my own concerns about whether her behavior was "crazy" or not. "Instead," he said, "try to see what she's doing from *her* point of view. Get inside her head and you'll understand that—in her mind, anyway—Susan has good reasons for her actions."

He also reminded me that, if I wanted to become a good doctor, my ability to understand irrational behavior would depend on my ability to respect and empathize with the patient. I had to see patients not as collections of charts in a medical file, but as human beings. As Dr. Bettelheim put it: "Treat the patient with common courtesy, as you would want to be treated, and you'll be doing the right thing."

Undoubtedly, a great deal of Bettelheim's sympathy for children, especially those who were outcasts or in pain, came from his own experience as a prisoner in Nazi concentration camps. But another part of it came from his innate gift of seeing the world as his patients saw it. He would sometimes say that if you wanted to see the world from a child's point of view, spend some time crawling around on your hands and knees.

Over the succeeding months I came to learn a lot about Susan's point of view. I realized that her life, which seemed so enviable from the outside, was filled with its own tremendous pressures and fears. I learned about the role her family and friends had played in causing her to transform one successful episode of dieting into a life-threatening condition. As Susan got better, she put on weight. Fittingly, as her body grew, so did her willingness to confide in me. She taught me a lot.

As beneficial as it is to understand anorexia and bulimia from the psychological vantage point, however, that alone is not enough. Eating disorders also result from physical malfunctions that have a powerful impact on thinking, feeling, and behavior. Starvation robs the body and brain of the raw materials they need to manufacture the chemicals that enable us to function. With these essential materials in short supply, depression and obsessional thinking increase. Starving people are less emotionally able to face their fears and overcome them, and to take the risks they must in therapy if they want to get better. Similarly, the impact on the brain of excessive dieting and disturbed eating patterns can lead to destructive cycles of bingeing and purging.

Disturbed physiology and psychology can thus combine to produce an eating disorder. But there's another essential piece to the clinical puzzle: understanding how the eating disorder patient fits into a family "system." A family may unknowingly perpetuate an eating disorder. Uncovering the hidden family meanings of a patient's anorexia or bulimia is often essential to her recovery.

Unless we physicians, in our search for answers, look at all aspects of our patients' problems—their bodies, their minds, their social world—we will be unable to free them from the tyranny of disturbed eating. If we take too narrow a view, we will be like the fabled blind men who tried to understand the elephant. In this book, we will look at eating disorders from many different angles to be sure we understand the true "nature of the beast."

In my current practice as a psychiatrist specializing in eating disorders, I see patients who span a wide range of ages and social backgrounds: dancers, homemakers, businesswomen, high school students. These people all have at least one thing in common: our culture. Through magazines, television, and movies, our culture sends a constant—and dangerous—message. That message, not so loosely translated, is, *"Only women who are thin are attractive."* For this and other reasons, the overwhelming majority of people with eating disorders are women. In this book, then, I will use the feminine pronoun in referring to my patients.

Physical changes are just part of the passage into adulthood. Social and cultural pressures also exert a powerful influence over the way we act, think, and feel. In my view, human psychological development has been studied too often from a predominantly male point of view. Recent work by Carol Gilligan of Harvard and other researchers has brought a new depth to our understanding of women's psychology, especially during the transition to adulthood. For example, studies have identified the pressure on women to be "nice" and to suppress their anger. Women are taught to value dependency and to define themselves through their relationships with others. The by-products of these pressures include depression, self-doubt, and decreased self-confidence.

Studies of how girls respond to questions on moral problems suggest one way this pattern evolves: At age ten, a girl is more likely to begin her answer with "I think." At age twelve, she is more likely to say "I don't know." And at age sixteen, she may say *"You* know." Over time, in other words, her ability to speak for herself is lost. In many cases, however, a woman will still feel compelled to express herself, and will do so by exercising control over one thing that is still within her power: her body. She decides to shape her body as a silent statement of autonomy. Achieving a sense of thinness can increase feelings of power and self-worth.

With the exception of obstetricians and gynecologists, perhaps no other medical specialist deals with so many female patients as one who treats eating disorders. How can I, a man, understand women's problems deeply enough to be of any use as a physician? The question is a fair one. Let me try to address it.

First, we men are human. I too struggle with occasional feelings of shame, anger, competitiveness, and loss of self-esteem—themes that crop up often in therapy with eating-disordered patients. Second, years of training and experience with hundreds of patients has helped to greatly sensitize me to the problems women face in today's society. Finally, and perhaps most important, a therapist's skill, sensitivity, and compassion are factors that can outweigh a difference in gender when it comes to helping patients get better.

My training in child psychiatry has taught me that, during the metamorphosis of adolescence, women's bodies undergo a much more radical transformation than do those of men. Changes occur not just in size, but in shape and, indeed, in function. Quite naturally, this greater degree of change also produces a wider range of emotional pressures, including everything from the monthly hormonal changes of menstruation to unwelcome attention from men on the street. But "body insecurity" is also directly related to centuries of discrimination and violence against women.

It's true that male therapists may be at some disadvantage in dealing with a largely female patient population. We men may not be able to provide adequate role models, or we may be less sensitive in working with women who have trouble dealing with their body image.

Strangely, these drawbacks may be partly offset by certain advantages. The presence of a male therapist may lead a woman to feel less competitive, which in turn can make therapy progress more smoothly. (As an aside, however, I should note that at some point the patient may need to confront issues related to competitiveness.) As a man and a doctor, I also have a kind of "double vision": I am able to compare and contrast the way men perceive women's bodies with the way women perceive their own bodies. From this perspective my sense is that women judge their own (and other women's) bodies much more harshly and hold a much stricter standard for "thinness" than do men. "Thin" to a woman seldom means the same as "thin" to a man.

The unhealthy pursuit of thinness is a problem that involves many issues besides the desire to attract men. As I've indicated, one such issue involves competition between women—including competition between mother and daughter. Another issue is that because women of this generation often take on roles formerly assigned only to men, they may feel they have to strive for bodies with a thinner, less rounded, and more "masculine" shape. (The perception is that a woman with a voluptuous figure may get less respect in the corporate board room.) Finally, many women pursue thinness as a means of distracting themselves from—or avoiding altogether—the uncertainties of forming real relationships with other people.

Over the years, I have become increasingly aware of the tremendous need for public education about eating disorders, as well as the need for greater awareness and sensitivity among members of the medical profession. I believe that people with these disorders suffer unnecessarily because the professionals charged with their care lack knowledge of effective treatment. This seems tragic, since sometimes, as a recent University of Toronto study has shown, a short lecture course about their illness is all some patients with bulimia may need to overcome it.

Anorexia nervosa and bulimia are curable conditions. They are not chronic illnesses that patients must live with for the rest of their lives. My belief tells me—and my experience confirms—that people with eating disorders and their families can change their lives for the better. My hope is that this book will help you make that change.

It's Not Your Fault

1

Eating Disorders in the Age of Biopsychiatry

"Why am I so fat?"

"Who made me such a pig?"

"Why is my child starving herself?"

"Why am I so disgusting?"

"How come I'm such a loser?"

"Where did I fail as a parent?"

"What did I do?"

"What *didn't* I do?"

If an eating disorder has shattered your life, questions like these constantly bewilder you. All of these questions derive from one dominating issue:

"Whose fault is it, anyway?"

The question is simple. The answer, however, is complex. We all want to know who's responsible. For every problem, there must be an identifiable cause, or someone to take the blame. At the end of our favorite television shows, guilty criminals always blurt out: "Yes, your honor, I did it! I killed the man!" Simple, tidy endings that resolve all the riddles and tie up all the loose ends make us feel better.

Eating disorder victims want desperately to solve the mystery of their illness. The urge to place blame is so strong that a bulimic often "confesses" to a crime she didn't even commit: "It's all my fault," she thinks. "If I were stronger, I'd be more in control. I'd be thin."

Others sometimes step forward to share the guilt. When a child develops an eating disorder, family members search frantically for information about it. They talk to friends, scan magazines at the checkout counter, or listen to health experts on radio and television talk shows.

Unfortunately, they often wind up with wrong information. They might read, for example, that children starve themselves because their parents give them too little attention, or too much attention, or the wrong kind of attention. Given such conflicting signals, who *wouldn't* be confused? The parent thinks, "It's all my fault. If I were a better mother [or father], I wouldn't have caused my child to act this way."

Or they might hear that children are more prone to develop an eating disorder if their families have a history of psychiatric disorders, such as depression or substance abuse. Parents naturally conclude that their child's illness results from their own troubled situation. They torture themselves by thinking, "It's all our fault—we should never have had children."

Round up the suspects, book 'em, and throw away the key.

Let me assure you: Self-blame is *wrong,* dead wrong. Such mistaken thinking only contributes to the severity of an eating disorder. Even worse, such attitudes can actually interfere with therapy, making it more difficult for a patient to seek, receive, and respond to treatment.

THE "NO-FAULT" APPROACH
OF BIOPSYCHIATRY

As a physician who has treated hundreds of patients with eating disorders over the past fifteen years, I much prefer the "no-fault" approach to managing eating disorders. Simply put, if you have an eating disorder, or if you are the parent of an anorexic or bulimic child, don't condemn yourself: *You are not to blame.*

"Fault" and "blame" are unnecessary—even harmful—concepts. They result in mental roadblocks, such as: "I am sick [or my child is sick] because I am a bad person [or parent]. If I could just snap out of it [or fix the problem], I could make myself [or my child] well."

Thinking in terms of "fault" is counterproductive. You don't suffer from an eating disorder because you are "bad" or because you are "not trying hard enough." On the contrary, I believe you are actually trying very hard to deal with the stresses in your life. Unfortunately, the method you have chosen—starvation or rigid dieting or purging—is just making your problems worse.

People who skip meals to lose weight often succumb to the urge to binge. They wind up eating more than if they had just stuck to the old three-square-meals-a-day formula. Learning to then purge as a way to exert "damage control" over bingeing makes it that much easier to binge in the future, leading to a vicious cycle. Some girls starve themselves as a way of coping with their fears of growing up. The damage starvation does to their bodies may delay their physical and emotional development, but it can't stop the process of growing older. Rather than helping to overcome the challenges of maturation, an eating disorder can cause physiological havoc that leads to disease, more mental turmoil, and sometimes even death.

Someone on the outside might wonder why people try to cope with their pain through such misguided means as disturbed eating. The answer, I think, is that often they fear their lives will just get worse if they don't do something—anything. The problem thus arises not from lack of effort but from using the wrong tools. In a time of stress and change, they seek to control one basic element in their lives—food—somehow believing that if they can control their eating habits, they can keep all their other troubles at bay. Attempting to force the body to ignore its inherent biological rules of eating, however, is like believing you'll always win at gambling in Las Vegas—eventually the "house" always wins.

I conceive of eating disorders as arising, not from some inherent flaw within a person, but from the *clash between social values and biological drives that exist within an emotionally vulnerable individual.* Let me illustrate.

A PARABLE

"Extra! Extra!" shouts the newsboy. "The President declares that every citizen of the country must now be exactly six feet tall—six feet, no more, no less. Extra!"

Grabbing the paper, we read that the penalty for failure to comply with this bizarre new law is severe: social ostracism. Gasp! People who are too short or too tall will be denied jobs or promotions. They will find it impossible to make friends. They will be regarded as failures, targets of ridicule, people to be loathed and avoided!

Imagine the chaos that ensues. Every television show, every magazine, is suddenly flooded with reports and advertisements showing how to increase (or decrease) your height. Phil and Oprah flog the subject to death. Revolutionary "Grow Tall Fast" exercise and diet plans spring up overnight. Movie stars release home videos endorsing the latest stretching strategy: "It worked for me, it'll work for you!"

Naturally, every law-abiding citizen tries to comply with the President's edict. But of course their efforts are doomed. No matter what exercises or eating plans or electronic devices they use, most people find their height is exactly the same as it was.

Some people are utterly crushed by the mere thought of not being six feet tall. To prevent being ostracized or ridiculed or branded as failures, they take extreme measures. People who are too tall undergo surgery to shorten their leg bones; those who are too short torture themselves on medieval-style racks, hoping to stretch a precious half-inch. Of course, such approaches result in permanent physical and mental damage. Some people even die in the process.

A ridiculous scenario? Of course. But substitute "weight" for "height" and you get some idea of what has actually happened to our society over the last thirty or forty years.

THE CULT OF THIN

Everywhere you look, the ideal of thinness, especially for women, is promoted as the ultimate goal. We've been brainwashed into accepting an artificial, impractical, even unhealthy image of the human form. Those who fail to achieve the ideal are mocked and scorned. People who are especially susceptible to social pressure—those who never developed a healthy sense of self-esteem—will go to extreme lengths to avoid ostracism and rejection. They will sabotage their own bodies for the sake of an artificial, unnatural concept.

But society's ideals are at war with our bodies' natural design. The war takes place on a vulnerable battleground: our minds. For some women, these conflicts may be temporary (a bout of crash dieting, perhaps) and will be followed by some kind of acceptable truce ("Okay, I'll eat normal meals, but no more desserts"). Other people, however, need additional support to resist social pressure. Without such protection, people become victims of a strange syndrome, one whose symptoms are a distorted body image, bizarre eating patterns, illness, and much unnecessary suffering.

How does our culture develop and transmit this deadly message about thinness? Why should thinness be the social currency we value? Let's look.

Envision the "ideal" female figure. What comes to mind? In this society, many people—men as well as women—probably conjure up an image of Miss America or a Playboy centerfold. Purely in the interest of science, a team of researchers carefully analyzed the body measurements of these icons of feminine beauty over the past few decades. They made a surprising discovery: As a general trend, each year the women chosen as these ideals have been thinner than their predecessors. This is odd when you realize that the average weight of the population has *increased* over the same time period. Thus there has been a widening gap between the "ideals" of female beauty and most women's actual weights. These beauty queens' relative body weights are actually lower than those of 95 *percent* of the female population!

My heart goes out to today's woman, whose body may be perfectly normal but who believes that she must compete against this absurdly distorted vision of ideal beauty.

Our culture's perception that the ideal female form should be abnormally slender is a fairly recent phenomenon. One of my bulimic patients, an eighteen-year-old college student, told me she had watched a Marilyn Monroe film on television. "Marilyn Monroe was such a pig!" she exclaimed. "She was so fat!" Strange to think that what was seen as sexy and attractive thirty years ago is now condemned as "fat."

Although there are some historical precedents for similar distortions of the feminine ideal, such as the Victorian eighteen-inch waist, never before have they had such an impact on the vast majority of women. Media, such as women's magazines, very often add to the confusion about body image. For example: The number of articles about dieting appearing in these publications has *doubled* every decade since World War II. Yet these same magazines present page after page of recipes for "luscious desserts" and "family-pleasing treats" illustrated with glistening, mouth-watering photographs. Mixed signals? You bet.

Since World War II, our food-buying and eating habits have also undergone a radical change. Food is plentiful, and its variety is enormous. Many of today's foods are very palatable but rich in calories due to their high fat and sugar content. Fast food—from chain restaurants to microwave meals in our own homes—has revolutionized how and what we eat. And in our sedentary society, the only exercise some people get is pressing buttons on their television's remote control. Given these facts, it actually does make some sense for people to be on their dietary guard.

For some people, however, an irresistible force (social pressure to be thin) meets an everyday temptation (tasty, abundant food) and produces an extreme reaction (an eating disorder). People at special risk include those who:

- have low self-esteem
- are overly sensitive to the opinions of others
- carry the concept of self-control to extremes
- have difficulty separating from their families
- work in occupations that require a high level of body-awareness, such as modeling, dancing, or acting

When people with these characteristics suffer stress—for example, the death of a relative, a move to a new school or city, or a personal loss such as the breakup of a romance—an eating disorder is sometimes the result.

THE SPECTRUM OF EATING DISORDERS

Most of us know people who exhibit what seem to be peculiar eating patterns, from self-professed "chocoholics" to the college student on a macrobiotic diet. Yet these unusual habits seldom represent a true eating disorder. Understanding just what qualifies as an eating disorder begins with basic definitions of the terms.

Anorexia—self-starvation—was first described as a clinical syndrome three hundred years ago. Yet only within the past few decades have eating disorders been widely recognized, not just by the public but by physicians themselves. Even as I write, controversy rages, here and abroad, over the exact nature of these disorders. This debate is more than mere medical hairsplitting; a precise understanding is crucial so that therapy can be developed and applied.

Anorexia and bulimia may appear to be different illnesses with different symptoms. Anorexia is characterized by starvation; bulimia is notorious for its cycle of bingeing and purging. While there are distinctions between the two conditions, it is also true that they have certain features in common.

Both anorexics and bulimics *overvalue bodily thinness.* The flip side of this attitude, and of equal importance, is an *exaggerated fear of fatness.* These highly prized but basically unhealthy concepts are constantly reinforced by social pressures and cultural signals.

Both disorders also involve an *obsession with food*. As the disease progresses, patients get caught up in the rituals of acquiring, preparing, and consuming meals. In time, thoughts of food come to dominate every aspect of their lives, at the expense of family, friends, careers, and, of course, health.

Eating disorders are "spectrum" disorders. Like the spectrum of light in a rainbow, anorexia and bulimia appear in a range of intensities. Think of anorexics as occupying the red end of the spectrum, with bulimics at the violet end. Both "colors" are highly intense but are of different hues. In between are many variations of the illness, each with a distinctive "color," or pattern of symptoms. There are several types of patients with eating disorders, especially among those with bulimia. The main difference between them may be simply the severity of their symptoms.

Looking at a rainbow, it is difficult to tell exactly where one color ends and another one begins. The colors seem to slide into each other, overlapping at certain critical points.

The same can be said of eating disorders. Women who start off with anorexia find it difficult to maintain constant starvation. So they eat. They then often adopt such measures as self-induced vomiting in order to keep their weight down. Conversely, patients who begin by bingeing and purging may eventually try starvation as their only means of restricting food intake. This passage from one kind of eating strategy to another affects the treatment they require. Anorexic patients, for example, fear that learning how to eat normally may result in urges to binge. As a doctor, I try to help patients confront, and conquer, this fear.

EATING DISORDERS AS DISEASES

To some extent, it helps to think of anorexia and bulimia in the same way as any other illness, such as diabetes or asthma. One advantage of this approach, called the medical model, is that it helps reinforce the "no-fault" concept I described earlier. A person with asthma is not responsible for the condition, but *is* expected to participate actively in managing the problem.

The medical model follows certain logical steps: evaluating the patient and the problem, arriving at a proper diagnosis, designing a treatment plan, then carrying out that treatment. This approach takes each person's individuality into account and looks at all the forces that may be contributing to the disorder. It also lets the physician choose from many therapeutic strategies to find the ones that have the best chance of working.

Such an approach is vastly superior to one in which a doctor assumes from the beginning that all eating disorders result from one cause—for example, a defective sense of self-esteem. Such restrictive, simple-minded thinking can lead to one-dimensional therapy that fails to address the multifaceted—perhaps I should just say human—nature of the disorder. As the saying goes, if all you have is a hammer, then every problem is a nail. It is better if the physician takes into account the nuts and bolts of the problem as well.

The medical model has limits. For one thing, anorexia and bulimia are not really like pneumonia. Most people would agree that there is nothing good whatsoever about pneumonia, unless you happen to be the bacterium that goes around causing it. Similarly, there is very little "good" about psychiatric disorders such as schizophrenia or depression.

However, I believe there is something positive that exists in the strangely inverted world of eating disorders. That positive element concerns the patient's attempt to exert her *willpower* to solve what she perceives as a problem. Rather than lying back passively and falling victim to the raging psychological and social forces that swirl around and inside her, she has adopted an active, even aggressive stance. She is taking a decisive course of action to achieve a goal—a goal she is willing to risk her life to achieve. While her goal is unreachable and her method is harmful, I feel her basic impulse is good and worthy of respect: She is trying to deal with a difficult situation by taking control and finding something in her life that makes her feel successful, special, and proud.

In a strange way, eating disorders express a very American kind of thinking: Pull yourself up by your bootstraps, get a hold of yourself, improve your life, set a goal and work hard to achieve it, distinguish yourself. However, the approach taken by the bulimic or the anorexic is too rigid, too extreme, and is completely out of harmony with the needs of the body and the mind. The strategy is doomed to fail. When it does, the patient will suffer guilt, despair, and a sense of worthlessness—the very feelings that precipitated the disorder in the first place.

My approach as a physician is to recognize the complexity of the problem and try to take into account the many psychological and social factors that affect a patient. I accept that she is trying to solve her crisis, and I will try to help her channel that energy in a healthier way. When this approach works, the patient changes her faulty patterns of thinking, alters her destructive eating behavior, and improves her relationships with other people. Ideally, she leaves treatment with the resources she needs to cope in healthy ways with the pressure to be thin, pressure that will undoubtedly continue over the years.

A WORD ABOUT BIOPSYCHIATRY

In the past thirty or so years, there's been a revolution in the way psychiatrists look at mental disorders and their treatment. The discovery of important new medicines of the mind, including antipsychotics and antidepressants, helped fuel this revolution. The study of neurochemistry reveals how tiny molecules interact with brain cells and trigger not just physical activity, but thoughts, moods, and feelings as well. Through these and other discoveries, we have become more aware of how the body's *biological* malfunctions can lead to *emotional* disturbances—thus the term *biopsychiatry*.

As a biopsychiatrist, I'm aware of the interlocking relationship between the healthy body and the healthy mind. I see people as biological organisms operating under certain physical rules that in turn affect mental function. Actually, *all* psychiatry is—or should be—"biopsychiatry." Psychiatrists can't afford to overlook the biological causes and effects of mental disturbance. If they do, they will inevitably misunderstand the problem and select treatments that will fail.

Eating disorders occupy a special place in the field of biopsychiatry. After all, eating is a basic and necessary biological function. The components of food—the amino acids that make up body proteins, for example—are the building blocks of the body. Thus it is quite literally true that you are what you eat.

A food imbalance can dramatically affect how we think and feel. Eating and weight also possess extremely powerful social and symbolic significance. Thus you are "how you eat" as well.

New research regarding weight control has recently become available. From this research has emerged a key concept known as the "set point model." The discovery of the set point has enormous implications for the biopsychiatric management of eating disorders, as we'll see later in this book.

Set point theory holds that your body has a certain predetermined weight range—the set point range—that it attempts vigorously to maintain. If anything threatens to disrupt this set point range—either overeating or starvation—the body will fight to stay at its preferred weight. In scientific terms, your body is a homeostatic system (*homeostatic* means "preserving the same condition"). If your weight drops below the set point range, your body becomes more efficient at retaining calories from the food you have taken in. Your body may also signal you to eat (possibly to binge) to get the weight back up where it should be. Mistaking these physical signals as simply "emotional" in origin neglects the complex feedback loops through which the body maintains its homeostasis.

TREATMENT OF EATING DISORDERS: REASON TO HOPE

Anorexia and bulimia are life-threatening conditions that must be treated aggressively and thoroughly. Fortunately, in many cases, they *are* curable.

No case is ever "hopeless." What is required in all cases is time—time to correct misconceptions about eating and weight, time to unlearn bad habits, and time to restore disrupted relationships with family, with friends, and with oneself. As a physician, I bring into play every resource that might have some chance of helping the patient get better, whether that strategy is labeled educational, behavioral, cognitive, medical, psychological, or interpersonal.

If you have an eating disorder, or know someone who does, this book will educate you about the condition, help you explore its causes, and tell you about the many different and effective ways it can be treated.

If you are the parent of a child whose eating appears to be dangerous to her health, you may find it reassuring to learn that *you don't have to wait for your daughter to ask for treatment.* You can intervene in ways that will help her realize the need for therapy. Intervention is necessary—indeed, lifesaving—especially if your daughter is very depressed, suicidal, or at a low weight. If as parents you are sufficiently united in your purpose, you'll succeed in helping your child.

When I treat eating disorders, I play the game to win. I suspect that because you are reading this book, you want to win too.

Good—welcome to the team.

2

Do You Have an Eating Disorder?

"It's so strange," said one mother. "Melissa turned into a vegetarian overnight. Now she won't eat any of the foods she always loved."

A father remarked: "Lisa seems to live at McDonald's. All that junk can't be good for her—can it?"

"Cookies! I think that girl exists on Oreos! What should I do?"

"I swear, she starts a different diet every week."

"She eats nothing all day, then gets ravenous just before bedtime. Is this just a teenage phase? Or should I worry?"

"I can't understand it. Every day she eats *exactly* the same thing. The same foods, in the same order, every meal. Even breakfast. Is something wrong?"

Adolescence: Spell it T-U-R-M-O-I-L. Hormones surge. Emotions run amok. Bodies change so fast that their owners don't recognize themselves in the mirror.

The physical transformation alone is hard enough to handle. But a teen's whole world is in upheaval. Socially speaking, the pressure's on. Suddenly a person whose age has barely reached double digits has to cope with enormous changes and choices. Sexuality. Dating. Demanding teachers. Those twin temptations, drugs and alcohol. New roles and responsibilities.

Some of this confusion and fear is bound to rub off onto the parents. They watch their sweet, obedient child transmute into an anxious, volatile creature from another world.

Everything in the kid's life is changing, and eating patterns are no exception. Unusual diets, strange menus, or just plain bad food habits do not always mean that an eating disorder has struck. Switching to vegetarianism or an occasional food binge represents nothing unusual.

Sometimes, though, there *is* cause for concern. Those habits may not be a phase, but a sign that something is wrong. The body could be changing so fast that it can't keep up with itself. Emotions may spin out of control. The pressure gets to be too much. For a lot of people, eating—or the discipline of not eating—provides relief, comfort, or just plain distraction.

You may think (or know) that something is wrong with the way your child is eating. Or you may be worried about a close friend or relative—or yourself. You may have witnessed bizarre behavior—for example, wolfing down a dozen bananas or six hot dogs in a row—that makes you suspicious. Maybe your daughter takes forever at the dinner table, picking at her food, eating nothing. Or she disappears into the bathroom two or three times during a meal. Or perhaps another person's casual remark—"Barbara's losing an awful lot of weight, isn't she?"—sets off an alarm in your head.

When does a "diet" become a disorder? What exactly are eating disorders, anyway? Why do they strike, and how do they affect the people who have them? This chapter will help you find out. To start, look over this list of warning signs that indicate something is wrong.

THE WARNING SIGNS OF EATING DISORDERS

Severe weight loss

Preoccupation with being thin and/or an intense fear of
being overweight

Severe diets or odd behaviors about food

Signs and symptoms of depression

Loss of menstrual periods

Hyperactivity, compulsive exercising

Distorted body image

Unexplained medical problems

Hair loss

Slow pulse (bradycardia)

Intolerance to cold (shivering, blueness of the skin and
fingers, etc.)

Edema (swelling of the ankles)

Low blood pressure

Low body temperature (hypothermia)

Dental damage (due to vomiting)

Weakness

Sleep disturbance

Now take the following quizzes. Answer each question as honestly as you can. Remember, *eating disorders can only be treated successfully if they are detected early, and the earlier the better.*

ANOREXIA INVENTORY

1. *Do you feel fat, even though you know (or others have told you) that you are thin?*

2. *Have you lost a significant amount of weight, especially recently?*

3. *Have you restricted food intake through dieting or fasting?*

4. *Do you burn off energy through excessive exercise?*

5. *Do you have urges to binge?*

6. *Have you "purged," either through vomiting or laxative or enema abuse?*

7. *Do you set dieting "goals," then reach them, only to set yet another goal?*

8. *Do you think about food constantly?*

9. *Do you feel uncomfortable eating in front of others?*

10. *Do you turn down spontaneous invitations to eat in places other than your home, say, in restaurants or at parties?*

11. *Do you have set routines you feel you must follow during a meal? If you don't follow them do you get angry or tense?*

12. *Do you take very small bites while eating, or do you count your bites?*

13. *Do you insist others eat while you resist eating?*

14. *Do you make a point of weighing yourself or looking in the mirror several times a day?*

15. *Does your mood depend on how much you have eaten? Are you happy if you eat nothing, sad if you eat anything at all?*

16. *Are you more socially isolated than you were, say, three months ago?*

17. *Are you a perfectionist? Are you overly critical of yourself?*

18. *Do you ever feel depressed or sad for a long time for no identifiable reason?*

19. *Are your menstrual periods irregular—not occurring every 25–30 days, or occurring an average of fewer than ten times a year for the past two years?*

20. *Do you feel cold all the time, or need extra layers of clothing?*

21. *Have you experienced low blood pressure, dizziness, or fainting spells recently?*

BULIMIA INVENTORY

1. *Do you binge often?*

2. *Do you feel your eating behavior is out of control?*

3. *Do you purge through vomiting, or using laxatives or enemas?*

4. *Do others in your household complain that you spend too much time in the bathroom?*

5. *Do you exercise excessively or use diet pills?*

6. *Are you constantly dieting or weighing yourself?*

7. *Are you preoccupied with thoughts of food or calories?*

8. *Do you plan binges or hoard food in anticipation of a binge?*

9. *Do you eat in secret or mislead others about your food intake? (For example, do you order a salad while eating out, but go on a binge once you are home and alone?)*

10. *Do you make excuses for the quantity of food you are buying—for example, telling the person behind you at the checkout stand that "company is coming"?*

11. *Do you spend large amounts of money on food?*

12. *Have you ever shoplifted food?*

13. *Are you very angry with yourself when you feel you have eaten too much, even if it is just an extra nibble?*

14. *Does feeling good about yourself depend on your ability to exert total control over eating or weight?*

15. *Do you isolate yourself from others if you feel a few pounds overweight?*

16. *Do you depend a great deal on others for approval?*

17. *Do you have difficulty asserting yourself even if you know you are right?*

18. *Are you excessively moody?*

19. *Are you excessively fatigued?*

20. *Have you noticed puffiness in your face or swelling in your neck glands?*

21. *Do you have trouble with your teeth, such as pain or discoloring?*

22. *Have people around you mentioned they have noticed unusual or offensive odors?*

23. *Has your weight fluctuated a lot recently?*

How did you score? In these inventories there is no arbitrary number of "yes" answers that would indicate the presence of an eating disorder. Instead, you can use these tests to raise your awareness about the possibility of serious problems. If there is reason for concern, I urge you to see your doctor for a complete evaluation. Don't put it off. The longer an eating disorder persists, the worse it gets.

THE NAME GAME, PART I: ANOREXIA

Before you can tackle a problem, you have to give it a name, but people often use the same words to mean different things. In medicine particularly, such confusion can be dangerous. Fortunately, in the last few years experts have begun to agree on the terms used to identify eating disorders. Such wasn't always the case.

The full name of the disorder of self-starvation, first coined by a Dr. Gull in the nineteenth century, is *anorexia nervosa*. While "anorexia"—Greek for "without hunger" or "lack of appetite"—is a real symptom of many illnesses, it's a poor label for people who are obsessed with food and who constantly fight the urge to eat. Only in the final stages of their illness do anorexics actually lose their appetites. A doctor who takes the word *anorexia* literally, who assumes that his anorexic patients have no desire for food, might give them appetite stimulants. For a woman with a constant, gnawing hunger, whose self-esteem depends on controlling her eating, such an approach spells disaster.

Experts spliced on the word *nervosa* to show that the illness involves not just a single symptom, but a whole range of psychological and physical problems. *Anorexia nervosa* describes a *syndrome*—a set of symptoms that occur together.

Not everyone is happy with the name. One English physician prefers *weight phobia.* Yes, anorexics do feel a powerful fear of fatness, but the disease is much more complex than that. Other fears besides that of weight may also be present—a fear of growing up, of maturity, or of separation from the family. Some writers like to use *self-starvation,* plain and simple.

However, *anorexia nervosa* is the name most professionals prefer, while laypeople use *anorexia* to indicate the whole syndrome rather than the single symptom of loss of appetite. In this book, for the sake of simplicity, I too will use *anorexia* to mean anorexia nervosa, unless I state otherwise.

THE NAME GAME, PART II: BULIMIA

A similar language problem exists with *bulimia*. The word comes from the Greek meaning "ox hunger"—certainly a vivid image. Before the 1980s, doctors used the term *bulimia* exclusively to mean a disorder of overeating. But, like *anorexia,* the word refers only to a particular symptom: in this case, binge eating. It doesn't include the flip side of the binge, the purge. The term is thus too narrow to describe the many different eating patterns that characterize the disorder.

For example, all bulimics eat large amounts of food, but there is a wide variation in weight. Some patients are exclusively bulimic, but roughly half of all anorexics also binge and purge. Their starving bodies scream for food; once they yield, they may consume an enormous amount at one sitting. To keep their weight down, these people desperately try to get rid of the meal. Still other bulimics were once self-starvers; they have returned to their normal weight but continue to binge and purge. It's important to recognize these variations, because they each call for a somewhat different treatment.

In the mid-1970s someone coined the term *bulimarexia* ("hunger/starvation") to describe the condition in which a purge follows a binge. Not a particularly graceful word, *bulimarexia* never caught on. British experts chose to use *bulimia nervosa*. As with *anorexia nervosa*, the term distinguishes the symptom from the syndrome and shows that the disorder has both psychological and physical elements.

Only in the late 1980s did doctors in this country accept *bulimia nervosa* as the best name. (Again, though, for simplicity's sake I will use *bulimia* and *bulimia nervosa* interchangeably, distinguishing between them when necessary.)

If this seems a bit confusing, take heart—even medical professionals are sometimes bewildered by the subtleties of these terms. I've mentioned the debate to show how our perceptions of eating disorders change as we learn more about them.

WHAT IS AN EATING DISORDER?

According to the textbooks, an eating disorder is a pronounced disturbance in the way someone eats. "Disturbance" means a change from the person's usual pattern, or a habit that poses a danger to health.

But such a definition isn't very helpful. Do people who switch to a macrobiotic diet, for example, have an eating disorder? After all, they have changed their eating habits. Moreover, for some people at least, such a diet may provide insufficient amounts of calories, protein, and other nutrients, thus putting their health in jeopardy.

In this book we'll confine our discussion to the two major eating disorders, anorexia nervosa and bulimia nervosa. Not covered are two other recognized but rare illnesses, *pica* (unusual food cravings, such as a craving to eat dirt or clay) and *rumination disorder* (a disorder in young children who regurgitate food without nausea). The third disorder we won't consider is obesity. Although there is some overlap between obesity and the other eating disorders, specifically in terms of problems with body image and self-esteem, the causes and treatment of this disorder are sufficiently different to require a separate book of their own. Experts generally consider obesity a physical disorder, not a psychiatric one, although it may have a psychiatric component to it.

The question of what is and what isn't an eating disorder is a common and sometimes baffling one. There are many areas of confusion and misinformation. In an effort to sort out this confusion, let me try to answer some of the most prevalent questions about eating disorders that I encounter as a physician specializing in the field.

Are eating disorders a recent problem?

No. Ancient Greeks and Romans wrote about abnormal eating patterns. Medical reports from three hundred years ago describe patients with anorexia. Only recently, however, have doctors tried to define these illnesses precisely, in order to better recognize and treat them. Bulimia, in fact, was only identified as a distinct disorder in the mid-1970s, although the problem existed long before then.

Don't eating disorders affect only rich white people?

No. Patients can be black, Hispanic, Japanese. Many are by no means rich. A small number are male. In one sense, though, anorexia and bulimia are economic in origin. They occur where food is plentiful, as in the industrialized nations of Great Britain, France, the United States, Germany, and Scandinavia. The incidence in Japan, a "Westernized" nation, is increasing. In areas where scarcity of food is a problem, such as parts of Africa, eating disorders are extremely rare.

Are all anorexics and bulimics women?

Most are, but about 5–10 percent of them are male.

Is a man with an eating disorder gay?

Not necessarily. An eating disorder may be just one facet of a complex personality problem. Some men with these disorders struggle with issues of sexual identity, including homosexuality. Others feel pressure because thinness is highly valued in their professions, such as sports, dance, fashion, or entertainment.

Are eating disorders caused by parents?

Family problems can *contribute* to the onset and severity of an eating disorder. But they don't cause it.

Aren't all eating-disordered families alike: upwardly mobile, with dominating mothers, and no independence for the children?

No. Research has shown that children with eating disorders come from many types of families, including healthy, functional families. It *is* true, however, that after years of struggling, families may begin to develop problems *because* of the eating disorder.

Are eating disorders all in the mind?

No. There may be a physical malfunction in the way the body regulates hunger. And the longer a disorder persists, the greater the damage it does to the body. The impact of starvation on the brain can lead to worsening mental and emotional problems.

Is an eating disorder a sign that some other psychiatric illness exists, such as a personality disorder?

Eating disorders are illnesses in and of themselves. They are not necessarily the product of some other illness. Of course, an eating disorder arising in a young person can affect the way her personality develops.

Do eating disorders cause depression?

Depression is a separate problem. A woman can be depressed *and* have an eating disorder; the former doesn't necessarily cause the latter. Some patients feel depressed because they are struggling with a chronic illness. However, there does seem to be a connection between a family history of mood disorder and the risk that a member may develop an eating disorder.

Will a teenage girl who worries about her figure develop an eating disorder?

Unfortunately, overconcern about one's body is normal in our culture. But when other emotional pressures bear down on a vulnerable person, the risk rises that she'll develop an eating disorder.

Does dieting lead to eating disorders?

Many patients did diet before their disorder arose, but others who diet never develop an eating abnormality.

Do food allergies, vitamin deficiencies, or improper diet cause eating disorders?

We need more research before we can answer this conclusively. Improper diet is destructive to a person's health, as are vitamin deficiencies and untreated food allergies, but there's not enough evidence to show that these in themselves can cause an eating disorder. However, there is evidence that imbalances in some vitamins or minerals may cause certain problems. Too much vitamin A, for example, can cause menstrual problems, while too little zinc can affect one's mood, appetite, and sense of taste.

Is it true that anorexics have no appetite?

No. Anorexics *do* experience hunger much of the time and need considerable willpower to conquer these feelings. The more they starve, the more their bodies crave food.

Do anorexics hate sex?

Better to say that most anorexics would rather *avoid* sex. Starving uses up all the patient's energy, leaving her none for any other activity, including but not limited to sex.

Are anorexics lying when they say they are fat but are obviously starving?

No—they mean it very sincerely, because the disorder has warped their ability to think and see accurately. The longer the illness persists, the more the patient misjudges her appearance and the more she feels compelled to keep starving herself.

Do an anorexic's psychological problems have to be cured before she can gain weight?

Absolutely not. This would be like trying to fix a broken leg by analyzing the hidden motivations behind someone's decision to go skiing. It won't work and it only delays therapy that might do some good. An anorexic is in danger of dying. Job One is to restore weight so that her body—and her ability to think clearly—can return to normal. Only at that point will psychotherapy have some chance of succeeding.

Do anorexics starve themselves so they can look good?

Looking "good" has a different meaning for anorexics than for normal people. Many anorexics know they look skeletal and emaciated. For them, starvation is a compulsion they can't control, not a plan to become more attractive.

Do laxatives and diuretics help control weight?

Not really. By the time food passes in a bowel movement, the body has absorbed most of its calories anyway. Any weight lost is probably just temporary "water weight" loss.

Who has an eating disorder?

Depending on the population studied, between .2 percent and 1 percent of teenage females have had anorexia. Bulimia is more common. Estimates range from upward of 1 percent of adolescent and young adult females in the general population to 4 percent of female college students.

Typically, anorexia strikes between the ages of fourteen and eighteen; most of my patients range between ages twelve and thirty-five. Yet anyone, from a small child to a postmenopausal woman, can become a self-starver. In these cases a metabolic problem other than anorexia may be present. The onset of bulimia usually occurs later in life than anorexia: The average age is around sixteen to twenty.

Statistics can give us some idea of how widespread these illnesses are, but there are problems with the accuracy of these numbers.

For one thing, as we'll see in Chapters Three and Four, the

criteria doctors use to diagnose eating disorders keep changing. As these guidelines narrow, the number of people who fit them changes. People with milder cases may be grouped with severe cases and thus distort the picture. Also, the incidence among certain groups of people is changing. True, many eating-disordered people fit the stereotype of the white, upper-class teenager, but a growing number of patients do not match this description. The disorders are now more equally distributed among social classes—evidence that cultural pressure to be thin permeates all levels of society.

Over the last decade, there has been greater public awareness about eating disorders. There may simply be more victims. Or perhaps the number is the same, but more people are seeking help, inspired by media coverage of these illnesses.

Another possibility is that the number of reported cases is lower than it should be. Many people think eating disorders, like other psychiatric illnesses, are shameful or embarrassing, not just to the victim but to the family as well. Some people with these problems, particularly men, may choose not to get help.

THE MEDICAL DANGERS OF EATING DISORDERS

Your body needs food to function. Poor eating damages the body in a host of different ways, and some of these medical complications can be fatal.

For example, gastric dilatation, in which the stomach expands and may rupture, can occur during a binge. Pancreatitis—inflammation of the pancreas—may also develop.

Starvation can lead to abnormal growth of fibrous tissue in the kidneys (interstitial fibrosis). Another risk is diabetes insipidus, which robs the body of its ability to conserve fluids.

Slowed heart rate (bradycardia) is a common effect of starvation. Potentially fatal heart arrhythmias may also develop, usually due to electrolyte imbalance, but sometimes occurring even when electrolytes are normal. Fatal cardiac failure can occur if weight is regained too rapidly.

Starving reduces the ability of bone marrow to produce blood cells. As a result, the white blood cell count may drop. (Surprisingly, this may not always lead to increased infections.) It also disturbs the blood's ability to form clots, which can lead to bleeding problems.

As the starving body "turns down the thermostat" to conserve energy, the thyroid reduces its functions. Other endocrine abnormalities also develop. Another major problem is osteoporosis, a decrease in bone mass that can lead to fractures of the ribs or spinal vertebrae.

These potentially fatal medical consequences may frighten you. However, sometimes it takes a good scare to break through the wall of denial that accompanies these illnesses.

WHY DO EATING DISORDERS ARISE?

That's the sixty-four-thousand-dollar question. Experts answer it differently, depending on their area of specialty.

The Biological Perspective

Biologists see eating disorders as a foul-up in the body systems that regulate hunger and eating, particularly the hypothalamus. This cluster of nerves in the brain controls many body functions, including intake of water and food.

By releasing hormones, the hypothalamus also regulates the onset of puberty—an important connection to eating disorders. Although we don't know exactly what "pulls the trigger," puberty may begin when the body reaches a preprogrammed weight and achieves a certain percentage of body fat. Starving makes both weight and body fat decrease. If the weight-to-fat ratio falls too low, metabolic changes—including the loss of menstruation, a kind of regression from puberty—occur.

Biologists also look for problems in the way the body converts food into neurotransmitters—chemicals that carry signals between cells. The brain "knows" when the body needs certain foods to make the neurotransmitters that are in short supply and tells us what we should eat next. Eating disorders may arise from a malfunction in this feedback system.

Other evidence of the biological basis of eating disorders comes from studies on twins. Identical twins, who grow from a single egg and share an identical genetic blueprint, have a higher incidence of anorexia nervosa than fraternal twins, who grow from separate eggs.

If we can identify the biological breakdown or the genetic glitch that causes an eating disorder, then perhaps medicine can correct the problem and offer hope for treatment.

The Psychological Perspective

Most experts feel biology alone can't explain eating disorders. The question then becomes, "What factors provoke abnormal eating in one person but not another?"

The answer, they believe, lies in a person's life experiences and the thoughts and feelings those experiences arouse. A loss or rejection, a death in the family, the act of leaving home, can all start the ball rolling. The anorexic may feel she is somehow not good enough, that she is a disappointment to everyone. She is a "failure" in every capacity except one: her ability to be thin.

In bulimia, some of the same psychological factors are at work. A bulimic also equates thinness with self-worth (although in this case the degree of thinness is less extreme than in anorexia). There are other pressures as well. As biologists suspect, there may be a physical urge to binge. Bingeing also serves as a kind of distraction, allowing a woman to push aside unpleasant feelings and focus instead on intense physical sensations. By overeating, a woman rebels against the limits society tries to impose. She conquers fear by withdrawing into the comfortable, dependable world of bingeing. (Patients occasionally refer to bingeing as their "friend.") Bingeing has much in common with the abuse of drugs or alcohol. By definition, however, a bulimic feels her behavior is beyond control. Purging thus becomes her way of regaining balance. She tells herself: "I overeat, but it's okay because I throw it up anyway." Bulimia lets her control at least one aspect of her life—eating—to make up for lack of control elsewhere.

The Family Perspective

I would be hard pressed to think of a patient whose family life had no direct bearing on the way her disorder developed. Volumes have been written on the role of family dynamics in anorexia and bulimia.

Some patterns that have been identified in certain eating-disordered families include an overemphasis on appearance, social isolation, emotional rigidity, and the inability to resolve conflicts. However, there is no such thing as a "typical" eating-disordered family. The same dynamic that triggers an eating disorder in one person may allow another to thrive. In Chapter Eleven we'll learn more about the family's influence on eating disorders, and how family therapy can be a vital component of treatment.

The Sociocultural Perspective

To sociologists, eating disorders result from the extreme value our culture places on *thinness*. Through advertisements, TV programs, and magazines, thinness has become a kind of social currency, a means of exchange between people. The hidden message: Thin wins.

The other side of the coin: Fat is failure. Chubby children suffer cruel teasing by their schoolmates—teasing that can become the trigger for an eating disorder. Fat people are the targets of jokes and whispered comments. Some find the doors to advancement closed. The cultural pressure to be thin can make feelings of insecurity, self-doubt, or unworthiness much worse.

Other trends stoke the fire. The modern changes in women's place in society and the lack of models showing how to fulfill those roles add to the problem. A girl whose mother was "just a housewife" may suddenly find herself, at adolescence, expected to become a "superwoman," adept at juggling career, family, and personal needs. Some women may lack the skills to cope with—or resist—these demands, including the demand that one must be thin. By submitting to these pressures, they hope to show they are worthy, that they can set and reach goals, and that they deserve respect.

ANOTHER POINT OF VIEW

Which of these views is right? All of them—to an extent. But a complete picture only emerges when experts pool their information and examine the problem from all points of view.

Most anorexics are teenagers, and I believe that for them anorexia represents a way to avoid maturity. By maturity I mean not just physical or sexual development, but psychological and social development as well. A woman can translate her fear of growing up into a loss of body weight. If she can keep the same weight she had at age ten, maybe she can stay ten forever. Achieving thinness lets her turn back the clock and revert to a childlike physical appearance. Even more important, loss of body weight causes the menstrual cycle to shut down. The patient gains control over one of the most powerful—and perhaps frightening—signs of womanhood. (For males, of course, the issue is different, as I'll explain later.) Thus *anorexia* can reflect problems in making the transition from *childhood to adolescence.*

In contrast, *bulimia* can reflect difficulty growing from *adolescence into adulthood.* Here the problem isn't so much one of achieving maturity, but of handling its responsibilities: separating from the family; controlling oneself and others; assuming an identity through marriage or career; defining oneself through relationships with others.*

A person with an eating disorder struggles with these deep and troubling issues. The pressures combine and drive her to create an identity based on her ability to control food and eating. Through such control she achieves something that everybody desires, something that society values: the ability to be seen as special.

Everyone wants to be special in some way. It's a natural human trait. We seek distinction through our talents, achievements, or personalities. Some of us take jobs and provide things that people want. Others express themselves through the arts. Still others

*This information has been developed by Dr. Susan Wooley at the University of Cincinnati.

devote themselves to the care of their families. Rewards for our efforts come in many forms: a paycheck, applause, a child's hug.

But victims of an eating disorder look for a *different* reward. They believe that the only way they can be special is to control their weight and eating habits—to starve themselves if they have to. An anorexic patient might say to me, "I want to be the thinnest person in my school," or, "the thinnest in the world."

Of course, many people realize that true self-esteem is based not just on physical appearance, but on other innate qualities. These are the people who answer the question, "Why must we be thin?" by saying, "I *don't* have to be."

As a specialist in eating disorders, I work to convince patients that *defining self-worth through abnormal eating is a dangerously unhealthy business.* To pursue the "ideal body shape" is to pursue a myth.

I see these myths every day in countless guises. I don't know how many times I have heard my patients say, "I always felt that if I was thin I would be happy," or, "If people really loved me then I wouldn't binge out," or, "Being fat lets people see me for the loser I am."

Some people believe that someone with an eating disorder won't get better unless she wants to. *Wrong!* For families to embrace this myth is to run the risk that their daughter will starve to death before she gets the help she needs. Many times, families refuse to get help for their daughter because they believe she can get better on her own. "Recovery is just a matter of willpower," they claim. People who believe this graduated from the "Just snap out of it" school of thinking. An eating-disordered girl can't "will" herself out of her condition any more than people can "will" themselves out of the flu.

Helping a patient to *want* to get better is actually part of the first stage of therapy. Once she has learned the importance of changing, she has reached a point where other types of therapy have a chance of succeeding. Patients need sensitive, thoughtful treatment to help them break the vicious cycle of disturbed eating, correct their faulty thinking, improve their eating behavior, and resolve their difficulties in relationships with friends and family.

To me, the most frustrating thing about these myths is how deeply rooted they have become. Many people accept them as reality. Thus the first important step in treatment is to uproot these myths and correct them.

No patient is "typical." Many share certain traits or experiences, but each patient has a different history—and a different future. Keeping that in mind, here are scenarios describing the course of these illnesses.

THE MAKING OF AN ANOREXIC

Before adolescence, the life of an anorexic-to-be seems pretty smooth. These people are often described as "model children": compliant, obedient, well-behaved. They carry out their duties at home cheerfully and willingly. At school, they are good students who are devoted to their work and usually get good grades.

In short, these people seem happy with their role as children. The demands made on them are easily met. They succeed at a level that fits their position in life, and thus feel good about themselves.

Come adolescence, however, the child is expected to function in new ways. Now an adolescent's identity derives more from relating to her peer group than from simply meeting the expectations of adults. An adolescent who has trouble with these new demands begins to feel inadequate, although she may not be able to put her feelings into words. Even the rewards for "good behavior" that the adolescent might once have expected from adults are now less tangible and less frequent. A twelve-year-old doesn't get a gold star for brushing her teeth every night; such behavior is now expected of her.

Feelings of inadequacy sometimes relate to the bodily changes of puberty, as the hormonal onslaught triggers a flood of new emotions. The onset of menstruation forces a girl to think about herself as a maturing woman, a sexual being. For some, the sudden awareness of sexuality may be more than they can bear. Many of my patients appear to weather the storm of puberty for some time, accepting menstruation as a natural part of their development. Often, however, it turns out that they have just been putting up a brave front. Deep down, they are terrified of what's happening to their bodies.

The fragile personalities these girls develop can be shattered by some devastating event. Such events take many forms, but they usually relate to a loss or a sense of failure.

For example, some anorexics have suffered the death of a parent or a particularly beloved grandparent. Sometimes the loss involves the breakup of the first (and most intense) romance. Some patients, about to enter college, are frightened by the thought of leaving the family or by the pressure to succeed. Divorce, relocation, marriage of a sibling, illness—any of these can shake her sense of security, challenge her ability to meet the expectations placed on her, and rob her of self-esteem.

Of course, the same can be said of anyone. The potential anorexic, however, lacks the inner strength necessary to handle loss, rejection, or change. She has aged, but she has not grown up. She has spent so much emotional energy pleasing others that she has none left to invest in understanding her own feelings. She has never learned to recognize the signals coming from her growing body, her brain, and, for want of a more scientific term, her soul.

Even if she does recognize these signals, she can't respond to them. Instead she has a vague sense that "something is wrong with me." She begins to mistrust not just herself but everyone around her. In such a state she can't make new friends or keep old friendships going. She withdraws further into herself.

Soon her insecurity, lack of trust, and inability to recognize feelings affect her perception. She can't even see what her own body looks like with any degree of accuracy.

Eventually, though, a kind of transformation takes place in her thinking. She gropes for an anchor to keep her from drifting into an emotional whirlpool. The notion that "there is something wrong with me" becomes "there is something wrong with my body—*it's too fat.*"

More than 6o percent of adolescent girls in our society believe they are "too fat." The difference for the anorexic, however, is the degree of distress this feeling causes, compounded by her inability to perceive her body accurately.

Ironically, her "realization" that she is fat, though distorted and incorrect, produces a tremendous sense of relief. At last she feels she has identified the problem. Now she can begin to manage it: She will diet.

The snowball has begun to roll. Any success at dieting—"Hey, I've lost two pounds in five days!"—provides a sense of accomplishment. Feelings of insecurity fade, replaced by a sense of mastery, competence, and self-control. Such emotions reinforce themselves. The greater the feeling of competence, the more she wants to feel competent. Success (weight loss) breeds the desire for more success (more weight loss).

Relief! No longer is she a passive, helpless victim of her inadequacy. Now she's regaining control over her life.

What's more, she feels relieved because weight loss reverses maturity. Menstruation stops. She becomes like a child again—physically, at least. Now she can "legitimately" avoid entering into more adult relationships. She reduces the risk of rejection and thus prevents damage to her fragile psyche. Preoccupied with her body, she focuses inwardly, avoiding the need to grow outwardly through interaction with other people.

The devastating effects of starvation are usually obvious. Sometimes, though, parents may be too close to the problem to see what is happening to their daughter until an outsider brings it to their attention.

Even if they fail to notice her weight loss, parents may find their daughter's eating behavior becoming increasingly strange. She dawdles over her meal for an hour, poking at her food, creating meticulous piles of peas or mashed-potato sculptures. She cuts her food into tiny pieces, nibbles one bite, then claims she is full. She puts herself in charge of all food shopping and preparation. She bakes cakes and cookies and insists that the family eat every bite, yet eats nothing herself. Eventually her preoccupation with food absorbs every waking moment. She may exercise compulsively for three, four, even five hours a day.

Starvation, though, is an unstable state. Besieged by hunger signals from her body, the girl must constantly resist the desire to eat. The longer she goes without food, the greater her hunger and the greater her preoccupation with eating.

In a weird way, this need for vigilance perpetuates the illness. Each victory over her appetite reinforces her sense that she is at last in control of her destiny. The thinner she gets, the higher her self-esteem; the higher her self-esteem, the greater her desire to be thin.

Sometimes, though, hunger becomes overpowering. The result: an eating binge. Horrified that she has failed, burdened by guilt over her weakness and loss of control, she resorts to drastic measures to purge herself of food.

In later chapters I'll pick up the scenario from this point and describe the physical, mental, and emotional impact of starvation. Briefly, though, I want to mention that at some point the body, robbed of a supply of nutrients, begins to steal from itself. That is, it "confiscates" essential chemicals stored in certain tissues, such as the protein required to keep muscles strong. Metabolism slows down to conserve dwindling fuel. Usually the anorexic begins to feel very cold; she may experience fainting spells.

Despite these warnings, the girl persists in her behavior, ignoring the pleas of family and friends and resisting the need for treatment. She sees as her enemy anyone who wants her to eat. I can't count the number of times I have confronted a patient with anorexia—a skeletal figure, pale, trembling with cold—who gazes at me through empty eyes and says, in effect: "Why do they want to take away the one thing that makes me special—my ability to be thin?"

How hard it is to convince these people of the one fact that everyone around them knows: Without treatment, they may die.

THE MAKING OF A BULIMIC

Bulimia may arise from anorexia; half or more of bulimics have a history of self-starvation. A traumatic event, such as a severe loss or change, may trigger the bulimic cycle. So too can an episode of dieting.

Binge eating is pretty common. Between 60 and 80 percent of American women report that they binge once in a while. Another 10 to 20 percent have weekly binge episodes. With statistics like these, we have to conclude that the *occasional* act of eating a lot of food in a short time is actually normal. Making a diagnosis of bulimia requires much more than that the person experiences an occasional binge.

As we have seen, different events can trigger increased bingeing. There may be a change in the chemical balance in the brain. We know that such changes occur in some types of depression and lead to the symptom of increased eating.

Psychologically, someone may use bingeing to control unpleasant or overwhelming feelings. Bingeing shifts one's mental focus. Eating a pound of cookies makes it easier to tolerate the anger one feels when denied a raise, for example. But bingeing then stirs up feelings of shame and inadequacy: "I *shouldn't* have done that." The binger thus takes the anger she feels toward her boss and redirects it toward herself. Eating also represents an act of revenge against the world; the binger knows she is doing something both forbidden and gratifying.

The intense sensory pleasure of (over)eating removes—or at least covers up—anxiety, such as dread of an upcoming school examination. Bingeing thus relieves tension in the same way as drugs or alcohol. Furthermore, bingeing produces chemical changes in the brain, changes that may have some direct anxiety-reducing effect.

Loss of control during a binge leads to self-disgust. Strangely, that self-disgust may also serve to reduce anxiety. Before the binge, the woman is haunted by the thought: "I may fail." Afterward, though, a new thought dominates: "I have *already* failed." Her burden is lifted; now she has little left to lose.

Bingeing also provides a familiar and dependable mental state, an escape from the emotional roller coaster. Many patients tell me they originally needed such an escape because of their chaotic family situation—for example, because the father came home drunk and abusive night after night. Others report that a binge provides "company" during times of painful loneliness.

Purging (vomiting, laxative abuse) or excessive exercise also has psychological meaning. Purging acts as "damage control"—a way of canceling out excessive calories. It also offers a way for the "child" part of the personality to return the good graces of the "parent" part by accepting punishment for being naughty.

Purging lets a woman think, "I can do something bad but it doesn't really count." In some patients, this thought comes to dominate the pattern—in other words, purging, not bingeing, becomes the goal. At first a woman may purge to "cancel out" her binge. Over time, however, she finds she must binge *in order to purge.* Calories are seen as "bad"; therefore, the emptiness produced by vomiting or laxative abuse is "good." Purging restores control to a life that feels out of control.

Often a bulimic sees her "discovery" of purging as a positive thing. At first it makes her feel calmer or better able to cope with stress. She may even feel happy because she loses some weight in the early stages of her illness. Such weight loss, however, is unstable. The metabolic and nutritional chaos that comes with bulimia usually leads to more bingeing, which in turn may lead to weight gain. (Even when someone vomits immediately, the body retains as much as 25 percent of the calories contained in the meal.) Moreover, many bulimics interpret purging as "permission" to engage in more bingeing.

Bulimics keep their binge-purge habits secret because they feel ashamed. What may initially have begun as a *response* to upsetting feelings now *produces* upsetting feelings. The pattern becomes a habit. Thoughts and feelings about bingeing and purging occupy more and more of the patient's time. In fact, she may structure her entire day around her habit. Some make an after-work ritual out of buying binge food, eating it, and purging. As with drug abuse, such devotion to ritual may increase the patient's isolation from other people and keep her from taking part in a more normal social life. This in turn leaves her with more empty time on her hands; usually she fills that time with even more bingeing and purging. If something happens to prevent her from indulging her habit—social obligations, work pressure—she grows increasingly anxious.

In severe cases, a bulimic purges so frequently that the mere feeling of having food in her stomach produces the overwhelming desire to get rid of it. Similarly, anxiety caused by the very act of eating may be severe enough to promote purging. Frequently, the bulimic tries to distract herself as she eats by reading, watching TV, and so on. Doing so just makes it easier to eat large amounts without being aware of it.

In bulimia, *overcontrol produces lack of control.* Trying to govern something that is ungovernable—the need to eat—just leads to the feeling that one is out of control. That feeling in turn drives a woman to exert even *more* control—and so the vicious cycle continues.

How does this happen? In several ways. After a binge-purge episode, a woman usually skips the next meal or two. Her hunger increases. Her body's cry for food grows stronger, pushing her closer to the inevitable binge.

Unrealistically strict diets have the same effect. Under such regimes a woman sets up rigid rules. She believes she must follow these rules *perfectly.* There is no margin for error. The trouble is that such rules are impossible to follow all the time. Once she breaks a rule, as she inevitably will, her thoughts spiral out of control. She thinks, "All is lost! I might as well go ahead and eat anything I want now, since I'm such a failure anyway." And voilà—a binge.

Some women go a step further. They try to hold off bingeing by distracting themselves through abuse of alcohol or illicit drugs. Unfortunately, these substances cause the woman to "let her guard down." Once she surrenders her willpower, the urge to binge takes over. Now she not only binges and purges, she suffers from substance abuse as well.

One last point: Many women create strict rules about their personal appearance. As one patient said, "If I weigh more than a hundred pounds I can't go out. I'll call in sick at work. And I won't be lying either—weighing more than a hundred pounds *is* sick!" The more such women stay home, the more isolated they become from other people. Lonely, depressed, and bored, they succumb to the temptation to binge.

The bulimic process, like the process of anorexia, eventually takes on a life of its own. The metabolic damage of purging impairs the ability to think clearly. Patients may describe themselves as being "in a fog" all day long. In time, the illness produces devastating feelings of depression, sometimes leading to thoughts (or even acts) of suicide.

There is much more to say about these illnesses, their patterns, and the impact they have on those who suffer from them. I include these brief sketches here hoping that you will recognize whether your own pattern, or that of someone close to you, reflects an eating disorder—and, if so, that you will recognize the stage the illness has reached.

Remember: The sooner you seek help, the greater the chance of recovery.

3

Anorexia Nervosa: Starving for Attention

Diagnosis—giving a name to a medical condition—is a critical moment in the process of helping a patient get better. Making this decision represents a moment in which the past, the present, and the future all converge.

The past is the patient's history: her background, the onset of the illness, and the course along which it has progressed.

The present is the patient herself, sitting before me here and now, a troubled and suffering human being.

The future depends on the accuracy of my insight and the wisdom with which I select the course of treatment.

The Greek roots of the word *diagnosis* mean "to perceive something apart from something else." When I diagnose an illness, not only must I *perceive*—recognize and identify—the signs and symptoms, I must also distinguish the disorder—*set it apart*—from the dozens of other conditions that might resemble it. The more precise and accurate our definitions, the easier my job becomes.

Let me illustrate this point by telling you about a patient I encountered in 1982. The year is significant, as I'll explain.

THE TROUBLE WITH PAULA

My interview with Paula was going nowhere. For nearly forty-five minutes this patient ducked my questions like a master politician. She refused to reveal her most precious secrets: her eating behavior and her attitudes toward food.

Paula appeared angry and was holding back because from her point of view I was trying to take away something valuable: her thinness.

Eighteen years old and standing five foot one, Paula weighed less than ninety pounds. She had lost twenty pounds in the past six months. Despite her haggard appearance and the fact that her menstrual periods had stopped, she continued to deny that anything unusual was happening to her. I was almost certain that she had anorexia nervosa, but I still needed to collect some more information before I could make a firm diagnosis.

Paula knew she had lost weight—it would be hard to ignore the evidence in her mirror, although a good number of anorexics manage to do just that. "I know I look thin," she remarked. "Everyone says so. But they don't understand—and you don't either. I *feel* fat. That's what's important."

I agreed with her that her feelings were important. But I also asked her, in light of her diminishing weight, what kinds of medical problems she had been experiencing.

"I don't have a problem!" she exploded angrily. "*You* have the problem! I was scared to death of turning into an immense fat pig, and so I decided to do something about it. *And I did.* Now everybody just wants to interfere—you, my parents, my stupid friends. I finally found something I could do to get control of my life, something I'm good at, and all you people want to do is mess it up. Why? *Why do you want to make me fat?*"

We sat in silence for what seemed like an eternity but was only a moment or two. Then, her eyes fixed on a spot on the rug, Paula muttered, "Go ahead. Put me in the hospital. Force me to eat. I'll just get rid of it."

"What do you mean?" I asked.

"Whenever I pig out, I just throw it up again anyway. That's another thing I've gotten very good at."

I sensed that Paula had said more than she intended to. Or, to put it differently, the part of her that wanted to get better and that realized what trouble she was in had just revealed one of her most important secrets.

As I said, my first guess was that Paula was anorexic. In writing up the notes of my interview, however, I hesitated when it came to entering the diagnosis. I had felt a similar hesitation in dealing with a number of cases prior to this one.

I took from my shelf the "cookbook" of psychiatric diagnosis, the *Diagnostic and Statistical Manual of Mental Disorders—Third Edition,* known as the *DSM-III,* published in 1980 by the American Psychiatric Association. I reread the list of the criteria for anorexia nervosa. Here they are in a somewhat abbreviated form:

1. *Intense fear of becoming obese that does not diminish as weight loss progresses.* (That fit; although losing weight, Paula herself had said she was "scared to death" of becoming a "fat pig.")
2. *Disturbance of body image.* (Yes, she "felt fat" even though she knew, objectively, that she was thin.)
3. *Weight loss of at least 25 percent of original body weight.* (Not quite; the figure was closer to 18 percent.)
4. *Refusal to maintain body weight over a minimal normal weight for age and height.* (True.)
5. *No known physical illness that would account for the weight loss.* (Her medical records, a thorough examination, and lab tests had revealed no disease or metabolic abnormality.)

Strictly speaking, Paula didn't meet the criteria for classic anorexia because she hadn't lost enough weight.

There was more, though. Something Paula had said just didn't make sense, didn't fit in with the way the illness was defined in these professional guidelines. She had inadvertently admitted that she would sometimes go on an eating binge ("pig out," as she put it). What's more, she claimed she was very good at throwing up her food when she wanted to.

But the manual didn't acknowledge this symptom as one of the diagnostic criteria of anorexia. Instead, binge eating followed by self-induced vomiting was included as part of the criteria for another disorder entirely: bulimia. The guidelines specified that the bulimic episodes *could not be due to anorexia nervosa* or any known physical disorder. In the section on anorexia nervosa, though, they stated that if an episode of self-starvation occurs in a person with *bulimia,* then it's acceptable to give both diagnoses.

This was like saying, "Cats and dogs have nothing in common, but some dogs have things in common with cats." A logical impossibility!

How was I to fill in the blank labeled "Diagnosis" on Paula's chart? Here was a woman whose symptoms in many ways fit the description of anorexia nervosa. Yet I could not enter this diagnosis because technically her weight loss wasn't quite severe enough. Nor did the diagnosis of bulimia fit very well. The guidelines clearly stated that the bulimia must not have been caused by the anorexia.

Again, this was in 1982. The edition of the diagnostic manual then in use was the first one in which bulimia appeared as an "officially recognized" psychiatric disorder—truly a step forward. But the description of bulimia, however well-meant, was little more than a first draft, based on early experience with a limited number of patients. The theory—the description of eating disorders in the *DSM-III*—didn't match the reality as represented by patients like Paula.

I was by no means the only physician who noticed this discrepancy. It was the subject of much heated discussion in the medical literature, at professional assemblies, and in countless private conversations.

For Paula, the best diagnosis available at the time was "atypical eating disorder." This catchall category included anybody who didn't quite meet the criteria for anorexia or bulimia. However, this diagnosis failed to provide much helpful information. It didn't specifically mention self-starvation, low body weight, or binging and vomiting. Like other physicians treating eating disorders, I was dealing with a patient who had a fairly common form of the illness but whose problem was not acknowledged in the official guidelines.

RECENT CHANGES IN EATING DISORDERS

I've told Paula's story to make the point that the definitions of eating disorders, and thus our ability to diagnose them, are only reflections of the degree to which we understand the disorders themselves. As our experience with these disorders broadens, our descriptions of them—and thus our diagnoses—become more precise.

Once the media got wind that a new eating disorder existed, they made bulimia into a kind of psychological superstar, one of the "fad" diseases of the decade. The whirlwind of attention produced a lot of misinformation about the illness. One positive aspect of this publicity, however, was that many people learned about the illness, recognized it in themselves, and sought help.

Almost immediately after the *DSM-III* appeared, psychiatrists began to revise it, not just to refine the information on eating disorders, but to reexamine virtually all the other diagnostic categories as well.

The results appeared in the *DSM-III-R* ("R" is for revised), published in 1987. The changes made in the criteria for anorexia and bulimia reflected the explosion of knowledge about these conditions and how they can affect different people in different ways.

If I met Paula today, I could "officially" indicate a diagnosis of *both* anorexia nervosa and bulimia nervosa—or what can also be called bulimic anorexia. In this way I could distinguish Paula from a patient who does not binge and purge, but who starves herself to the point of emaciation—a condition which could be referred to as "restricting anorexia." This refinement in our perspective has powerful implications for the course and outcome of treatment.

Let's take a look now at how the new, improved *DSM-III-R* describes anorexia nervosa. In the next chapter we'll do the same for bulimia.

DIAGNOSTIC CRITERIA FOR ANOREXIA NERVOSA

A. Refusal to maintain body weight over a minimal normal weight for age and height, e.g., weight loss leading to maintenance of body weight 15 percent below that expected; or failure to make expected weight gain during period of growth, leading to body weight 15 percent below that expected.

B. Intense fear of gaining weight or becoming fat, even though underweight.

C. Disturbance in the way in which one's body weight, size, or shape is experienced, e.g., the person claims to "feel fat" even when emaciated, believes that one area of the body is "too fat" even when obviously underweight.

D. In females, absence of at least three consecutive menstrual cycles when otherwise expected to occur (primary or secondary amenorrhea). (A woman is considered to have amenorrhea if her periods occur only following hormone, e.g., estrogen, administration.)*

The first guideline, Criterion A, gives physicians an objective means of measuring the degree to which a person is emaciated: 15 percent below minimum normal body weight. The question of what constitutes "normal weight" is tricky, as I'll explain later in

Diagnostic and Statistical Manual of Mental Disorders (Third Edition—Revised). Washington, D.C.: American Psychiatric Association, 1987, p. 67.

this book. This 15 percent figure (a somewhat arbitrary number, but still useful) is considerably less than the 25 percent given in the earlier edition. The change reflects the reality: Like other clinicians, I have seen numerous patients who seem to have anorexia but who, like Paula, haven't lost enough weight to meet the criteria.

You might be puzzled by the use of the term "refusal to maintain body weight." Doesn't the word "refusal" suggest that the patient has made a *conscious* decision to act (or not act) in a certain way?

Yes, that's true, but it still doesn't mean that the anorexia is the patient's fault. You have to think of the "decision" to lose weight as one made under duress. In a sense, the brain is held hostage to the disease and can't think clearly. Anorexia is not a well-thought-out, rational plan; it's more like a compulsion.

Still, such refusal makes life difficult for doctors as well as patients. Many a hospitalized patient declares war on the doctors and the staff. She sees them as members of a conspiracy whose evil aim is to force her to become fat. Patients may feel that they are being hunted down and annihilated by the "fat-doctors." The patients, who see themselves as valiant rebels fighting to preserve freedom, will do anything to thwart this scheme: hide butter under the tray, spit out bites of food into their milk glass, exercise frantically while lying in bed, even run away from the hospital. Naturally, it's hard to build a sense of trust and mutual cooperation under such circumstances.

One more point. The first diagnostic guideline lets us think of body weight in one of two ways: either as *weight actually lost* or *weight never gained.* The difference is important. Some anorexics feel fat *now,* and thus want to shed pounds. Others, particularly the younger ones, fear becoming fat *in the future,* and thus starve themselves to keep from gaining weight in the first place. It's not necessary for a woman to reach a certain weight and then lose it in order to be considered an anorexic.

Criterion B mentions the intense fear of becoming fat. The earlier *DSM* specified that this fear doesn't diminish even as weight loss progresses. The new version lets us acknowledge the presence of anorexia even in those cases where the woman reports that the fear does lessen as her weight shrinks.

Criterion C expands the concept of disturbed body image. The disturbance might now reflect the patient's perception of her body size or shape, as well as her weight. It also identifies a common anorexic symptom: the tendency to isolate and focus on one part of the body in particular.

Not long ago I visited a patient named Caitlin in her room at the hospital. In the course of our conversation, I indicated that she was making progress and was now eligible to go for short walks outside the hospital.

"I can't do that!" she wailed. She threw back the bedclothes to reveal her legs, each of which wasn't much thicker than a baseball bat. She pinched the skin between her fingers—she had to try a couple of times before she could actually grab anything—and shouted, "*Look* at this fat thigh! I can't go out in public looking like this!"

The final criterion, D, acknowledges a feature of anorexia that the previous guidelines ignored: the loss of menses (menstrual periods), specifically three periods in a row, at some time during the course of the illness. In about four out of five cases, the loss of menses (also called amenorrhea) occurs as a direct result of starvation. Without proper nutrition, the brain senses that there is not sufficient energy for menstruation and doesn't supply the "on" signal to the reproductive organs. (In male anorexics the equivalent problem is a loss of interest in sex, usually due to a reduction in the amount of testosterone produced.)

In another 20 percent of female patients, however, amenorrhea occurs *before* significant weight loss—that is, before starvation takes its toll. Sometimes a report of skipped periods is nothing more than a figment of the patient's faulty memory. But not always.

The fact that some anorexics stop having periods *before* they lose weight may be evidence of a biological problem, at least in some cases. Because the hypothalamus regulates both eating and the reproductive system, any malfunction may affect both systems.

Other problems can also cause the loss of menses before weight loss occurs. In order to menstruate, a woman's body needs not just sufficient weight, but a certain reserve of energy as well. Female athletes, for example, may eat adequate meals and maintain proper weight. But they may expend so much energy during exercise that they deplete their reserves. Menstruation then stops. Also, through chemical changes we don't yet fully understand, emotional stress can interrupt the monthly cycle.

ANOREXIA: A CLOSER LOOK

The *DSM-III-R* is more than just a psychiatric cookbook. No mere list of diagnostic criteria can describe the many ways a mental disorder affects people, while diagnosing by symptoms alone will not fully explain a condition. To enhance its usefulness, the manual describes some of the other features of anorexia nervosa.

For example, it notes the different ways weight loss can occur. One woman might rely on reduced food intake alone. Another might reduce intake but exercise excessively as well. Others use self-induced vomiting or laxatives or diuretics. The manual thus acknowledges that bulimia and anorexia may indeed coexist, as we saw in Paula's case.

The compulsion to exercise is very common in anorexia. Even doctors a century ago recognized the symptom. Today I see this trait in patients such as Roberta. Several times a week she would go into the bathroom in her hospital room and stay there for a suspiciously long time. The nursing staff would grow concerned, wondering if perhaps she might be trying to induce vomiting. As it turned out, Roberta used the bathroom as her personal gym, sneaking in a few more sit-ups and push-ups.

Many anorexics feel they have to *run* everywhere, that walking is just a missed opportunity to burn off more calories. Parents often tell me that their anorexic daughter "never stands still" or that she "always runs up the stairs" or that she "pedals her exercise bike until after midnight."

Anorexics aren't driven to exercise because they want to be physically fit. They simply want to burn off energy (and thus weight) in any way possible. Excessive exercise may also trigger some pleasurable changes in brain chemistry, producing effects such as the "runner's high" that many joggers report. Thus anorexics may exercise to experience a neurochemical "reward."

Besides exercise, other weight-loss methods include use of laxatives to stimulate bowel movements or diuretics to decrease water in the body. Anorexics frequently resort to such tricks to speed up the removal of food from the body.

The results can be disastrous. Many patients—some of whom use between thirty and a hundred laxative tablets *a day*—report cramps and abdominal pain. What's more, the body, robbed of its ability to regulate elimination on its own, can become dependent on a laxative. I find that weaning patients from laxatives is one of the hardest tasks in treating eating disorders.

Laxatives and diuretics can produce severe dehydration and electrolyte imbalance. Electrolytes are chemicals such as sodium and potassium that help transmit electrical signals within the body. An insufficient supply of electrolytes puts tissues and organs, particularly the heart, at risk of failure. Patients who abuse laxatives and diuretics risk problems with their hearts and other organs, problems that in some cases lead to death. Ironically, laxatives don't even help that much. A laxative abuser loses no more than 10 percent of available calories through this method, and most of the weight loss is merely "water weight" anyway, as I mentioned earlier.

Of course, the problem with starving yourself is that you're always hungry. No matter how carefully you defend yourself against food, sooner or later you will have to eat something or die. Because the hunger can be overwhelming, eating even small amounts can trigger a binge.

For people with these disorders, eating anything, especially when it leads to a binge, represents loss of control. Vomiting restores control—at least until the next urge to eat comes along.

About half of all anorexics practice self-induced vomiting. I'll have more to say about the physiological impact of vomiting in the discussion about bulimia in the next chapter.

By acknowledging these weight-loss practices, the *DSM-III-R* recognizes the differences between anorexics who attempt to starve themselves exclusively through reduced food intake (restricting anorexics) and those who reduce weight by extraordinary means (bulimic anorexics).

The manual goes on to describe some of the other common features of anorexia nervosa—for example, the "magic power" that food has over its victims.

Once I discovered that a patient named Debbie had stuffed whole packages of cookies, cheese, fruit, and candy into her underwear drawer in her hospital room. When I asked whether she was preparing for an eating binge, she replied, "Oh, no. I'm not going to eat that stuff. I just keep it there to show myself how much control I have over it. The more food I can lay my hands on, the greater the temptation to eat. And the more I can hold out and not eat, the stronger I feel."

Like Debbie, many anorexics exhibit peculiar behavior connected to food. They imbue food with enormous, almost supernatural force. Some prepare elaborate meals for their families, but eat nothing themselves. Or they toy with the food on their plate, poking it around with their forks, and finally throwing the whole meal away.

As Paula's case demonstrated, anorexics often deny that they have any problem whatsoever. They see their starvation not as a defect, but as something that makes them *special*. "Look at me," they seem to say. "See how much control I have over my body." Almost every one of my patients, at one time or another in the course of her illness, will feel something to the effect that "Not everyone can do this."

Because they deny the problem, anorexics feel that therapy, or any attempt to intervene, constitutes a deadly threat, a plot to rob them of their "specialness." Needless to say, such an attitude makes my job as their doctor much more difficult.

SPLITTING HAIRS: THE DIFFERENTIAL DIAGNOSIS

Of course, features of any one particular illness often occur in other conditions as well. Colds cause runny noses and watery eyes, but so do allergies.

The same principle—the crossover of symptoms—applies to eating disorders. In fact, one expert referred to anorexia nervosa as one of the "great pretenders."

An endocrinologist might conclude that weight loss results from hyperthyroidism or Addison's disease (a malfunction of the adrenal glands that results in inadequate supplies of hormones). A gastroenterologist might suspect a disease of the bowels that prevents adequate absorption of nutrients, a neurologist might wonder about a defect in the hypothalamus or the possibility of epilepsy, and so on.

As a biopsychiatrist, I look for signs that some organic illness or abnormality is causing the patient's eating problem. A physical examination and lab tests will usually reveal whether some underlying illness, perhaps a tumor or some other condition, is causing the weight loss, the swelling of the ankles, the low blood pressure, and the extreme sensitivity to cold.

Many psychiatric and physical illnesses cause weight loss. With other illnesses, however, the patient usually complains about the problem, or is at least indifferent to it. In contrast, *the anorexic takes inordinate pride in her thinness.*

Depression—a symptom of anorexia in a certain number of patients—is also widespread. Depression can exist as a disorder of its own, with its own defined set of features, or it can arise from many organic illnesses. Sometimes feelings of depression are a natural, even healthy response to a troubling situation, such as the loss of a loved one.

Prolonged depression can lead to weight loss. But depressed individuals do not usually experience disturbance of body image or fear of fatness. Such attitudes signal the presence of anorexia.

People with schizophrenia often experience warped beliefs

and behaviors related to food and eating. Typically, schizophrenics might maintain that their meal has been poisoned, or that "Martians have put aphrodisiacs in the water supply." They might also eat in weird ways that resemble the bizarre habits of an anorexic. But a schizophrenic usually will not meet the full set of criteria for anorexia. In rare cases, however, both disorders can be found in the same individual.

The behavior of the anorexic often suggests the presence of an obsessive-compulsive disorder. To illustrate, let me tell you about an anorexic patient named Sonya.

The day Sonya arrived at the hospital, I stopped by her room and saw her unpacking her suitcase. I saw that she had wrapped *everything* she had brought—toothbrush, underwear, books, a favorite cuddly toy—in aluminum foil. She had then placed each foil ball in a separate plastic bag.

Sonya noticed the somewhat startled look on my face. "Germs," she said tersely.

In my years of experience with eating disorders, I had never seen anything like it. She seemed to be laying in a year's supply of foil-wrapped baked potatoes. It's possible that even before her anorexia struck, Sonya, like some other eating disorder patients, may have had an obsessive-compulsive disorder. This is a very hot area of current research, and there seems to be more of an overlap than was previously thought between anorexia nervosa and an obsessive-compulsive disorder (OCD). Medications that are useful in OCD, such as Prozac (fluoxetine), may prove quite helpful in treating anorexia nervosa. It is important to remember, however, that starvation itself will increase obsessional thinking.

A WORD ABOUT ANOREXIA IN MALES

Although self-starvation in men is rare, it does occur. In fact, a paper published in 1694 by the physician Richard Morton—generally recognized as the first unequivocal description of anorexia—describes two cases, one of whom was a sixteen-year-old boy. As the author stated:

[The boy] fell gradually into a total want of appetite, occasioned by his studying too hard, and the passions of his mind, and upon that into a universal atrophy, pining away more and more for the space of two years . . . I advis'd him to abandon his studies, to go into the country air, and to use riding, and milk diet (and especially to drink Asses milk) for a long time. By the use of which he recovered his health in a great measure, though he is not yet perfectly freed from a consumptive state . . .

The criteria for diagnosing anorexia are virtually the same in both sexes. Like female anorexics, male anorexics starve themselves and may or may not use self-induced vomiting or some other extreme means of weight control. Males experience fear of fatness related to loss of control over eating. Paralleling the female's loss of menstruation, there is a disorder in the activity of the reproductive hormones. This leads to a decline of interest in sex and a decrease in ability to perform.

The pattern that anorexia follows in men and women is also similar. Although the illness occurs in people from all social levels, there is a disproportionately high incidence among the upper classes. Depression is more common in families with a male anorexic member; his siblings are also more likely than average to have anorexia nervosa. Some anorexic males are involved in activities in which low weight or weight control is valued. Those at particular risk include jockeys, ballet dancers, wrestlers, flight attendants, and models.

The illness usually begins during the boy's adolescent years. The trigger is often an attempt at dieting, although it may also be a stressful life event, a disappointment caused by failure at school, or a social loss such as rejection by a girlfriend. Sometimes a prolonged illness leads to weight loss. If the boy sees the loss as desirable for some reason, he may decide to continue starving himself.

Homosexuality is *not* a criterion. Part of the tragedy of eating disorders is that they strike vulnerable individuals at a time of life—adolescence—that is already fraught with enough emotional and physical turmoil to last a lifetime. During the teen years, young people have their hands full trying to recognize just who they are and to incorporate that awareness into their personalities. Confusion reigns—confusion about gender identity, social roles, self-worth. Youngsters who start out with low self-esteem and poor ego defenses may feel successful in achieving thinness. That feeling then escalates into a vicious cycle of anorexia.

These young men, like anorexic young women, are literally starving for attention.

A DIAGNOSTIC SUMMARY

Arriving at a diagnosis of anorexia nervosa is not just a matter of looking at an emaciated teenage girl and filling in a line on a medical chart. As a physician, my task is to look at the whole context of the problem: her past history, her family and social milieu, and her present physical and emotional signs and symptoms. Were you to come to me, I would carefully evaluate you, medically and psychiatrically, to rule out the presence of another disorder that would require a different therapeutic strategy altogether.

Most important, my goal is to understand you as a human being suffering from a distorted perspective on life. I look at the problem from *your* point of view. A person with anorexia invariably feels she has a *good reason* for doing what she does. I hope to learn why you feel compelled to solve your problem through dangerous control over your eating behavior.

As we have seen, though, a patient's very ability to reason and to think clearly is diminished by both the presence of disease and the effects of starvation. It does no good, as her family has already discovered, to argue with her, to tell her to change or to "just snap out of it." It's better if I try to connect with her by showing that I understand how she feels and thinks. Sometimes a simple comment—"I won't argue with you; many anorexics feel that way"— opens doorways into her mind.

In my practice, a diagnosis means more than just giving a name to the disorder. It is also the beginning of the effort to find out why the disorder exists in this particular person at this particular time in her life. Once we have discovered *why,* the patient and I can then begin to find out *how* we might solve the problem.

4

Bulimia Nervosa: The Dirty Little Secret

Gina cried as she recalled her fourteenth birthday party. At the time, she told me, she stood five foot six and tipped the scales at 150 pounds. She felt that she was heavy, but up until that afternoon she had never paid much attention to her body size. "I'm just big-boned," she would think, or, "It'll be different when I get a little older."

But suddenly, during her party, things changed. She had just finished cutting the cake and was handing out plates. One of the guests, thinking he couldn't be heard, whispered to the girl next to him: "I'm surprised she didn't eat it all before we got here."

Gina remembers how her face flushed and her head began to pound. She tried to pretend she hadn't heard the remark.

But she *had* heard it.

And those words continued to echo in her head as she spoke to me in my office on a spring day nearly four years later.

Through her tears, Gina told me that from that moment on all she could think about was how *fat* she was.

She started to believe that whenever people looked at her, they thought, "What a pig!" If she went to a restaurant, she "just knew" that everyone noticed what she ordered. Gina imagined their conversations: "That blimp. She doesn't need that. Why do people like her eat in public? You'd think she'd realize . . ."

Gina started dieting and managed to lose a few pounds. Somehow, though, she "just couldn't keep the weight off." She imagined that her body was somehow *determined* to weigh a certain amount and that it was fighting her every effort to shed pounds.

She realized that she'd have to do something drastic, although she wasn't sure what that would be.

Then one night she watched a TV program that described people who went on eating binges and then induced vomiting to rid themselves of the food. As she remembers, "I was disgusted but fascinated at the same time. Something tingled inside me. I knew I would have to try it."

Try it she did. Within a year she was vomiting every other day.

To lose even more weight, she skipped breakfast. Eventually she omitted both breakfast and lunch. Ironically, she took a job in a fast-food restaurant near her home. From three o'clock, when classes ended, until her shift was over around ten, she was surrounded by greasy, high-calorie foods. Despite not having eaten since the day before, she suppressed her appetite until her dinner break at six o'clock.

At first she snacked on small amounts of french fries and onion rings. When she'd eaten enough she ducked into the bathroom and threw up.

Arriving home late in the evening, she would fix dinner for herself, the rest of the family having eaten hours before. Alone, she raided the kitchen, consuming whole packages of cold cuts, potato chips, cookies—"whatever was there."

She told me that she always ate "just as fast as I could, before anyone could catch me." She then ran to the bathroom, stuck two fingers down her throat, and puked. She began to follow this routine daily.

The pattern persisted for some time. After a while, thoughts of food and eating filled her every waking moment. She still skipped breakfast and lunch, but by mid-afternoon hunger overwhelmed her. She sneaked food at work, even though she knew that she could be fired if she got caught. Regardless, she scarfed down bags of french fries, three or four chicken and cheese sandwiches, onion rings—even cold sausages from the refrigerator. Once back home she ate leftover steak, rice, potatoes, salad, and several scoops of ice cream.

None of this stayed down for long; she made herself vomit as soon as she finished.

Then the stress level rose. Her grandmother, with whom she was extremely close, died. Her best friends left for college. Her boyfriend began working two jobs and had little time for her.

At home, Gina's parents began arguing more than usual. Her father took a position with a trucking company that required him to be away from home for a week at a stretch. Sobbing, Gina told me that during this time, "everyone left me."

Although she denied any connection, Gina soon experienced a huge increase in the food she consumed. At work she ate "anything that wasn't already in the customer's hand. I was out of control. I poured scoopfuls of french fries into my gullet—I didn't even bother chewing. I ate six pieces of chicken and hardly stopped to breathe."

She now vomited two or three times per shift. So adept had she become at inducing vomiting that any food—"even an animal cookie"—was enough to trigger a purge.

Vomiting is an exhausting activity. After her shift Gina would go home and fall into bed. After a few hours, though, she would awaken ravenous, and clean out the cupboards. If there wasn't enough food, she went to a friend's house and ate cheese sandwiches and snack foods.

About this time she became increasingly obsessed with her weight. She stepped on the scales three or four times a day. If she registered a gain she would nibble on a cookie merely to trigger the urge to vomit. Even when she had dropped to 115 pounds, she still "felt fat."

In the three months before I saw her, Gina deteriorated. She was sleeping poorly at night—a common problem with eating disorders—and began sleeping more during the day. She couldn't concentrate, nor could she enjoy anything except the act of eating and purging.

With these pressures increasing, Gina got into a big fight with her boyfriend and he suggested they end the relationship. Furious, she went home and took a handful of antibiotic pills—nothing deadly, but a threatening gesture of suicide nonetheless.

The next day at school she appeared pale, weak, and distraught. A concerned friend asked what was wrong, and Gina, weeping, poured out her story of bingeing and purging. The friend spoke to their high school counselor, who informed Gina's parents and recommended that she be checked into our hospital.

Gina's friend was a friend indeed—she probably saved her life.

I've told Gina's story in such detail because she illustrates so many features of bulimia nervosa. I hesitate to call Gina a typical bulimic, however. There are so many different ways the disorder can affect people that the word *typical* loses its meaning.

DEFINING BULIMIA NERVOSA

In the previous chapter I mentioned that bulimia first appeared in the list of "official" mental disorders only as recently as 1980, and that the original criteria for diagnosing the condition served as little more than a well-intentioned first draft. The *DSM-III-R*, published in 1987, substantially improved its definition of bulimia, largely because physicians had had time to study many more patients with the condition. The revised definition reads as follows:

DIAGNOSTIC CRITERIA FOR BULIMIA NERVOSA

A. Recurrent episodes of binge eating (rapid consumption of a large amount of food in a discrete period of time).

B. A feeling of lack of control over eating behavior during the eating binges.

C. The person regularly engages in either self-induced vomiting, use of laxatives or diuretics, strict dieting or fasting, or vigorous exercise in order to prevent weight gain.

D. A minimum average of two binge eating episodes a week for at least three months.

E. Persistent overconcern with body shape and weight.*

One subtle but significant change appears in the very name given to the illness: from bulimia to bulimia nervosa. Such a change, never made lightly, was the result of intense debate by experts on both sides of the Atlantic.

When the disorder first attracted notice, experts focused attention on the single *symptom* of bulimia—"ox hunger," or uncontrolled bouts of overeating. Bulimics resemble anorexics in many ways, especially in their attitudes about body shape and weight. The main difference, however, is that a bulimic's weight is more likely to fluctuate—sometimes wildly—yet on the average it tends to stay within the normal range. An anorexic, by contrast, falls considerably below even a minimal normal weight.

Different experts proposed a variety of terms to identify these patients. A British physician, Gerald Russell, introduced the term *bulimia nervosa* in 1979. The name identifies more than just the symptom of overeating and helps forge a link with anorexia nervosa. Of course, you can't please all the people all the time, espe-

Diagnostic and Statistical Manual of Mental Disorders (Third Edition—Revised). Washington, D.C.: American Psychiatric Association, 1987, pp. 68–69.

cially when those people are doctors. The controversy over the name continues.

The first criterion in the *DSM-III-R* attempts to define an eating binge. Even so, the definition is somewhat vague: What exactly constitutes "a large amount of food"? How rapid is "rapid"? And what qualifies as a "discrete period of time"?

Actually, this vagueness is purposeful and has its advantages. It grants physicians some leeway in applying the standard to different patients. Sally might eat half as much as Shirley, but both their meals might be considered "large."

"Rapid" simply suggests that the food is consumed quickly. A normal person might eat a normal meal in, say, half an hour. At a formal dinner she might eat a larger amount of food, but that dinner might stretch out over the entire evening. In contrast, a bulimic will often gorge herself as quickly as she can, sometimes eating a day's worth of food within fifteen minutes.

"Discrete time" sidesteps the need to specify the period over which the patient eats. This is an improvement over the 1980 version of the *DSM,* which stated that the binge usually takes "less than two hours." True, most binges occur within that time, but I treat patients who get home from work around six o'clock and begin eating whatever they can find. When that's gone they send out for pizza. Finally, around ten o'clock they make a beeline for the convenience store, where they buy as much ice cream and as many cookies as they have money for, then dash home and continue eating. These people qualify as bulimics, even if their eating binge doesn't quite match the original guideline.

The second criterion makes the crucial point that the bulimic feels her eating behavior is out of control. In this way she resembles alcoholics or drug addicts who also can't control their behavior. Her lack of control produces strong feelings of shame and inadequacy. To compensate she goes to extreme lengths to regain mastery, but as we have seen, such actions just perpetuate the vicious cycle.

The third criterion identifies the flip side of binge eating: weight control through extraordinary means. The authors of these revised guidelines felt that purging or other similar behavior was such a cardinal feature of the syndrome of bulimia that it deserved a listing of its own. The guideline also helps differentiate between bulimics, who tend to be of normal weight, and people who just overeat. This latter group may be overweight, a problem that requires a different therapeutic approach.

I should note, too, that this criterion doesn't necessarily mean that a bulimic will use only one method of weight control. Many patients, particularly those in the more advanced stages of the illness, combine several techniques. Vicky, for example, induced vomiting several times a week. She also exercised for at least an hour a day, ate only one meal a day, and took diuretics if she felt she was gaining weight.

The fourth criterion specifies that the pattern of bingeing and purging must reach a certain severity before medical intervention becomes necessary. By stating the frequency with which binges occur and by indicating that the behavior must persist for a certain period of time, the *DSM-III-R* helps differentiate those people with a severe disorder from those who might binge only occasionally. The actual figures (at least two episodes a week for three months) are useful but somewhat arbitrary.

The last criterion, addressing the bulimic's distorted attitudes about her body, appeared in the manual only after a lot of wrangling. Some physicians felt that bulimics showed their "overconcern" about the body simply through the extraordinary measures they use to control weight. Surely, they argued, self-induced vomiting *by itself* reflects overconcern about the effect of food; another criterion would just be redundant.

However, other experts felt that the extreme importance bulimics (and anorexics, for that matter) attach to body shape and weight is an *essential feature* of the illness. In fact, without evidence of these distorted attitudes, some physicians are reluctant to enter a diagnosis of bulimia, choosing to classify the problem as a type of depression or some other variety of disturbed eating.

In my practice, almost all of the people I see for bulimia express concern about body shape to one degree or another. If a patient doesn't appear to have these attitudes, I attribute their absence to my inability to perceive them, or to the patient's skillful ability at disguising them.

Some final notes. The 1980 criteria stated that depressed mood was an essential component of the illness. The new version drops that requirement. Many patients do have depressive symptoms. The strong association between eating disorders and depression suggests a possible link somewhere in the brain: The cause of one may be the cause of the other. In the past, some experts thought of eating disorders as just one subtype of depression.

Another change between the two versions eliminated the prohibition on diagnosing bulimia nervosa if the patient also had anorexia nervosa. Thus we can now indicate both diagnoses when it's appropriate to do so.

BULIMIA NERVOSA: A CLOSER LOOK

The *DSM-III-R* provides more than just a list of diagnostic criteria. It also describes other typical features of the disorder. For example, it notes that eating binges may occur either spontaneously or as a result of a breakdown in control. Many patients tell me that just *tasting* a desired food can start an avalanche of eating. One woman said she made a point of memorizing the locations of all the bakeries in her town, so that she could arrange her routes to avoid accidentally smelling fresh-baked doughnuts and pies.

On the other hand, the bulimic may devote a lot of time to planning her binges. A patient named Winnie told me that every Sunday morning she pored over the newspaper to look for food bargains at the local grocery stores. She always set aside several hours every weekend to trek to the store and stock up for the week's binges. Doing so evoked a whole range of emotions, from the pleasurable anticipation of eating such tasty foods to the worry about the effects of self-induced vomiting on her digestive system and the guilt about her behavior.

The food consumed during a binge is often high in calories, sweet, and able to be eaten rapidly—even without being chewed.

However, bulimics will eat almost any food—even salad or "health foods"—during a binge. A typical menu for one patient's binge might be two pounds of peanut M&M's, a gallon of ice cream, half a chicken, a package of raw Pillsbury chocolate-chip cookie dough, a microwave pizza, a tub of yogurt, and a box of Pop-Tarts. Studies show that the major difference between binge meals and normal meals is often the quantity of food consumed, not the type.

Patients often look on their bulimia as their "dirty little secret." Most go to great lengths to keep their bingeing and purging hidden. Often this means arranging circumstances so that the patient is alone when she eats. As we saw in Gina's case, her work schedule meant that she got home late in the evening. Once alone in the kitchen, she would eat the leftovers from the family meal. Many times, a bulimic turns down dates or refuses to join her friends at a restaurant because she feels she mustn't eat in front of others, lest her secret be revealed.

Other patients know they must conform to their family's schedules so as not to attract undue attention. They thus eat a normal meal, but may excuse themselves several times during the meal or immediately afterward to go to the bathroom and throw up. If questioned about their behavior, they'll blame the problem on a "urinary tract infection" or a "stomach virus." Although I've been in practice for a long time, the sheer ingenuity with which bulimics conceal their behavior never ceases to amaze me.

Interestingly, a binge does not necessarily stop when the food disappears—not as long as pizzas or Chinese food can be ordered by phone and grocery stores stay open twenty-four hours a day. Even the feeling of being full won't do it, a sign some experts believe means that something is wrong with the way the patient's brain perceives the feeling of fullness. No, the binge might continue to the point of physical pain, when it's no longer possible to cram in more food. Sometimes the binge stops only when the patient falls asleep. In some cases a family member might enter the room, or a visitor might come to the door, at which point the patient stops eating.

Self-induced vomiting often marks the end of the binge, the

return of control. The "punishment" has fit the "crime." For some bulimics, however, an empty stomach and the relief of abdominal pain mean that they can then turn around and begin all over again.

Surprisingly, vomiting itself can become habitual. Patients believe (wrongly) that because they are throwing up, they aren't absorbing any calories. Overeating becomes "okay" since it won't result in weight gain. They also learn the degree to which they can control vomiting. Some patients learn to trigger vomiting simply by applying a little pressure to the abdomen—an act that gets easier over time. For some patients, merely the sensation of having food in their stomachs can trigger intense urges to vomit. Others, however, need a full stomach in order to vomit, and thus need to eat large amounts before they can purge.

In terms of family background, a significant percentage of parents of bulimic children are obese. Obesity in childhood or during the teen years may predispose a girl to develop bulimia; the story of Gina illustrates this point. The incidence of depression is also higher among members of families with a bulimic child than in the population as a whole.

An eating binge can be seen as one kind of impulsive behavior. Many bulimics are unable to control other types of impulses as well. A considerable number have a history of stealing. One patient revealed that she sewed pockets inside her coats so she could shoplift food and other items more easily. Sometimes the stealing is motivated by the high cost of eating food in such quantities; sometimes it just reflects the way the patient interacts with her world. Some bulimics engage in promiscuous sexual behavior, having a large number of partners in short-term relationships. The incidence of alcoholism and abuse of illicit drugs is also higher than in nonbulimic populations.

SPLITTING HAIRS, PART II:
THE DIFFERENTIAL DIAGNOSIS

As with anorexia nervosa, the symptoms of bulimia nervosa might appear in a number of other physical and psychiatric conditions.

Take, for example, the problem of overeating, technically known as hyperphagia. The urge to consume excessive quantities of food can arise when the hypothalamus becomes damaged due to a head injury, tumor, or some other cause.

Endocrine disorders, such as diabetes or hyperthyroidism, can disrupt metabolism, causing the patient to burn energy at an abnormally high rate. When energy stores are depleted, the body, in a kind of metabolic panic, turns on the hunger drive to compensate.

Prescribed medications and illicit drugs also affect eating behavior. Some antidepressants and antipsychotic medications may increase appetite and lead to weight gain. Marijuana is a well-known cause of binge eating. In some patients, frequent abuse of marijuana contributes heavily to the bulimic cycle.

The congenital defect known as Prader-Willi syndrome causes ravenous appetite with poor ability to feel full; the eating thus continues unabated and leads to massive obesity. Abnormal eating occurs in the Kleine-Levin syndrome, which is also marked by periods of extreme sleepiness.

In most of these cases, it's easy to spot the cause of overeating. Sometimes, though, the cause is more subtle. One of my patients, a sixteen-year-old named Sarah, suffered from a form of epilepsy that produced certain kinds of brain seizures. Two years before, she had started dieting to become thin. She developed anorexia and later became bulimic as well. During a seizure she flew into a rage at any object that happened to be in sight at that moment—a lipstick container, a telephone, whatever.

Sometimes the focus of her rage was the food on her plate. Because food enraged her so much, she stopped eating, eventually losing so much weight that she had to be hospitalized. Specialized brain-wave recordings revealed that her seizures occurred in the part of the brain that controls emotional states, rather than in the part responsible for muscle activity. In Sarah's case, an anticonvulsant drug played a vital part in treating her eating disorder.

As in anorexia, the distorted attitudes and bizarre behavior caused by bulimia may be confused with other psychiatric illnesses such as schizophrenia. In rare cases, a patient may indeed have both an eating disorder and schizophrenia. Recognizing the presence of both conditions is crucial, since therapy designed to correct one problem may have no effect—or an adverse effect—on the other.

THE MEDICAL COMPLICATIONS OF BULIMIA NERVOSA

Bulimia does not produce physical symptoms in the same way that chicken pox does, for example. But there *are* physical consequences, most of which are actually side effects of overeating or vomiting. These complications can be grouped as follows:

Digestive Tract
   Stomach pain
   Abdominal swelling
   Pancreatitis
   Cramps
   Nausea
   Vomiting (involuntary)
   Rupture
Malnutrition
   Electrolyte imbalance
   Hair loss
   Softening or discoloration of fingernails
   Weakness
   Dental decay
Neurological Changes
   Depression
   Mood changes
   Disturbed sleep
   Abnormal brain waves
   Muscle spasms
   Tingling sensations

Endocrine Changes
  Thirst
  Dehydration
  Amenorrhea (absence of menstruation)
Due to Vomiting
  Fluid loss
  Edema
  Burning sensations in the mouth and esophagus
  Dental decay
  Electrolyte imbalance
  Scars on the hands (When fingers are thrust in the back of
    the throat to trigger vomiting, they can involuntarily
    be bitten.)
Due to Laxatives, Diuretics, Diet Pills
  Malabsorption
  Cramps
  Kidney damage
  Swelling in the fingers
  Withdrawal symptoms (constipation)
  Increased (rebound) appetite
  Mood swings, increased irritability
Death

When you eat vast amounts of food in a short period of time, you place a severe strain on your body's ability to function. The stomach is only so large; when stretched too far, pain and nausea may result, as may involuntary vomiting. There are rare reports of people who have died when their stomachs burst from overfilling.

As food enters the body, the gastrointestinal organs begin the process of digestion and send feedback signals to the brain to regulate the process. However, overstimulation caused by a food binge can disrupt body function. The pancreas, for example, secretes some of the enzymes necessary to break down food in the stomach. When forced to overproduce, such as during a binge, the pancreas becomes irritated. The resulting condition, known as pancreatitis, causes abdominal pain, abdominal distension, nausea, and vomiting.

Binge eaters, of course, don't worry too much about a balanced diet, but the consequences of malnutrition also include hair loss, discoloring or softening of the fingernails, and weakness. And of course, just as you've been told since the age of two, eating too many sweets can indeed ruin your teeth. Two pounds of M&M's and a gallon of ice cream a day won't win you many points with the American Dental Association.

After a year or two of constant vomiting, a patient may end up with crumbling, ugly teeth. The most common symptom is perimolysis—dental erosion due to calcium loss brought about by the acid in the vomitus—but patients wind up with a lot of cavities as well. Some report that their teeth are abnormally sensitive to temperature changes. Many bulimics, aware of the danger, try to compensate by brushing vigorously after each vomiting episode. Ironically, overenthusiastic scrubbing only hastens erosion. Eating-disordered people may eat a lot of citrus fruit or candy to stave off hunger, which further damages teeth. Starvation and malnutrition also weaken the bones of the jaw.

Disordered eating and purging may lead to chemical imbalances in the brain. Consequently, bulimics may experience sleep difficulties as well as mood changes such as depression. In Chapter Five we'll take a closer look at the physiology of eating and its regulation by the brain.

Vomiting does more than just remove food. The bitter taste of vomit comes from the mix of stomach acid and other digestive juices secreted during the process of eating. Your body works hard to make that juice. Like little factories, the pancreas, the liver, the gallbladder, and other organs manufacture different enzymes and other substances to enable you to break down fats and absorb calories. Those substances are made up of proteins, minerals, and other elements that were absorbed from previous meals and stored in these organs.

Thus, when you throw up, you not only remove nutrients you need now, but you also deplete the reserves of those nutrients absorbed during previous meals. Without these life-giving substances, your heart can't function properly, nor can your other muscles and tissues. As a result you may experience weakness, fatigue, constipation, depression, even heart failure. Another serious complication can arise for those patients who use ipecac to induce vomiting. Ipecac is a nonprescription medicine used to trigger vomiting after accidental poisoning. Unfortunately, repeated use of ipecac may weaken muscles (including the heart); fatal heart difficulties have occurred in a number of bulimic patients who abused this drug.

The loss of chemical building blocks also makes it harder to manufacture the hormones needed to regulate various body systems, including the reproductive system. By definition, all anorexics experience loss of menstrual periods; about 20 percent of bulimics become amenorrheic, while about 50 percent experience menstrual irregularities.

Poor eating habits affect the brain and the nervous system. Some eating-disordered patients show abnormalities on brainwave (electroencephalograph, or EEG) tracings. Just what this means medically, however, is not yet clear. Sleep is affected too; bulimics may enter the rapid-eye movement (REM) phase of sleep sooner than normal. Disturbed sleep at night means fatigue the next day. Some patients report feeling muscle spasms or tingling sensations.

Vomiting removes a lot of fluid. So does abuse of laxatives and diuretics. Such practices can lead to chronic dehydration, which in turn poses the risk of permanent kidney damage.

Using laxatives is like locking the barn door after the horse has escaped. By the time food enters the large intestine, nearly 90 percent of its calories have already been absorbed anyway. In the course of a day, laxatives might help you get rid of the caloric equivalent of one measly candy bar.

But is it worth it? The risks of laxative abuse include dehydration, poor absorption of food and its nutrients, abdominal and muscular cramps, mineral imbalances, and swelling or clubbing of the fingers. Some of my patients admit taking anywhere from four to a hundred(!) laxative tablets every day.

Abuse of laxatives can cause the bowel to become dependent on these substances to function normally. The bowel loses its ability to contract in a coordinated way to move the fecal material along. A kind of backup in the biological sewage system results, leading to bloating and abdominal distension. When the patient stops taking laxatives, severe constipation may occur, in some cases requiring surgical intervention.

Some bulimics try to control appetite through excessive use of diet pills, which may contain the stimulants known as amphetamines. Side effects of these substances include mood changes, irritability, fatigue, and insomnia. The attempt to suppress appetite artificially only works for so long; eventually, the desire to eat becomes overwhelming. Thus, ironically, the use of appetite suppressants might actually lead to an eating binge. Another stimulant widely abused by bulimics is caffeine, both to suppress appetite and to improve mood and energy level.

THE MANY FACES OF EATING DISORDERS

In struggling to identify precisely the different subtypes of patients with eating disorders, writers have spilled a great deal of ink in the pages of medical books and journals. I'm about to spill a little more, but it's worth it, because identifying these illnesses and their effects on patients points the way to appropriate treatment.

Case 1: Hannah

Hannah reported that one day she was suddenly overwhelmed by the idea that she was fat. At the time she weighed 110 pounds—by no means an abnormal weight for a girl of thirteen who stood five foot two. Nonetheless, the notion that she was overweight consumed her. She had always been active, but she stepped up her daily exercise to over an hour a day.

When her weight failed to fall fast enough, she began decreasing her food intake. At first she did feel hungry, but she just "trained herself" to ignore the feeling. She denied ever inducing vomiting or using laxatives or diuretics.

Strangely, Hannah told me that she believed she "did not deserve food," and that she wasn't "good enough" to be allowed to eat. She saw her excessive exercise as a way to "earn" what little food she did consume.

Despite her refusal of food, she began taking over the job of making meals for her entire family. She grew irritable, experienced suicidal feelings, and had trouble sleeping. She never menstruated.

After a couple of months, Hannah said, she was no longer hungry. She managed to get by on as little as one candy bar a day. Although she lost nearly forty pounds over the course of a year—36 percent of her body weight—she felt as though her weight had never changed.

Hannah's case is a classic example of *restricting anorexia*—weight loss through self-starvation exclusively, without bingeing and purging. Restricting anorexics are perhaps the most easily recognized and well-defined of all patients with eating disorders.

Case 2: Yvonne

Believing that her parents never loved or wanted her, Yvonne began to "bust her butt," as she put it, to find emotional gratification through success at school. She studied long hours and became involved in as many after-school activities as she could manage. She joined the track team and worked out every chance she could.

After she dropped from 124 to 109 pounds, Yvonne's menstruation ceased, yet she continued to exercise compulsively and still perceived herself as overweight. Her concentration began to fail, which was particularly troubling, given her desire to stay on the school honor roll. She hoped that academic success would make her parents love and respect her, and thus allow her more social freedom. Sadly, though, her father regarded the weight loss as deliberate misbehavior, and began hitting her as a form of punishment.

She showed him, though. She lost more weight. She was hospitalized at a mere hundred pounds.

Ironically, while in the hospital, Yvonne learned about laxative abuse from her fellow patients. She ate voraciously just so she would be allowed to leave the hospital. After discharge she returned to her old habits; she restricted food intake, some days ingesting nothing but diet soda, and continued to exercise throughout the day. She also began to induce vomiting and to take laxatives. It wasn't long before she had to be hospitalized again.

Once released, Yvonne remained fearful of food. Oddly, she seemed to be particularly phobic about bread, terrified that even the slightest crumb would make her fat. She took a job as a waitress, but reported that she never felt hungry at work. Periodically, she succumbed to her desire to binge.

Eventually, though, she began to feel depressed, lonely, even suicidal. Although her parents tried to help lift her spirits by giving her more freedom, she was frightened by the idea of social interaction, and became even more withdrawn.

At home, Yvonne's father lost his job, her sister developed a serious illness, and her parents fought more. As the level of stress in her family rose, so did Yvonne's use of laxatives. Despite an occasional binge, she dropped twenty pounds in less than a month. She felt weak and fainted several times at school.

One time she fainted but didn't come to. Rushed unconscious to the hospital, she was treated in intensive care until she revived the next day. She then agreed to be transferred to a specialized eating-disorder program.

Yvonne, like Hannah, had anorexia nervosa. But as you've just seen, the illness affected these two young women in radically different ways. In addition to restricting food intake, Yvonne resorted to other measures to reduce weight even further: constant exercising, laxative abuse, and self-induced vomiting. Her diagnosis, then, was *bulimic anorexia*. Bulimic anorexics have been shown to be more social, depressed, and impulsive, with greater family difficulties and family histories of depression and obesity.

Case 3: Irene

Twenty-six-year-old Irene worked as an executive at a major cosmetics firm. Part of her job was to entertain clients, which she did two or three times a week. Usually the entertainment took the form of elaborate buffet dinners at fancy restaurants. For Irene, these meals were a form of delicious torture.

During her teen years, Irene became concerned about her weight. She tried restricting her eating, skipping meals and nibbling on salads for dinner, and managed to lose a few pounds.

She couldn't keep it up for long, though. Feelings of hunger would overwhelm her, and she would rampage through the house, eating anything in sight. After the binge, she felt such revulsion and self-loathing because of her lack of control that she induced vomiting. This cycle—attempted self-starvation leading to bingeing and purging—recurred once or twice a year for several years.

Eventually Irene gave up attempting to lose weight. The bingeing continued, however. She eventually developed a routine in which, *every night,* she would come home after work and drink an entire bottle of wine. One effect of the alcohol was to lower her inhibitions so that, at some point, the urge to binge would take over. She would then gorge herself on sweet foods, such as cookies and ice cream.

Often, too, she stocked her refrigerator with leftovers brought home after her business-related dinners. Although she exercised restraint during dinner, she always asked to take food home "for her dog." Of course, there was no dog, and her refrigerator was thus always filled with a supply of binge food.

Shortly after eating she would flee to the bathroom, where she vomited into the toilet. With a perverse sense of pride, she told me that she had become so adept at inducing vomiting that all she had to do was think about it, bend over, contract her stomach muscles, and—boom.

If you were to meet Irene, you wouldn't think she had a weight problem at all: At five foot six, she registers 135 pounds. Yet she is convinced that unless she vomits virtually everything she eats, she will turn into a "fat sack of lard."

I listed Irene's diagnosis as *bulimia nervosa.* Certainly she fit the *DSM-III-R* criteria to a tee.

Let's stop for a moment. On the surface it would seem that in order to diagnose anorexia there must be low weight, whereas the essence of a diagnosis of bulimia is bingeing and purging. If both of these symptoms are present, then we can diagnose *both* anorexia and bulimia.

In reality, however, things are not so simple. Many patients with what we call "normal-weight bulimia" have lost as much weight as, or even more than, an anorexic—they just started at a higher weight to begin with. The body senses that its weight is too low and starts sending out powerful "feed me" messages. Often the person responds by bingeing.

This raises a logical, but complicated, question: What is normal weight? It's easy enough to establish what the average weight is for a given population. But the average weight for a group of people is not the same as the normal weight for a particular individual.

Research has confirmed that there is a tremendous range in people's natural weights. We know, too, that a person's weight, determined largely by heredity, tends to be remarkably stable over time. In other words, if your body's weight-regulating mechanism is set at a certain point, say, 120 to 125 pounds, then you will probably remain at that weight for years unless such factors as exercise or diet are significantly changed. In the next chapter we will discuss this concept, known as the *set point model*. We'll also talk about how the body works to maintain a stable weight and ways we can influence our set point weight.

5

Half the Picture: The Physical Side of Eating and Hunger

Long ago, in the Far East, a monk went to his teacher and asked, "What is the secret of life?"

The teacher replied, "When hungry, eat. When full, stop. When tired, sleep."

The monk was puzzled by this response. "That's *it*?" he thought as he left. Only after years of study and meditation did the wisdom of the teacher's words finally dawn on him.

The philosopher taught a valuable lesson, one that still applies hundreds of years later: *Listen to your body*. Struggling to control natural impulses leads to turmoil and conflict. It is better to be in harmony with your body.

We eat to live. Food supplies the organs and tissues with the fuel they need to function. Without food we die. An obvious truth, perhaps, but one worth stating.

Because its survival depends on eating, the body acts as a kind of biological food processor, one that is programmed to seek, consume, digest, and eliminate meals. When it senses that its fuel reserves are low, the body trips a "hunger" alarm. This alarm in

77

turn triggers behavior whose goal is to find and consume food. At some point, when we've eaten enough, "fullness" signals reach the brain and shut off the urge to eat. Even before this point the process of digestion begins as the various organs secrete enzymes and acids to break the food down into its nutritional components.

In many ways this system operates automatically, on a purely physical level, without any need for conscious control. We don't, for example, have to bother ourselves thinking, "Ah! I've just eaten a jelly doughnut! Time to tell my pancreas to produce insulin so I can deal with all that glucose." If we did, we'd have no time or brainpower left to do our jobs, watch television, or talk to a friend on the telephone. And given the human capacity for error, it's likely that we'd sometimes make the wrong decision anyway and wind up suffering from self-induced indigestion.

Yet anorexia or bulimia reflects just this kind of misguided attempt to overcontrol the physical process of eating.

Sometimes a physical malfunction—a chemical imbalance, for example—may trigger or contribute to abnormal eating behavior. Like other bodily systems, the one responsible for eating can break down in many different ways. Disease, physical damage, or a genetic defect can cause malfunctions at one or more points along the way and prevent the body from generating the proper signals. Our very diet affects behavior in direct and specific ways, as we'll see shortly.

But a person with an eating disorder has, in a sense, declared war on the automatic aspects of the process of eating. *She* will now decide when to give in to hunger; *she* will now decide when and what she will eat. She declares her independence from the forces that govern from *within.* Doing so will show the world just how strong she is at resisting the forces that she fears are attempting to control her from *without.*

If the secret of life is to eat when hungry—that is, to respond to the body's inner wisdom—then the anorexic or bulimic has set out on a difficult and dangerous road indeed.

THE EATING PROCESS

Stripped to its essentials, eating is the process by which we bring life-supporting chemicals into our bodies, an act that occurs at reasonably predictable intervals over the course of a day. Once the food is ingested, acids and enzymes in the stomach break it down, after which it passes into the intestine.

The nutrients, such as glucose, fatty acids, and proteins, pass into the bloodstream and float along until they reach their various destinations: the liver, the muscles, and so on. The body uses some of the nutrients immediately. Others pass into reservoirs, such as the fat cells, where they bide their time, waiting for the metabolic call to duty. That call comes from hormones—insulin, for example—and other chemicals. These chemicals escort the nutrients into the cells and tissues, where, broken down to their component parts, they help fuel the engines of life.

Eating involves not just internal processes but external ones as well. When we eat, we literally absorb part of the outside environment and incorporate it into ourselves. Eventually we return part of the meal to the environment and the process repeats itself. No wonder then that food, serving as a direct link to the "outside world," can have such power over us! It's not surprising that some people begin to use food and eating in abnormal ways, as weapons in the battle to gain control over their environment.

Eating behavior is partly biological, governed by the physical needs of the individual. It's also partly social, determined by our interactions with other people. The way we think about food also affects the way we eat. For example, knowing that eating a candy bar at five o'clock could spoil her appetite for a big meal at six might affect a person's choice whether to snack or not. Emotional factors also come into play; the sheer pleasure of tasting or smelling food can determine the content, timing, or size of our meals. Even though our bodies may not be sending hunger signals, the very presence of a scrumptious chocolate cake may make us want to eat.

Eating behavior, then, may occur in response to forces that

have nothing to do with our bodies' current nutritional needs. In treating the eating-disordered individual, there are two relevant questions to ask: "What biological abnormalities may be present?" and "Why have the nonbiological factors that affect eating behavior come to dominate the biological factors?"

THE BRAIN

The brain acts as the central processing unit for all these various forces and influences. Different parts of the brain control responses to different stimuli.

Perhaps of greatest interest in a discussion of eating is the hypothalamus. This cluster of nerves, located near the front of the brain and surrounded by the hemispheres of "gray matter," is astonishingly powerful given its tiny size. The hypothalamus, serving as a kind of gatekeeper between the brain and the rest of the body, coordinates many activities, including the central nervous system, the endocrine system, and the autonomic nervous system that governs, among other things, breathing and digestion.

The hypothalamus receives signals from the body about the state of energy supplies, decides what has to be done, and issues orders accordingly. For example, "hunger" signals sent from one part of the brain to other areas propel us toward the refrigerator. During the meal, various feedback loops change the concentration of certain brain chemicals. The hypothalamus records all of these changes and signals other parts of the brain to stop the eating. You put your fork down and push yourself away from the table. This is a "satiety" response. Without it we would continue eating to the point of physical pain.

Although small, the hypothalamus is divided into several discrete areas. Since the 1940s, we have known that damage to one area can disturb metabolism, resulting in overeating and obesity. Such results led to the early conclusion that the hypothalamus housed the central mechanisms in charge of hunger and satiety. We have since learned, however, that the eating process is much more complex than this simplistic explanation would allow. Hunger signals are now thought of as "decentralized," traveling not just from the brain to the body, but from the body to the brain as well.

Research has also revealed that the hypothalamus, like the rest of the brain, is awash in a biochemical bath. The different areas of the hypothalamus are studded with specific receptors geared to respond only to certain neurotransmitters.

OTHER ORGANS

The brain is just one of the links in the chain of the eating process. Other links include the nose, mouth, esophagus, the digestive tract, the bowels, and the kidneys.

Until recently, people tended to look on the stomach as just a passive bag that received food, broke it down, and passed it on. New discoveries indicate that the gastrointestinal system plays an active role in regulating the intake of food.

Food landing in the stomach sets in motion a series of events. The stomach and small intestine react to the size of the meal and the type of nutrients contained in the foods—fats, carbohydrates, and so on—by releasing the right mix of acids and other compounds necessary for digestion. Various gastrointestinal peptides are released in response to feeding, which in turn signal the hypothalamus to "terminate eating." (A peptide is a compound of two or more amino acids; proteins are long sequences of amino acids linked together.)

THE CCK STORY

One of the best-studied gastrointestinal peptides is cholecystokinin, or CCK. After you eat, the small intestine releases this hormone, which stimulates pancreatic secretion and gallbladder contraction. It also sends satiety signals up to the hypothalamus.

Women who have bulimia may have a malfunction in their CCK system. In one study, bulimic women tested before a meal had the same amount of CCK as normal women. Yet after eating they had a significantly smaller increase in CCK than did normal women. They also reported fewer feelings of fullness than the normal women did. Treatment with tricyclic antidepressants not only reduced their bingeing, but also helped their CCK levels return to normal.

This important new research doesn't necessarily mean that a faulty CCK system *causes* bulimia. But decreased CCK, and thus the decrease in satiety signals, may reinforce a woman's urge to keep eating.

Such findings have led to a revolution in the way we think about the digestive system. As one expert put it, rather than being a passive system, the gut now appears to be a "great sensory sheet extending from the mouth to the small intestine." This sheet is exquisitely sensitive not only to the presence of food, but to its exact chemical composition as well.

THE BIOLOGICAL THERMOSTAT

Think of the thermostat in your home. You set the dial to maintain a constant temperature of, say, seventy-two degrees. When the furnace has put out enough heat, the thermostat switches it off for a while. If someone leaves the front door open and cold air rushes in, the thermostat kicks on again, staying on until the temperature returns to the desired level.

Your body works in a similar way. Earlier, I used the term *homeostatic* to describe how your body tries to maintain its equilibrium. The biological "homeostat" responds to changes in the environment to keep your metabolism working on an even keel.

Currently, one of the most exciting fields in medicine involves research into the fascinating and complex ways the body responds to such signals. We are beginning to learn that a number of subsystems work together to control eating as well as other types of behavior.

These subsystems operate on the feedback principle: Signal A activates process B, which in turn sends signal C to shut off signal A. These signals are carried by hormones or other chemical messengers that activate nerves or stimulate other responses. Many of these processes are triggered, not just internally, but by physical and social cues from the outside world. Just about anything, from contact with other people to the amount of daylight you receive in a twenty-four-hour period, can affect your body's function—your homeostasis.

The concept of feedback is important to eating disorders for several reasons. For example, your body tries to keep weight at a constant. If you start weighing too much, your metabolism speeds up to burn off the excess pounds. Conversely, should your weight drop, so will your metabolism, to conserve dwindling energy supplies.

Another series of feedback loops involves your body's cravings for certain nutrients and its response to the nutritional content of the food you eat. Studies on animals (and simple observation of humans) shows that at times we prefer to eat carbohydrates, for example, and at other times we choose protein-rich foods. The menus we choose can have a tremendous impact on our moods and our behavior.

HUNGER AND SATIETY

When the brain detects the need for food, it presses the body's hunger button. We respond by eating. The swelling stomach eventually sends a chemical message to the brain: "Enough already!" When this feedback message arrives, the hunger system shuts down until the process begins again a few hours later.

At one time, scientists believed that eating was a single process. Hunger and satiety were thought of as opposite sides of the same coin, just as inhaling and exhaling form one complete breathing cycle. In the past few years, however, we have come to look at eating as a series of processes that operate somewhat independently of one another. Hunger, in other words, is a somewhat separate system from satiety.

The discovery of these separate systems changed the way we think about eating disorders. Experts used to believe that anorexia involved a malfunction only in the *hunger* feedback loop. Although patients usually admit feeling hungry, they somehow condition themselves to ignore those signals. Perhaps the signals are faulty in some way—they may be too weak or are sent along the wrong pathway.

But we now have evidence that anorexia also involves malfunctioning *satiety* feedback loops. For example, an anorexic's stomach will often be slow in passing food along—a condition known as delayed gastric emptying. It has been well demonstrated that the slowing of stomach emptying in anorexia increases the perception of fullness or satiety. Thus in these people even the presence of a small amount of food in the stomach may trigger satiety signals. Other studies confirm that an anorexic's feelings of hunger and satiety do not necessarily correlate with the actual amount of food in her stomach. Bulimia, too, may arise from abnormalities in both the hunger and the satiety systems.

NEUROTRANSMITTERS

So far we've taken a broad look at the eating process and the different feedback loops involved. But how do those loops actually operate? How do messages travel from one site to another, and how do they communicate their information? The answers reveal the fascinating complexity of the body's design. More important for our discussion, they indicate how a chemical disturbance in the brain can contribute to the abnormal eating behaviors seen in anorexia and bulimia.

Not so long ago, biologists conceived of the brain as a kind of computer, a machine that generates and processes electrical signals. New discoveries forced us to revise that model. We now think of the brain more in terms of a chemical factory. Chemical "messengers" travel across the gap between nerve endings, and when they reach the proper receptors they trigger electrical signals.

Without the presence of a neurotransmitter, an electrical impulse comes to a biological dead end—its message can't get through. Too much or too little of a given chemical can also affect the rate and the clarity with which the signal is carried. That's why we speak of chemical *imbalance* as the cause of a number of mental and physical disorders.

Sitting within the skull, the brain is enmeshed in an intricate network of blood vessels. Before blood can reach the brain, it must pass through a kind of filter known as the blood-brain barrier. This barrier acts, quite literally, as a bodyguard, preventing potentially harmful molecules carried in the blood from gaining access to the brain. For example, the blood-brain barrier will not permit certain drugs to enter the brain and wreak biological havoc.

Blood contains the red cells, which transport vital supplies of oxygen to nourish the brain cells and keep them functioning, and the white cells of the immune system, responsible for protecting the body from invaders. These cells are suspended in plasma, the fluid portion of blood made up of water, minerals, glucose, fats, proteins, and other substances.

The exact composition of plasma is determined in part by the types and amounts of food you eat. Following a meal, the chemical makeup of plasma changes. For example, if you've eaten a large steak, the presence of certain amino acids—the building blocks of protein—may increase. When blood containing this particular plasma mix reaches the blood-brain barrier, the different amino acids compete with each other to squeeze through the openings in the filter. Like shoppers clawing their way to reach a K-mart blue light special, only a few can get through.

Different chemical mixtures trigger the manufacture of different neurotransmitters. Let me give you an example. (Bear in mind, however, that not all the facts are in on this intricate process.)

Eating carbohydrates stimulates the pancreas to release insulin, in turn lowering the blood levels of most amino acids. The amino acid tryptophan is unaffected by this process. More tryptophan enters the brain, since there is less competition at the blood-brain barrier from other amino acids. In the next step of the process, tryptophan is converted to a powerful neurotransmitter called serotonin. The higher the tryptophan level, the more serotonin the body can make.

Serotonin circulates in the blood, eventually reaching a certain part of the hypothalamus. When the serotonin level is high enough, it triggers a message that speeds to the other parts of the brain. The message reads something like: "Stop eating carbohydrates now and look for food with other nutrients." Thus it may be that the specific foods you have already eaten may lead to cravings for other types of foods.

Experiments have shown just how powerful these neurotransmitters can be. For example, animals who normally eat a balanced diet will turn into voracious carbohydrate-cravers, even to the point of endangering their health, if their brains are flooded with certain chemicals that stimulate carbohydrate ingestion.

There are actually three main groups of neurotransmitters involved in the regulation of appetite: the monoamines (of which serotonin is one), the amino acids, and the neuropeptides.

At this point let me introduce the term *macronutrients,* a word that refers to the major components in food. The three types of macronutrients are carbohydrates, proteins, and fats. Each of these supplies a different type of energy to the body. A balanced diet contains a healthy mix of all three macronutrients. As a rule, animals and most humans will seek out foods that, over the course of time (say, a day) will supply the macronutrient blend their bodies need.

Macronutrients affect the production and release of neurotransmitters. As we saw in the above example, carbohydrate consumption may lead to increased serotonin levels. Similarly, sweet or fatty foods lead to production of certain neuropeptides.

Like a biological traffic cop, the hypothalamus directs all this activity, and it's a particularly busy intersection. Signals coming from the brain affect the diet, while diet in turn affects the signals heading for the brain. Should something go wrong, a neurotransmitter disturbance might trigger an abnormal pattern of eating. This in turn might worsen the already existing neurotransmitter disturbance, causing more abnormal eating, and so on.

Such findings underscore how chemical messengers spark specific behavior. Controlling the balance of these chemicals through medications might ultimately enable us to bring abnormal eating patterns under control. To understand how, let's take a closer look at one of the systems involved.

ENTER THE ENDORPHINS

One of the most fascinating avenues of biochemical research over the past few years led to the discovery that the body manufactures its own natural painkillers. These substances became known as *endorphins,* from *endo* (meaning "arising from within") and *morphine.* Evidence suggests that endorphins play a direct role in regulating appetite and affect other functions such as pain relief, memory—even blood pressure.

Like a lock that accepts only a certain key, cells of the central nervous system have receptors that accept and respond only to particular endorphins. For example, it appears that one receptor involved in stimulating appetite (called the "kappa" receptor) is designed to work only with the substance known as dynorphin. Dynorphin molecules fit into the kappa receptors. Nerve impulses then travel to the hypothalamus, which interprets and relays them as hunger cues. Appetite is thus stimulated, particularly for sweet-tasting foods.

Scientists soon found that rats given morphine (which increases endorphin activity) and allowed to choose from among the macronutrients tended to increase their fat intake while ignoring the carbohydrates. The investigators then administered drugs known to *block* the opiate receptors. Doing so, they found, tended to suppress eating. They found the same effect in humans. They then theorized that use of opiate blockers (also known as opiate antagonists) suppresses appetite by producing feelings of fullness or satiety.

But what triggers the release of endorphins in the first place? Further experiments found that food deprivation or stress can play a role. In other words, if you are under stress—pressure at work or school, for example—your body secretes endorphins to control the damage. Some of those endorphins ease any physical pain you might be feeling, while others work to stimulate your appetite, especially for sweet foods. You may respond to these signals from your hypothalamus by gobbling down a slice of pie, for example.

But why should eating sugar help relieve stress? Why doesn't lettuce (to pick a food at random) have the same effect?

As it turns out, the very act of eating sugar stimulates the opiate-releasing process even further. Not only does sugar make the body release more endorphins, it also enhances the ability of the receptor to bind with the substance—like oiling a lock to make a key work better. Thus, eating sweet foods does indeed relieve stress, producing feelings of relaxation and contentment by enhancing the amount of natural painkillers floating around inside the body.

You might have spotted the flaw in this otherwise tidy little system. Here's the problem: When a person is under stress, the body releases endorphins that stimulate the appetite for sweet foods. The person then eats a candy bar. The sugar in turn stimulates further secretion of endorphins, triggering greater appetite and leading to more consumption of sweets. Where does the cycle end?

As you might have suspected, it may *not* end. Theory has it that some people with bulimia might be caught up in the vicious cycle represented by the opiate-receptor feedback loop.

A bulimic will typically skip meals in the belief that doing so will keep her weight under control. But skipping meals only defers appetite; it doesn't eliminate it. Eventually the urge to eat becomes overpowering, leading to a binge. Food deprivation itself can trigger the release of endorphins, which in turn stimulate appetite. Thus a bulimic who deprives herself of meals causes her body to produce a powerful natural appetite stimulant.

Many a patient reports that her binges occur in times of stress. Research has shown that stress also cranks up the endorphin system. Finally, when a binge leads to consumption of high-sugar items—ice cream, cookies, candy—even more opiates are released, stimulating appetite even further, and the vicious cycle kicks into high gear. For many, the only thing that disrupts this process is a drastic measure: self-induced vomiting.

BRAIN CHEMICALS AND MOODS

Brain chemicals do more than regulate behavior. They also determine our moods. An imbalance—too much or too little of a given substance—can produce symptoms of mental disorder ranging from depression to the abnormal elation and hyperactivity known as mania.

As we have seen, the incidence of depression in relatives of eating-disordered people is higher than the rate found in the general population. Researchers have long been intrigued by this apparent connection between eating disorders and affective disorders (mood disorders, such as depression and mania). Is it possible that both types of illnesses arise from a common source?

We don't yet have all the evidence we need to answer this question with confidence. However, there is no doubt that disruption along certain neurochemical pathways can lead to disturbed moods of varying severity.

Consider, for example, some of the fairly common syndromes in which feelings of depression play a part. The first, and most widely known, is PMS—the premenstrual syndrome. Symptoms of PMS include sudden mood swings, irritability, anxiety, feelings of hopelessness, difficulty concentrating, sleep disturbance, food cravings, and physical problems such as headaches or joint pain.

Another illness that has received considerable publicity in recent years is SAD, or seasonal affective disorder. With the onset of winter and its shorter days, people with SAD begin to feel depressed, hopeless, and lethargic. The illness is particularly troubling because during the summer these same people are lively, outgoing, and energetic. The contrast can be confusing, not just to the patient, but to family, friends, and co-workers as well.

Less familiar is the syndrome known as CCO, or carbohydrate-craving obesity. The name is self-explanatory: Patients with this condition overeat carbohydrates to the point of severe, health-threatening obesity. A variant of this illness is a form of bulimia in which patients, usually mildly obese women, engage in severe bingeing, often involving carbohydrate-laden foods, but with little or no vomiting.

These conditions share certain symptoms, including depression, lethargy, difficulty concentrating, and periodic bouts of overeating leading to weight gain. People with these disorders seem specifically to prefer carbohydrates above all other foods. One of my patients, who as it turned out had SAD, described herself as a "bread and pasta fiend" in the winter, while in the summer she ate more protein.

Bouts of depression in SAD, as its name suggests, appear in a cycle determined by the changing seasons. PMS strikes regularly every month (though it is worse for some people during the winter months). CCO, however, seems to trigger abnormal eating virtually every day, most often in the late afternoon or early evening. It's this regular rhythm—seasonal, monthly, daily—that caught the attention of investigators concerned with the ways our bodies change over the course of time.

We now know that many of our bodily functions operate on what is known as a circadian cycle. *Circadian* means "about a day." The word refers to the fact that many natural functions—sleep, hunger, sexual arousal—are not discrete events but rhythmical processes that continue over a period of approximately twenty-four hours, with peaks and valleys that occur at different times. As a rule, these processes are regulated by the hypothalamus.

Noted brain experts Richard Wurtman and Judith Wurtman conducted experiments with CCO patients. Their work demonstrated how the urge to consume carbohydrates strikes predictably during the late afternoon. But why should this be so? If a person has a disorder that compels her to eat huge quantities of food, why should her appetite be greater at certain times of day? And why is it limited to a certain type of macronutrient? Not all of the answers are in yet. However, some evidence points to the neurotransmitter serotonin—or rather, a defect in serotonin secretion—as one possible source of the problem.

A normal person who feels the urge to eat something sweet might be satisfied with a couple of cookies or a candy bar. In contrast, a carbohydrate craver continues to eat beyond the point of satisfaction. As we learned earlier, serotonin usually acts to suppress eating. The Wurtmans believe that carbohydrate-craving behavior suggests something has gone wrong with the feedback loop that signals the brain when enough food has been taken in.

There's another level to the problem as well. When asked why they succumbed to such dangerous eating practices, carbohydrate-craving people reported that they weren't interested in the taste of the food. Instead they ate as a means of fending off tension, anxiety, or mental fatigue. In other words, carbohydrate cravers seem to use food as a kind of self-prescribed regimen of antidepressant therapy. Earlier we saw how carbohydrates lead to increased serotonin levels. Could a defect in the serotonin system be a common link between these disorders?

Knowing that a faulty serotonin system may underlie certain kinds of abnormal eating has led to the use of medications to correct the problem. A chemical called d-fenfluramine, for example, acts as a kind of biological boxing coach. It calls on serotonin to get out there and fight by triggering its release from nerve cells. Then d-fenfluramine prolongs the bout by blocking reabsorption of serotonin back into the cell—in a sense, keeping the boxer from returning to his corner before the fight is over. The popular antidepressant Prozac (fluoxetine) also increases serotonin levels by blocking the reabsorption of serotonin by the nerve cells.

Through this one-two punch, d-fenfluramine helps serotonin do the job it was designed for: control appetite. Use of this and other similar compounds can help some carbohydrate-craving patients enjoy more normal moods and in some cases lose weight. There has also been some success in using these medications for PMS and SAD. Recent research in patients with PMS has also shown that consumption of high-carbohydrate meals (which increases serotonin) can help improve premenstrual depression, tension, and fatigue.

Let me take a moment to recap some of what we've discussed so far in this chapter.

My main point is that eating is not just a simple process. A complex network of signals exists between the brain and the rest of the body. Some of these signals arise from within. Others—anything from the amount of daylight outside to a friend's invitation to go and grab a burger—come from the outside world.

These signals trigger the release of biochemicals that stimulate appetite. The digestive organs respond to what we eat by releasing still more chemical messengers that report to the brain. The brain processes the information and issues orders to stop, continue, or eat something different next time.

Although social cues play a role, eating is largely a self-sustaining physical process. Disruptions can occur at any point in the system. There may be insufficient supplies of a certain brain chemical or a defect in an organ's ability to respond to a neurotransmitter's message. Fortunately, our growing knowledge of how physical problems contribute to eating disorders points the way to new and effective biological treatments. We'll learn more about such strategies in Chapter Seven.

PHYSICAL ASPECTS OF ANOREXIA NERVOSA

Some of my anorexia patients tell me that they rarely feel hungry. They are so good at starving themselves, they say, because they've trained themselves to suppress hunger.

I've dealt with enough patients to know that's not always the case. These people may be frequently hungry. Their illness is such that they must stand guard at all times lest hunger overwhelm them and they give in to the urge to eat even a mouthful of food.

Their claim that they don't experience hunger may be in part a product of selective inattention. They don't *want* to be hungry; therefore, eventually, they fool themselves into believing that they aren't. They convert a hunger pang into a signal that they must work harder at being thin, through exercise or some other means. In part, however, their starvation may biologically decrease their perception of hunger.

Hunger denial isn't present in all anorexics, though. A patient named Jackie often remarked that yes, she did indeed feel hungry—a feeling she began to display as a kind of badge of valor. I once heard her remark to a fellow patient, "I could eat a horse—but of course I won't." Later, during a therapy session, I probed a little deeper into what she meant. Jackie replied, "If I can keep from eating even though my appetite is so huge, I know I'm succeeding in my quest to be thin. That success makes me feel very proud."

Jackie thus revealed that she believed her extreme hunger (and her ability to resist it) marked her as a skilled soldier in the fight against fat. She actually cultivated her hunger because being aware of it helped make her feel thinner.

Some anorexic patients report that their efforts to starve themselves spring from their fear that they will eat beyond the point of fullness. For these individuals, a full stomach becomes a source of horror. If they eat enough to feel even a little full, they panic. They fear they have gone over the edge, that they have lost all control.

I treated a sixteen-year-old patient named Zoe, who had been anorexic for three years. Long after she began to improve, Zoe was still terrified that she might eat too much. Over the course of her illness, she said, "I think I've lost the ability to know how much food is enough." Zoe's satiety feedback loop had malfunctioned. It took months of treatment for this patient to relearn correct eating behavior.

Laboratory studies on anorexia patients often reveal that the hypothalamus isn't functioning the way it should. Less clear is whether a defect in the hypothalamus causes the anorexia, or whether the effects of starvation have in turn affected the hypothalamus. Without going into detail, suffice it to say that, to different degrees in different patients, starvation and loss of body weight disrupt endocrine functions ranging from the thyroid to the liver to the reproductive organs.

These endocrine changes in anorexia occur along several body networks. Amenorrhea, loss of interest in sex, and reduction in breast size are all symptoms related to the pathway connecting the hypothalamus and the pituitary gland with the reproductive organs.

Other pathways link the hypothalamus to the nerves regulating blood pressure and heart rate, or to the body engines that turn our sleep cycles on and off.

There may even be a physiological network that governs one's ability to perceive the body accurately. If so, disturbance of body image, one of the key symptoms of anorexia, may result from abnormalities in the neurotransmitter system.

At some point, the anorexic's illusion that hunger doesn't exist becomes a reality. In the terminal stages of the illness, hunger does indeed disappear. Without sufficient food, the body withers. The stomach shrinks, as does the small intestine. The ability of these organs to function shrinks as well. The stomach pumps out less digestive acid, and is thus less able to break down what little food is available. Eventually the stomach muscles may atrophy and lose their ability to pass food into the small intestine, a medically serious condition known as gastric dilatation.

PHYSICAL ASPECTS OF BULIMIA NERVOSA

Laboratory tests on bulimics reveal various endocrine abnormalities. Most of these, however, reflect the impact of bulimic behavior—bingeing and vomiting—on the body. They are the effects of the disorder, not the cause.

As we saw in Chapter Four, the act of vomiting depletes the body of essential fluids and chemicals. The passage of stomach acid up through the esophagus and out the mouth can burn or deteriorate the lining of the throat and causes tooth erosion. Loss of certain minerals threatens the ability of muscles to function properly. The heart is at high risk of developing an irregular rhythm or of stopping altogether. Affected by fluid imbalance, perhaps made worse by the use of diuretics, the kidneys malfunction. Menstruation becomes irregular, or stops altogether, due to changes in the body's ability to manufacture and secrete hormones. The list—a sad one—goes on.

BODY DEVELOPMENT

Of course, our bodies are changing from the moment we are born to the moment we die. We grow, we become ill and get well, we exercise or stop exercising, we age.

By definition, adolescence is a difficult time, a period of rapid growth and development. No big revelation there, but a point worth keeping in mind. Hormones flood the body, triggering an incredible number of physical and emotional responses. A young teenager's body grows in all directions—taller, wider, thicker. The overall shape changes too. Most of these changes are directly related to sexual development.

For boys, maturity means broader shoulders, facial hair, deeper voice, and genital enlargement. Each of these is basically a desirable event, serving to enhance the boy's feelings of masculinity. One other point: Nobody *sees* the changes in a boy's sexual organs. They are—no pun intended—a private matter.

Maturity is a different experience for a girl. The physical changes are more obvious to everyone. Her breasts develop, her hips widen. The reproductive organs mature and menstruation begins. Her sexual growth takes more of a psychological toll. Girls can't help comparing themselves to their peers; boys can't help noticing the change.

With the onset of menstruation, a girl comes to associate maturity with perhaps excruciating pain, blood, uncontrollable mood changes, and the "hassle" of dealing with menstrual flow. The female body needs a certain percentage of fat tissue before menstruation can begin and continue. Maturity is thus directly tied to an increase in body fat.

The massive physical overhaul of adolescence requires an enormous amount of energy to sustain it. That energy, of course, comes from food. No wonder teenagers are always hungry!

As a rule, kids handle the trauma of adolescent development surprisingly well. It is, after all, an exciting time. The thrill of

95

dating, the sense of growing independence, and the incredible energy of being young compensate, at least to some degree, for the stress of change.

Not everyone, however, is well equipped emotionally and psychologically to adjust to these physical and social demands. For some young girls, this sudden awareness of their sexuality, plus the pressure to develop new kinds of relationships with boys (and with other girls, for that matter) is too much. Add to this mix a family situation that fails to prepare the girl to cope with such changes and you have a recipe for trouble.

Whether consciously or unconsciously, some girls connect eating and body development. They think, "If I could just control my eating, I can control the changes in my body." Doing so means they can avoid all the problems of puberty.

A recent incident illustrates the point. One of my patients, a fourteen-year-old girl named Kate, reached 112 pounds. She then became anorexic and starved herself down to 83 pounds. During treatment she agreed to return to a weight between 101 and 105, which was the range at which menstruation had stopped. She stated adamantly that she "never wanted to get back up to one hundred and twelve again."

We explored the reason for her attitude. It turns out that, shortly before her illness began, she had walked past a construction site. In typical fashion, the construction workers whistled at her; one yelled out, "Nice ass, baby!"

Unfortunately, this type of emotional harassment exists everywhere, and I think it's disturbing to every woman. Teenagers, sadly, are often least able to cope with it. Kate felt humiliated and embarrassed. Later she began to sense, more or less consciously, that if her weight dropped she wouldn't have to cope with that kind of abusive and unwanted sexual attention. A girl of eighty-three pounds, whose body has the silhouette of a ten-year-old, is at very low risk of being told she has a "nice ass."

Of course, girls are often flattered at being noticed by people they know and like. They appreciate compliments from people they trust. But for a girl who is overwhelmed by such attention, or who is unprepared to deal with it, the "safer" option might be to starve herself and avoid such confrontations entirely.

That option—anorexia nervosa—is anything but safe.

SET POINT

Anyone who has ever been on a diet knows it is extremely difficult to keep weight off once it is lost. Sure, she might shed a few pounds in the first weeks or so but, try as she might, that weight almost invariably returns. When it does, the person usually blames the diet or, more typically, herself. "It's my fault," she wails. "I have no willpower. I'm a failure—a washout."

When I hear such remarks from a patient, I tell her as emphatically as I possibly can: "It is *not* your fault." And I proceed to tell her about a scientific discovery that has revolutionized the way we think about body weight.

Simply put, that discovery—known as the set point model—has revealed that each person is biologically programmed to reach and maintain a body weight that falls within a certain, relatively narrow range. Within that range, body weight is strongly guarded against either increasing or decreasing substantially.

For the individual, the actual weight range is not a matter of personal choice or aesthetic preference, nor is it a response to cultural pressure. It is part of our genetic, physiological destiny (with perhaps some influence from the way we are fed in infancy). Just as we have no control over whether our eyes will be brown or blue, we have no choice over the body weight that our DNA says will be right for us.

The human body is an organic system that takes in and expends energy. Like the coal that stokes the furnace, food in the form of calories provides energy. Metabolism determines the rate at which our bodies convert the food into energy.

Normally, the metabolic rate represents a balance between intake and expenditure. If we consume roughly two thousand calories a day, we will usually burn off roughly two thousand calories a day. Such burning occurs actively, through work or exercise, or passively, through sweating or regulation of body temperature. The very act of thinking burns calories. Even when we are sitting or sleeping, we are burning energy at a certain rate. Our metabolic balance is controlled by interaction among a number of different factors, including hormones and their receptors in the cells, neurotransmitters, diet, amount of exercise, our genetic inheritance—even the temperature of the air around us.

The set point model, supported by much scientific evidence, shows that metabolism tries to reach and hold a certain weight level. Some people are naturally skinnier and others are naturally heavier. The set point model implies that *different body weights are appropriate and healthy for different people.*

A person biologically programmed to weigh 160 pounds is healthy and normal at that weight. If she suddenly dropped thirty pounds, her metabolism would react as though the body were in a state of siege—which, in a sense, is what starvation is. Her metabolism would slow down tremendously—by as much as a whopping 30 percent—to help conserve energy. Her body would take the few calories it gets and use them more efficiently until it returned to its higher weight. Conversely, someone who should weigh 100 pounds and who balloons up to 140 will experience an acceleration of metabolism, a cranking up of the physiological furnace in an effort to burn off the unwanted weight.

You can see the vicious cycle. A person decides to diet—say, by cutting down her food intake by 20 percent. She loses some weight. Her body senses the change and reacts as though it is in danger of starvation. Her metabolism then drops as the efficiency by which her body converts food to body weight increases.

Thus, although the dieter eats less food, her metabolism also decreases. A recent study on a group of women found that after nine weeks of dieting they had lost an average of 3 percent of their original weight. Yet their consumption of oxygen—which the body uses to burn energy and which thus fuels metabolism—dropped by a substantial 17 percent.

When weight rises beyond the set point range, the body burns off energy—by raising body temperature, for example. Conversely, loss of too much weight triggers a kind of biological blackout. The person will feel fatigued and may begin to sleep more. Body temperature may drop to conserve calories. As we have seen, anorexics often complain of feeling cold.

Menstruation also stops. There is genetic wisdom—I'm tempted to call it "bio-logic"—behind this development. A starving woman can't spare the energy needed to build another human being. In the interest of survival of both the mother and her future children, the reproductive system shuts down.

By undergoing this radical energy-conservation program, the body struggles to push weight back up to the right level for this particular person. But when her weight starts to rise again—as it inevitably will—the dieter begins to panic. She may take even more drastic steps to lose weight, triggering further metabolic disruption. And so on.

In fact, repeated cycles of dieting may actually increase the body's metabolic efficiency and make it even harder to lose weight. Such cycles may also change the way fat is deposited, with more fat being laid down in the stomach region.

There *are* certain factors that can modify the set point weight to some degree. Exercise has been shown to lower set point. In other words, regular exercise doesn't just burn calories; it actually seems to shift the regulation of body weight to a lower level. Similarly, certain drugs can lower set point. Anyone who has stopped smoking cigarettes and subsequently gained weight can attest to the effects of nicotine in keeping set point weight down. What's more, evidence suggests that long-term response to a high-fat diet can *raise* set point. Thus, lowering the percentage of fat in your diet may help you lower set point.

The set point model has much to tell us, not just about obesity, but about the eating disorders as well. For the anorexic, self-starvation and severe weight loss cause the metabolism to slow to a crawl. The greater the loss, the more the body fights to return to its preprogrammed level. This explains why a person with this illness feels she must maintain such vigilance against hunger. Her body is fighting for its very life, and will muster all of the available resources to defend its existence.

Although they may have lost as much weight as an anorexic,

bulimic women may be at a statistically "normal" weight or above. But the set point model suggests that "normal" can't be defined by referring to some chart, such as the Metropolitan Life tables of height and weight. *Normal weight can be defined only for a particular individual.*

In fact, I would throw out the word *normal* altogether and substitute *natural* instead. To illustrate: Woman A may be five feet four with a small frame and a set point range of 114 to 120 pounds. Some insurance-company chart somewhere probably says this particular woman is "average." But woman B—same height, same frame—may have a set point range of 130 to 136 pounds. She's above the statistical average, but she is at a good and healthy weight *for her.* Each of these women has a set point range that reflects her natural weight.

But now Woman B reads an article that says her weight is "above average." She feels compelled to diet and loses twenty pounds. She now weighs about the same as Woman A, around 116 pounds. No one would consider her emaciated, yet she has lost 15 percent of her body weight—the same percentage required for a diagnosis of anorexia! Although statistically "normal," her body may be in a state of semistarvation. Because she needs more food than she is eating, she is at risk of developing uncontrollable binge urges, thus triggering the vicious cycle of bulimia.

To break the cycle, people may need help. They need a teacher who will show them the way to regain a healthy balance between the mind and the body.

6

Getting Help

When I first met Lisa, in the winter of 1987, she had been bulimic nearly half her twenty-seven years.

During the previous two years—*two years,* four times a week, forty-four weeks out of the year—she had lain on a psychoanalyst's couch, burrowing to the bottom of her soul to find the key to her suffering.

She got nowhere.

In fact, she got worse. Although she kept her weight at a steady 120 pounds, she was now bingeing and purging at least two, and often three, times a day. Alcoholism further complicated her problem.

Then, in the fall of 1987, a crisis occurred. As assistant creative director at a New York advertising agency, Lisa had sweated over a campaign for a line of designer jeans. She was about to explain her concept to a roomful of clients. Rising to make her presentation, Lisa felt ready and eager.

"Things went fine at first," Lisa told me. "But then, when I lifted my hand to point to a chart, I accidentally whacked the display easel and it just collapsed. My diagrams and paste-up boards scattered all over the floor. I was very angry—and totally humiliated."

As she scrambled to restore the display, she recalled, her thoughts spiraled out of control: "I'm such a jerk . . . they think I'm a total fool. My ideas are stupid. They hate this ad campaign. They hate *me*. They're sitting there thinking, 'How dare this disgusting fat slob tell *us* how to sell clothes? What's she doing in this business anyway? Who does she think she is?' "

Somehow, Lisa said, she managed to finish the presentation. She even forced herself to sit through the luncheon that followed, nibbling on her salad, poking at her peas. Excusing herself to go to the bathroom, she noticed a tray loaded with pastries. "Something possessed me," she recounted. "I grabbed two pastries in each fist, locked myself in a restroom stall, and crammed the pastries into my mouth. As if *food* would make things better."

After she swallowed the last bite, she stuck her fingers down her throat and threw up. Then she felt a crush of guilt, shame, and self-loathing. Exhausted and miserable, she sat sobbing in the stall.

A colleague from the agency, concerned about Lisa's absence, came to see if she could help. Smelling vomit, she realized what had happened. "She told me I needed help," Lisa recalled with a bitter smile. "I told her I'd *had* help. I'd spent thousands of dollars on analysis, and look how much good it had done me." With concern and urgency, the colleague told Lisa how her sister had been helped by an eating disorders program at a local hospital.

The next day, Lisa said, she went to her psychoanalyst and talked about terminating therapy. She then made an appointment and came to see me.

"How can I help?" I asked.

Lisa started crying. Through her tears she said, "I feel so frustrated. It just seems so hopeless. I've tried. God knows I've tried. But if I can't get some control over this problem, I'm not sure life will be worth living."

During the rest of our first session I learned more details of her story: how her dietary chaos began when she was a teenager, became entrenched during college, and persisted into adulthood. During the next few sessions it became clear to me that, as an outpatient, Lisa wasn't making much progress with her bulimia and her alcoholism.

I told Lisa our task was to break the pattern of abnormal eating, and that hospitalization offered the best hope of doing so. I emphasized how hospitalization was not a cure, but a beginning. I explained that gaining control while in the hospital was something like jump-starting a car—and that she would continue her journey on the road to recovery as an outpatient.

With some hesitation, Lisa entered the hospital. At the end of four weeks she was well enough to leave.

I bring up this case not to stress the benefits of hospitalization, but to make an important point, which the following story also illustrates.

One night a police officer saw a man down on all fours beneath a streetlight. "Is everything okay?" he asked.

"Oh, sure," replied the man. "I dropped my car key back there in the alley and I'm just trying to find it."

"But if you dropped it in the alley, how come you're looking for it here?"

"The light's better," he replied.

Like this misguided individual, Lisa's psychoanalyst used an ineffective approach to her problem. He thought that the light of analysis—a very good technique for certain problems—would help. Because of the limitations of this approach, he couldn't see that the key to the problem lay in another direction entirely. Again, if the only tool you have is a hammer, then every problem becomes a nail.

TREATMENT IN THE AGE OF BIOPSYCHIATRY

Eating disorders can arise from biological imbalances, emotional turmoil, and cognitive distortions. The best treatment is one that takes all of these components into account. Let me illustrate. Imagine a car with bad brakes careening out of control down a steep hill during the middle of a rainstorm. Behind the wheel is someone who never learned how to drive a car. A formula for disaster! Given unrestricted powers, how might someone intervene to restore control of the car?

Well, if we could somehow level out the hill so it was no longer as steep, the car would eventually roll to a stop. Perhaps, too, a mechanic could leap aboard and fix the brakes. At the same time we could broadcast a quick course in driver education over the car radio, teaching the driver how to relax and ease up on the gas. And by setting up a giant canopy, we could keep off the rain and reduce the slipperiness of the road surface.

As a biopsychiatrist, I see parallels between this scenario and the treatment of eating disorders.

The slope of the hill represents the physical, or biological, component. If I can "level off" the peaks and valleys (reducing the chemical imbalances, or decreasing the starvation or the bingeing and purging), I can return the patient to a more even course of eating. *Medical therapy*—the use of everything from controlled nutrition to certain medications—comes into play here.

Behavioral and cognitive therapies work to fix the way a patient behaves and thinks by showing her how to apply the brakes and bring her disordered habits under control.

By teaching her about the dangers of starvation or self-induced vomiting, *educational therapy* equips her with the strategies she needs to make sensible eating choices.

Individual and group therapies that address her feelings help her to ease up on the gas and stop supplying the emotional fuel that propels her erratic behavior.

Last, by improving her relationships with significant people in her life, for example, through *family therapy*, we might provide her with a dry surface, a road through life on which she can maneuver with greater confidence and stability.

Lisa's story shows this principle in action. Medications helped her deal with the biological issues, including her depression. Behavioral therapy showed her how to change bad habits. Cognitive therapy helped her learn new ways to handle stress. Through individual and group therapy she explored her feelings and improved her relationships, and the "twelve-step" approach of Alcoholics Anonymous and Overeaters Anonymous reduced her dependencies on alcohol and food. Though family therapy wasn't an option in her case, many patients do benefit from this approach.

Treatment that focuses on one element and ignores others may be ineffective. For example, "talking" therapy in which disordered eating behavior is not addressed may lack a crucial ingredient for success. The twelve-step approach of Overeaters Anonymous (see Chapter Ten) may be doomed to fail if the patient has a biologically caused depression. For an anorexic, restoring weight without altering distorted attitudes may merely be a "quick fix" whose results won't last over time. Similarly, fad diets or the megavitamin and food-allergy approaches may seem to work, at least temporarily, but their results are only a placebo effect that provides the passing illusion of a successful cure.

GETTING HELP

If you have an eating disorder, or know someone who does, the time to get help is *now.* Don't wait. The longer the disorder persists, the harder it is to eradicate.

By reading this book you're taking a crucial step: You're educating yourself about the disorder. You know the dangers, you know the warning signs. You are also learning about treatment options.

You know, too, that the end point of self-starvation or dietary chaos is chronic disability—or even death.

If your child has an eating disorder, you may feel you are helpless. Not true! You have more power than you realize. No matter how chaotic your family life, you are very important to your daughter. Use that importance to assist your daughter in getting help. The same holds if you are the husband or roommate of the person with the disorder.

Sometimes, disturbed eating can actually be a *cry for help.* Does your daughter parade her skeletal form in front of you? Does she leave the table often during a meal to visit the bathroom, or does she "forget" to clean up after she vomits? She is sending a signal: Help me!

Children need limits. They trust parents to set limits, to reassure them that the world is a safe and loving place. Sometimes a girl is just waiting for her mother or father to confront her about her disorder, to ask *what's wrong* and to insist on treatment. She can't bring up the subject herself; she's too consumed with guilt or shame.

That's why you need to act. Sometimes just showing that you care enough to intervene can have a powerful therapeutic effect.

It won't be easy. There may be denial, bitterness, angry confrontations. Expect these reactions. It's natural that a threat to your daughter's very identity should provoke resistance. But stay focused.

Here are some practical tips on how to intervene.

Plan your strategy: Think about who should approach your daughter. The mother alone? The father? Both? Whatever your plan, be sure you present a strong, unified front.

Get your facts straight: Be sure your daughter does indeed have an eating disorder, and isn't just spending too much time in the bathroom combing her hair. If you have doubts, bring them up in a nonjudgmental way. Keep at it until you are satisfied that your daughter is not endangering herself.

Know the problem: Bone up on the subject. Become as well informed as your daughter is.

Know the solution: Find out about treatment facilities in your area and meet with caregivers. If you don't like their approach, keep hunting. A list of resources appears on page 216.

Choose your words: Think about what you will say. Rehearse it. Imagine the conversation and prepare answers to any objections.

Set the stage: Decide when and where to confront her. Don't act on impulse. Wait for a moment of calm, a time free from distractions—not, for example, ten minutes before Thanksgiving dinner.

Plunge in: Once you've made your plan, stick to it. Every day you delay, the disorder gets worse.

Show your concern: Make it clear how you feel. Tell your daughter you love her but are concerned. Tell her she needs help, and why. If she says, "There's no problem," you can say, "I don't accept that. I'm worried, and I just can't look the other way when I see that you are hurting yourself."

Make "I" contact: Focus on how the problem affects *you* personally. Say, "I notice that you spend a lot of money on food," or, "I've heard you vomiting after dinner, and I feel very concerned." Show her how you feel. Doing so, rather than telling your daughter that she is "weak" or "bad," can reduce her tendency to be defensive.

State the goal: Your goal is to get help; stay focused on this goal. Tell her, "I have looked into it and I know help is available. If you'll see an expert, I'll do everything I can to support you." No matter how carefully you word it, however, an anorexic child will probably think you just want to make her fat. Reassure her that the goal is to overcome her fear of fatness and help her cope with difficult feelings.

Don't criticize: Avoid commenting on her appearance. You may think you are making helpful statements, but she may take them as criticisms. For example, when you say, "You're looking healthier," she may interpret your remark as, "You're getting fatter."

Listen!: Listening is hard work. Your feelings may be so strong that you have to resist the temptation to interrupt or make judgments.

Acknowledge her fears: For her, gaining weight may be scarier than dying. She may be terrified of being cooped up in a hospital or of being force-fed. Don't say, "There's nothing to be afraid of." Better to say, "I understand how you feel. A counselor can help you conquer those fears." Denying her feelings is something she does too much of already.

Be realistic: Treatment won't necessarily cure the disorder. It *can* teach other ways to think and behave. "Cure" comes as the patient applies those methods over time in different situations. Also, some anorexics fantasize that they can eliminate symptoms without restoring weight. Not true.

Keep plugging: You may not succeed at first. Be patient. Don't let the subject drop. If you keep at it, you add to your chances for success. Sometimes the danger to your daughter may warrant taking increasingly serious steps. Cut off her allowance; ground her; keep her home from school. If this doesn't work, you may find it helpful to get professional guidance to develop another strategy.

Stop "enabling": If you're not helping your daughter, then you are *enabling* her to get worse. Shift the responsibility to her. If she binges, she must replace that food. Make her pay for it, too. If she makes a mess of the bathroom, she must clean it up.

Make yourself available: Make sure she knows you are there to help. Open the lines of communication—not just about her disorder, but about anything that concerns her. Tell her, "I know you're going through a hard time, I'm here for you, I want to help." Of course, families who aren't very supportive can't change overnight. They may need therapy themselves. But it's worth the effort.

RESISTANCE

Dealing with eating disorders would be easy if all we had to do was say, "Eat normal-sized, healthy meals at regular times and you'll be fine." While the prescription is basically correct, nothing is that simple.

Remember, anorexics often don't think they are sick. Instead, their illness *is* their identity. Thinness makes them special. They are thus poorly motivated to accept treatment. Patients often agree to gain weight just so they can get out of the hospital. Once out, they may starve themselves all over again.

Also, although thinness makes them proud, many anorexics feel that at their core they are rotten, unlovable people. Therapy might mean exposing the horrible "truth" of their rottenness to an unsympathetic stranger. Given this fear, who *wouldn't* resist treatment?

Bulimics are often more receptive. As Lisa's story indicates, a bulimic's loss of control often impels her to seek help. Many welcome the chance to learn how to restore control over themselves and their eating.

Resistance springs not just from poor mental attitudes but from the physical consequences of the disorder as well. In anorexia, for example, the starvation itself may cause disturbed thinking. And some bulimics are so uncomfortable with any amount of food in their stomachs that even a small meal triggers the urge to vomit. Therapy that requires her to eat can cause physical as well as emotional discomfort. It takes time to get used to eating correctly again.

You need to work through the problem of resistance with your daughter. You both need a lot of support to reduce your fears— fears that are very real for both of you.

TREATMENT

The process of treatment begins at the first moment of contact. Because such contact usually comes by phone, treatment can start before the doctor and the patient have even met face-to-face.

As a doctor, I try to plant the seeds of success during those first, critical moments. If I create an atmosphere of *trust*, of caring, then there's hope. If my tone is judgmental or threatening, then the process may be doomed.

The next step is to meet with those involved. If the patient herself asked for help, then the first appointment is with her; when the parents make the call, I may ask to see them first. In other cases it may be best to see everyone at the same time.

The initial evaluation may take one or more meetings. However, if the situation is life-threatening and the patient needs to be hospitalized, I don't wait.

Every situation is different. If in your search for help you don't feel the caregiver is responding to your needs, discuss the problem with him or her. If you are still not satisifed, keep looking.

The Initial Assessment

I perform a complete assessment of the problem *before* the patient and I agree on a plan for treatment. Too many professionals say, in effect, "Welcome to our facility, here's how we'll treat you, now tell me all about your problem."

Typically I start by asking, "How may I help?" Patients often seem surprised that I play the role, not of adversary, but of collaborator on a joint project—as indeed I am.

The patient's initial response is most revealing. Here are some examples drawn from recent cases:

"You can't help me. My parents are the ones with the problem." This comment is typical of anorexics, who feel they aren't sick at all and have come just to get people "off their backs."

"My father called me fat, so I started losing weight." People with low self-esteem are very sensitive to such remarks. One fifteen-year-old patient, inspired by the Olympics, demonstrated a gift for gymnastics. When her coach said she might do better if she "lost a little weight," she began to diet. Unfortunately, she focused on weight loss at the expense of everything else. If starvation had been an Olympic event, she would have qualified for a medal.

"I look in the mirror and I get scared. I want to find some peace inside." Some patients know they are hurting themselves and want help in stopping. Especially in anorexia, the more distress the patient feels, the more motivated she is to get treatment.

Follow the Leader

In conversation I follow my patient's lead. Following someone's concerns, hopes, and resistances is more productive than a mechanical, by-the-numbers interrogation.

Sometimes when I ask, "How can I help?" she replies, "You can't help. I don't want to be here." I may then say, "Well, someone is concerned enough to insist that you come here. Maybe we need to look at what's going on in your life that makes you feel you need to starve yourself almost to the point of death." Or she may say, "I don't think you can help—nothing has worked so far." I might then ask, "What have you previously tried?" and explore why other efforts have failed. And because words mean different things to different people, I would explore what she means by certain terms. Does "desperate," for example, mean "confused" or "suicidal"?

Many times, the most telling clues come from something a patient avoids saying, or hesitates over. If a patient tells me something is none of my business, I'll respect that. But later, when we've established a higher level of trust, I may ask again.

Trust is crucial. It takes time to build trust, to demonstrate concern and show that my intention is to heal, not to harm. When I show a patient that I accept her feelings as valid—although I don't necessarily accept her way of dealing with those feelings—I send the message that the patient herself is worthwhile.

Areas of Focus in the Initial Assessment

After basic demographic questions—age, family status, and so on—I ask about eating behaviors. I also explore her social life, sexual history and attitudes, and her use of illicit drugs or alcohol. In later conversations we take a closer look at her answers.

Weight: One important area to explore is the patient's *weight history.* I ask patients about their "desired weight." When a patient who weighs 150 pounds says her ideal weight is 110, I will pursue the matter, asking how realistic she thinks that goal is. Often she responds, "Well, I'd *like* to hit one hundred and ten, but probably the best I could hope for is one hundred and twenty-five. I did get down to one hundred and twenty once, but only for three days. I felt miserable when I started gaining again."

Patients often recount their weight history in enormous detail, which is not surprising considering they focus on eating every waking moment. Actually, the ability to recall weight history often provides me with a vital number for anorexics: the *weight at which they stopped menstruating.* In restoring weight, the target weight needs to be above this level if patients are to overcome their phobia about resuming menses.

I also want to learn about her *attitudes toward weight*. Does her family comment frequently on weight and appearance? One patient traced her disorder to the fact that whenever her father saw a fat woman he said, "Look at that tub of lard!" She was so concerned he would say that about her—and thus stop loving her—that she began to starve herself.

And what about *mealtime behavior*? What is dinnertime like? Who is present? What turns does the conversation—if any—take?

I also explore her *attitude about her body*. What is her body image? Is it accurate or distorted? Does she focus on a particular area? Is there a clash between perception and reality?

Behavior: Next I'll look at the patient's behavior related to food and eating. What about *dieting*? Are certain foods "forbidden"? What are her attitudes about *weighing herself* and looking in the mirror?

Historical context: In family therapy, it is sometimes said that the calendar tells the story. I look to see how the problem evolved over time, and to find events that might have triggered the disorder. These events may include a loss (death of a relative), change (divorce, relocation), or rejection (breakup of a romance). Some details may emerge in conversations with parents. This isn't to say that the adults' perspective is better or more accurate than the patient's. Both points of view are often needed.

Family: I also want to know the patient's family background. Does she view her parents as strict or uninvolved? Is she starving for attention? Have there been traumatic events—death, separation, loss of a parent's job?

Thinking patterns: People with eating disorders often display black-and-white thinking: Everything is all one way or the other, with no room for subtle shadings. During the assessment, I listen for such clues so I can orient therapy to correct distorted ways of thinking.

Social milieu: How well does the patient function outside the family? Does she get along at school or on the job? Does she have friends? A lover? What else is there in her life besides the eating disorder? Obviously, if there *is* nothing else, giving up her behavior will be that much harder.

Substance abuse: Use of illicit drugs and alcohol severely complicates an eating disorder. I will always ask: Do you use alcohol or drugs? How often? How much? I try to avoid sounding like a prosecutor, but I have to know the facts if I am to be of any help. Detoxification is a critical element in managing eating disorders.

Suicidal feelings: As with substance abuse, if a troubled patient doesn't bring up the subject of suicidal thoughts, then I will make a point of asking about them directly.

Physical Examination

If the patient's primary physician hasn't already done so, I order a detailed medical workup, including complete blood count, blood chemistries, thyroid-function tests, urinalysis, and electrocardiogram. Even though a problem may appear to be psychological in origin, I have to rule out potentially treatable *physical* causes, such as a brain tumor.

For example, many anorexics suffer from intolerance to cold. They shiver all the time, despite the fact that they wear several layers of clothes, drink hot liquids constantly, and keep the heat turned up. Such sensitivity can also be a sign that the thyroid isn't up to par. I thus order thyroid-function tests to rule out this cause of a common anorexic symptom. It is important to distinguish between thyroid abnormalities that *result* from the body's attempt to compensate for the eating disorder from those that *cause* disordered eating, hyperactivity, or weight loss.

I also look for signs of possible vitamin and mineral deficiencies. A recent study by Dr. Richard Hall and associates at the University of Florida showed that a phenomenal 25 percent of hospitalized eating disorder patients, regardless of their diagnosis, have severely low levels of magnesium. Patients with low magnesium may develop difficulties with cardiac arrhythmias (posing the risk of sudden death), restlessness, diminished concentration and memory, hypertension, muscle weakness, leg cramps, and decreased feelings in the arms and legs. It's not necessarily hard to correct a magnesium deficiency—a few days or weeks of oral magnesium preparations should do it. But if the problem isn't corrected, it can result in fatal cardiac difficulties.

Electroencephalogram Tracing

EEG tracings have some value in the eating disorders workup. However, such tracings measure the patient's brain waves only at one point in time. They can thus fail to detect a seizure disorder even if one is present. If I strongly suspect a seizure disorder, I may order a twenty-four-hour continuous recording. Contrary to previous speculation, there doesn't seem to be a higher incidence of seizure disorders among patients with anorexia or bulimia than in the general population. A recent study by Dr. Harrison Pope and his colleagues at Harvard University showed no significant differences in the brain-wave abnormalities spotted on the EEGs of bulimic patients compared to depressed patients.

Psychological Tests

These broad-ranging tests reveal how the patient's mind works and may provide clues to the thinking patterns that contribute to the disorder. Such tests are certainly useful for inpatient treatment, where the expense and intensity of treatment calls for as rapid and complete a workup as possible. They may also be useful for an outpatient when there are questions about her cognitive functioning or the dynamics of her personality.

The Treatment Formulation: Putting It All Together

Each component—interviews, physical exam, tests—adds to understanding and reveals the direction treatment should take. However, it's not necessary, and may even be harmful, to wait for all the pieces to fall into place before treatment begins. If I see that a patient needs to be hospitalized *now,* I take immediate action.

Developing the treatment plan is a collaborative effort involving the doctor, patient, and family. Together we look at the problem from many angles, decide on the goals, and develop the approach that stands the best chance of working. Sometimes this involves drawing up a treatment contract that explicitly spells out goals and methods. More on this in Chapter Eight.

THE GOALS OF TREATMENT FOR ANOREXIA NERVOSA

The aim of any therapy is to help the patient return to a normal life. The anorexic needs to learn there are ways besides starvation to cope with the problems of growing up.

The first step is to *return the patient to a healthier physical condition.* The patient is not likely to benefit from psychotherapy if her starvation is too severe.

Let's disgress for a minute to look at the difficulties that starvation itself (that is, starvation not necessarily caused by anorexia) can cause. In a famous study by Ancell Keys at the University of Minnesota, thirty-six carefully screened normal males voluntarily decreased their food intake over six months. They each lost an average of 25 percent of their original body weight. The experimenters monitored their progress carefully.

The symptoms produced by starvation were the same we now know as the classic symptoms of anorexia. The men became preoccupied with food—reading cookbooks, collecting recipes, dreaming about food. They reported more depression and noticed that their ability to concentrate was impaired. They developed bizarre eating habits, such as mixing unusual types of foods together, creating superstitions surrounding certain foods, or stretching out their meals for extended periods of time. They noticed increased irritability, difficulty sleeping, a loss of interest in sex, and social withdrawal. After the experiment ended, a few of the men actually went on to become chefs.

The Keys study reveals why restoring weight is such a priority for treatment of anorexia. Extremely low weight, no matter what the cause, results in such severe disturbances in thinking and feeling that any form of therapy is unlikely to be successful until there is some degree of return to a healthier weight. Additionally, in some ways anorexia represents a phobia about mature body weight. As with other phobias, the fear won't go away until the patient confronts the things she fears most.

Once weight increases to a healthier level, we can start to address other aspects of the illness. We now begin to *resolve the underlying psychological issues* that contribute to the disorder. The task involves showing the patient how to accept herself and like herself. We help her build a new identity that isn't based solely on her ability to starve. In so doing, we loosen her grip on childhood and help her make the passage into adolescence and adulthood.

Through family therapy and social-skills training, we work to *improve the patient's relationships.* Anorexic girls are so focused on themselves and on their condition that they lose the knack of dealing with other people. They are scared of reaching out for fear they'll be rejected. As her peers grow and mature, the anorexic is left behind and now has a lot of catching up to do. Treatment focused on social-skills training can help.

THE GOALS OF TREATMENT FOR BULIMIA NERVOSA

Treatment of bulimia has a different focus. For one thing, anorexics need to do *more* of something—eating—while bulimics need to do *less* of something—bingeing and purging.

Rodney Dangerfield, the comedian, tells about the time he went to his doctor with a sore shoulder. Raising his arm, he said, "It hurts when I go like that." The doctor replied, "Don't go like that."

Unfortunately, breaking the binge-purge cycle is rarely that easy. Instead of just telling the patient, "Don't go like that," one must reduce the forces behind the urge to binge and purge. These forces include the physical effects that are caused by an irregular pattern of eating or trying to maintain a weight that is too low.

Another goal of treatment is to change the patient's characteristic cognitive distortions and disturbed emotional responses. For example, learning how to be more assertive can be a key element in recovery. A binge is frequently triggered by anger that the patient feels powerless to express. One woman told me her boss demanded that she work on a Saturday when she had made other plans. She suppressed her fury, telling herself that "I'm lucky to have this job, no one else would hire such a worthless person." She worked that Saturday, then went home and pigged out for two hours. After assertiveness training, such patients find it easier to "just say no" without feeling guilt or self-hatred.

Finally, improving family relationships can be very helpful, especially for patients living at home. But because bulimic families can vary widely in their dynamics, therapy must address the particular family pattern involved.

IN OR OUT OF THE HOSPITAL?

One crucial decision is whether the patient should be hospitalized or whether she can be managed as an outpatient. There are advantages and drawbacks to either approach.

It's generally better if treatment can take place outside the hospital. The patient won't be snatched out of her familiar surroundings and plunked down into a strange environment. Yet sometimes those "familiar surroundings" are contributing to her disorder.

And, of course, it's easier to monitor and control behavior in the hospital. Often the hospital provides a kind of safe haven in which a patient and her family can begin to gain control of the problem.

Realistically, you can't "cure" an eating disorder in the hospital. People have to eat every day for the rest of their lives. They have to learn how to function on their own, in the "outside world," without supervision. A bulimic woman usually has to keep wrestling with the urge to binge and purge even after she leaves the hospital. In follow-up counseling, we continue to work on controlling these urges.

Inpatient care is *required* when:

- There is a medical emergency—the patient is severely emaciated, has a severe electrolyte imbalance or arrhythmia, is blacking out, or is otherwise unable to function
- She can't keep any food down

- She is unable to break the binge-purge cycle
- She is severely depressed or suicidal
- She is so obsessed with food that she can't function
- She is a substance abuser and can't break the habit
- She is a severe laxative or diuretic abuser and can't stop as an outpatient
- She has a severe personality disorder that complicates her ability to be treated outside the hospital
- Her personal situation is so unstable that treatment outside of the hospital is impossible
- Her family can no longer cope with the problem
- A careful program of outpatient care fails to work
- Adequate outpatient care isn't available

Although hospitalization is expensive, it is certainly more effective—in terms of both symptom improvement and cost—than a prolonged, unsuccessful outpatient treatment, such as Lisa's psychoanalysis.

Now then: We've made the diagnosis, assessed the patient and her problem from many angles, considered the therapeutic options, and decided on the treatment formulation and setting. What actually happens in treatment?

7

The Medical Method

Eating disorders push patients to extremes. The anorexic girl becomes *severely* emaciated. The bulimic eats *huge* amounts of food and then takes drastic measures to rid herself of it. Treatment tries to restore moderation, to even things out once again.

Think again of the image of an out-of-control car careening down a hill. One way to help restore control would be to steer onto a more level driving surface, to flatten out the hill—in other words, to somehow *change the physical component of the problem.*

That's what I mean by medical treatment: therapy designed to correct the *physical* things that have gone wrong.

The body is a biological organism. Each function operates within a certain range. For example, a person normally breathes between ten and twenty times a minute. The heart beats between forty and seventy times a minute. The exact numbers depend on a lot of variables—activity, stress, overall health, and so on. At certain moments these rates may speed up or slow down, but over time they stay pretty much the same. The slope of the "biological hill" is gentle.

Not so in someone with an eating disorder. For her, the slopes labeled "hunger" and "satiety" are pretty steep. It doesn't take much of a push to set her rolling down that hill. As we have seen, the push can come in the form of emotional stress or a neurochemical imbalance. Medical treatment brings the biological problem back under control.

In anorexia, the first medical priority is to *stop weight loss*. The patient needs enough calories, not just to keep the body working, but to stop depleting its energy reserves.

Ideally, the patient will agree to eat voluntarily. As her doctor, I work with her to design a diet she can tolerate, both in terms of types of food and amounts to be consumed. Refeeding at too fast a pace can cause heart problems. Moderation is the key.

An anorexic girl who is not in immediate medical danger and who agrees to begin eating may be treated outside the hospital. Should she continue to lose weight or fail to gain enough weight during the next phase of treatment, she may require hospitalization.

The next step is to begin restoring weight. Unless starvation is reversed, its effects on behavior and mood—bizarre eating habits, impaired concentration, social withdrawal, and so on—will only persist. As long as they do, other forms of therapy don't stand a chance.

Restoration is also necessary because, as we have seen, anorexia reflects a phobia about weight. The fear won't really diminish until the patient confronts the very thing that makes her afraid. Unless and until she actually gains weight, any therapy directed at helping her cope with her fear is all theoretical—just talk.

Restoration doesn't mean the patient has to return to the highest weight she reached before the disorder took hold; it might be about 90 percent of that figure. Together we hammer out an agreement for weight gain. This agreement includes a list of the rewards granted for success and the consequences imposed for failure. Consequences include confinement to her bed, no social activities, and so on. I'll discuss this agreement, known as a behavioral contract, in Chapter Eight.

Weight restoration means eating enough calories so that excess energy can be stored in the body. It also involves eating the right balance of nutrients. Sometimes dietary supplements can be very helpful if the patient isn't yet eating enough of certain foods. There are some medications that in a few cases might help speed up a return to normal weight, either directly, by affecting eating-control centers in the brain, or indirectly, by reducing the anxiety surrounding eating. We'll look at some of these options in a moment.

Bulimia is a different story. Patients are at risk not from starvation but from the metabolic havoc their eating patterns cause. Changing the slope of the hill means breaking the cycle of bingeing and purging.

Bulimic behavior often arises from, or is reinforced by, bad habits. Therapy shows the patient how to break those habits. It teaches her the facts about food and helps her explore her feelings about eating and her body. Many patients can work on these goals without being hospitalized.

Sometimes, though, patients need the tightly structured medical environment of a hospital. Such an environment allows them to focus on their problem with the help of an experienced and supportive staff. They can work on the basic changes in thinking and lifestyle needed to free themselves from their habit.

No matter where treatment occurs, some patients may benefit from the careful use of medications. The rest of this chapter will look at what these medicines are and how they work—or don't work.

One caution: There is no "magic pill" for eating disorders. Much as I might like to, I can't sit down and write you a prescription guaranteed to cure your disorder in two weeks or even two years. Medications may help—sometimes they help a lot. But they aren't enough by themselves. At best they are just one part of a complete program of therapy.

Each patient is unique. Her illness springs from specific biological, social, and familial circumstances. Her thoughts and actions, and thus her symptoms, are hers alone. Similarly, she may respond to certain medications differently from another patient who has what appears to be the same disorder.

Some doctors believe drugs play only a minor role in treating eating disorders, but as a clinician, and as a practical person, I believe in using all the tools that work. In more than a few cases, I've seen medications produce a great deal of improvement over a fairly short time.

DRUG THERAPY FOR BULIMIA NERVOSA

Antidepressant Medications

The discovery that antidepressants can help relieve symptoms of bulimia represents a major medical success story. Treatment with antidepressants is one of the few drug strategies shown to be of any value in managing this illness. In fact, scientific studies have found that *use of these medications can reduce bingeing frequency by as much as 70 percent.*

As we have seen, there are connections between eating disorders and depressive disorders. Studies have shown that between 25 and 80 percent of eating disorder patients have major depression either currently or as part of their history. Of course, the distress of bulimia, like any chronic illness, can *cause* its victims to feel depressed. That's a normal reaction, but feeling sad because one is struggling with an illness is a totally different problem from clinical depression. In fact, studies show that in about half of the cases, depression starts a year or more before the bulimia even shows up.

Also, when we look at the relatives of eating-disordered people, we find a much higher incidence of affective disorders than in the normal population. Such findings suggest that susceptibility to these illnesses runs in families.

It's tempting to conclude that antidepressants only *seem* to work on bulimia because they treat the underlying mood disorder that so many patients also suffer from, but the evidence shows otherwise. Several studies specifically screened out those bulimic patients who also had depression. Even in the nondepressed group, the medications produced good results. For that matter, some studies found that depressed patients using these medications actually improved less in their eating disorder symptoms than the nondepressed group.

In Chapter Five we saw how the hunger and satiety feedback loops, and other biological systems as well, involve some of the neurotransmitters also involved in depression. Thus, even though these medications are called "antidepressants," it doesn't mean that eating behavior improves because depression lifts. There may be some bulimic people who benefit because the medications change the chemical systems that regulate feelings of hunger and satiety.

Which Antidepressant to Use?

Of all the classes of antidepressants, the tricyclic antidepressants, or TCAs, have been studied most. ("Tricyclic" refers to the drug's three-ring chemical structure.) The TCAs shown to work best are desipramine, imipramine, and amitriptyline. All of these products have some troublesome side effects—sedation, dry mouth, lowered blood pressure. Because it has the lowest incidence of side effects, desipramine is usually my first choice for treatment if I am using a tricyclic antidepressant. If a patient has trouble sleeping, I will consider prescribing a product that is more sedating, such as imipramine or amitriptyline.

Of course, because of her purging, a bulimic patient may have trouble keeping anything in her stomach. Medicine won't do any good if it doesn't get absorbed. I therefore ask my patients to take their medication just before bedtime, so the drug has time to work.

Sensible practice means giving the lowest dose of medication that still has a chance of producing benefit. Doing so minimizes the risk of side effects. If the patient doesn't seem to be responding, I gradually increase the dosage. We usually see results within a week or two, but, as in treatment for depression, an adequate trial of these medications often needs a good six weeks.

During the course of therapy it's necessary to monitor the levels of the medication in the patient's body. We do so by analyzing blood samples. This step is important because different people metabolize medications at different rates. Two people on the same dosage regimen may show very different plasma levels, and may thus have completely different responses to the medicine. We try to achieve the same plasma levels in bulimics as we do in depressed patients who use the medication.

Getting the right concentration of the drug can mean the difference between therapeutic success and failure. One study showed that a group of patients with a plasma level of desipramine that was below the therapeutic range noticed no improvement in their bulimia. But when the concentration was raised, four out of six patients stopped bingeing.

Some patients incorrectly think that "if a little medication works, then taking more should work even better." Nortriptyline (another tricyclic), for example, has what we call a "therapeutic window." This means there are both minimum and maximum levels of concentration that will provide benefits. Above or below those levels, the drug loses its effectiveness.

I also discuss the possible side effects with my patients before I write the prescription. Doing so helps prepare them for any problem they may have with the medication. This in turn improves compliance. If the patient is suicidal or psychotic, or if she abuses drugs or alcohol, antidepressants must be used with extreme caution.

As I've said, medications are just part of an overall treatment plan. Prescribing antidepressants without setting up a solid psychotherapeutic relationship with the patient may hurt her chances of getting better.

Monoamine Oxidase Inhibitors (MAOIs)

Like the TCAs, antidepressants of the MAOI class raise the levels of crucial neurotransmitters, but they do so in a different way, by inhibiting the action of an enzyme called monoamine oxidase. This enzyme breaks down certain compounds in the blood. By keeping monoamine oxidase from doing its job, the drug allows higher levels of certain neurotransmitters to circulate.

Studies show that two MAOIs, phenelzine and isocarboxazid,

effectively reduce or elminate bingeing. The dosages are the same as those used in treating depression. Drugs of this class pose a somewhat greater risk of side effects, such as lower blood pressure, agitation, or sleep disturbances, than do the TCAs.

There's another problem with MAOIs. Because they interfere with enzyme action, they affect the body's ability to break down an amino acid called tyramine. Too much tyramine floating around in the bloodstream can cause problems related to high blood pressure, such as excruciating headaches, internal bleeding and even death.

Certain foods contain high amounts of tyramine. The list includes cheeses, wines, beers, pickled herring, liver, yeast extract (including brewer's yeast), salami, pepperoni, bologna, yogurt, and fava beans. A patient should only take an MAOI if she understands the risk involved and agrees not to eat any foods containing tyramine.

A New Antidepressant

The most popular antidepressant in the United States these days is Prozac, the brand name of fluoxetine. Part of the reason for the enormous success of this medicine is that its side effects, when present, are often less troublesome than those of other antidepressants. While many antidepressants act on a variety of neurotransmitter systems, Prozac appears to work exclusively on the serotonin system. While some other antidepressants can cause weight gain, Prozac seems less likely to do so—a feature of particular interest for people with eating disorders. In fact, some people taking Prozac experience a decrease in weight.

Another interesting feature of Prozac is that it seems to reduce obsessive thinking in some patients. There is growing research on the overlap between obsessive-compulsive disorder and anorexia, and Prozac is being evaluated for its effectiveness in both of these disorders.

Current evidence seems to show that Prozac is as effective in reducing bingeing in bulimia as other antidepressants. Side effects can include agitation, nausea, fatigue, and insomnia. But on the whole, it is well tolerated by most patients.

When to Use Antidepressants?

Different doctors use medications differently. Some feel confident that these drugs work and should be tried first. Doing so, they feel, is cost-effective, and produces the most benefit in the shortest time. Other doctors prefer to use the various forms of psychotherapy described in the next part of this book. Then, if those strategies fail to produce enough improvement, they'll decide whether to step up to the use of medications.

Although I am convinced antidepressants can work, I am not so sure they result in long-term improvement once the patient stops taking them. If the patient's psychological, social, and family pressures haven't changed, then it's possible that her illness will persist or return. Of course, I will usually not hesitate to use antidepressants in patients who also have a clinical depression.

Research hasn't yet shown how long a bulimic patient should keep using antidepressants. As a rule, if the patient shows improvement during the initial six-week trial, we continue with the drug for at least six months. Doing so decreases the possibility of relapse.

Many patients fear using medications. They are afraid the drug will make them "high," like cocaine, or that they will become addicted. I try to reassure patients that such fears are groundless. While antidepressants do help a depressed person return to a normal mood, they do not produce a "high" in someone who is already at a normal level. They are also not addictive.

Other Medications

Fenfluramine: This product also enhances serotonin activity and is widely used to promote weight loss in obese people. Recently a study found that fenfluramine may significantly reduce symptoms of both bulimia and depression.

Opiate antagonists: In Chapter Five, we talked about the role of endogenous opiates (endorphins) in regulating eating. Certain drugs can block these opiates and thus reduce their effect on behavior. One of these products, naltrexone, is used to treat heroin addicts. Theory has it that naltrexone may also have a role in managing eating disorders. However, clinical results so far are mixed. One study turned up no evidence that naltrexone led to weight loss in obese people. And a study at the usual dosage level failed to show any impact on bingeing behavior, although a study at a dosage four times as high saw a significant reduction in bulimic symptoms. Unfortunately, such high doses also resulted in a high rate of nausea and a serious risk of liver toxicity.

Anticonvulsant drugs: In some ways, bulimia resembles a seizure disorder such as epilepsy. Seizure disorders involve misfires in the electrical system of the brain. Like seizures, bulimic binges are episodic—that is, they occur at unpredictable intervals rather than constantly. Both binges and seizures make their victims feel out of control. Many bulimics look on their binges as repugnant or inconsistent with their true personality—in other words, they feel their binges are somehow foreign, not really a part of themselves. People with seizures often make similar remarks.

To find out whether eating binges were the result of faulty brain wiring, some researchers studied the electroencephalograph readings of bulimic patients. Because they found brain waves similar to those seen in epilepsy, these researchers tried giving their patients phenytoin, an antiseizure medication (sold under the brand name Dilantin). They reported that the drug was effective. Unfortunately, subsequent studies, failing to replicate these findings, indicated no more than mild results with phenytoin.

Another study looked at carbamazepine (sold under the brand name Tegretol), an anticonvulsant related to the TCAs that is used to treat seizure disorders and manic depression. Results showed that carbamazepine had a profound effect on a bulimic woman who also suffered from a mood disorder that resembled manic depression, but had no effect on five other patients in the study.

Thus the notion that bulimia is primarily a form of seizure disorder, and that antiseizure medications can help, hasn't won many supporters over the last twenty years or so.

Antianxiety medications: Anxiety can set the binge-purge cycle in motion. Because therapy must address the patient's anxiety, naturally it's tempting to consider using one of the many antianxiety drugs on the market.

Perhaps the most widely known of these are the benzodiazepines such as diazepam (sold under the brand name Valium). We used to call these "minor tranquilizers" because they seemed relatively safe compared to the "major tranquilizers," such as chlorpromazine.

We now realize there's nothing "minor" about them. These powerful medications have a high potential for abuse and can lead to dependency. In the state of New York, for example, the law now requires that doctors follow the same procedures in prescribing benzodiazepines as they do when prescribing narcotics, another class of drugs with high potential for abuse. As we have seen, bulimics have a high incidence of substance abuse, and may misuse an antianxiety drug. Side effects include drowsiness, disorientation, and headaches.

Antianxiety medicines do have a specific use, however. I may prescribe them for a limited time when a patient knows she is about to face a highly stressful situation, such as a family reunion or a trip home for Thanksgiving.

Stimulant medications: Although amphetamines may help reduce appetite and produce antidepressant effects, these drugs have a high potential for abuse and are almost never appropriate for use by bulimics.

Lithium carbonate: Some physicians have given lithium, commonly used in treating bipolar disorders, to bulimics. A few of those treated, including some who didn't respond to other antidepressants, noticed a drop in their bingeing and purging episodes. We don't yet have good controlled studies proving the effectiveness of this medication. Lithium has a serious drawback: It depletes the body's supply of potassium. As we have seen, bulimics who vomit a lot or who abuse laxatives or diuretics are already at risk of low potassium. The medical literature contains at least one report of a bulimic woman who died of cardiac failure caused by the combined effects of vomiting and lithium.

DRUG THERAPY FOR ANOREXIA NERVOSA

Antidepressant Medications

Unfortunately, the few good studies on the use of antidepressants in treating self-starvation have produced nothing like the results seen in bulimia. The specific antidepressants studied so far include clomipramine and amitriptyline. Clomipramine, recently approved for use in this country and sold under the brand name Anafranil, is used to treat obsessive-compulsive disorder, which has some features in common with anorexia. The theory was that the same drug might prove effective in both. So far, however, results have been inconclusive. We need more studies, especially ones looking at the use of clomipramine in higher doses.

If we can one day find the right antidepressant, we may help anorexics in two ways. First, these medications can improve depressed mood. When that happens, the patient's attitudes may improve not just about eating but about life in general. Second, such drugs may correct the underlying biological malfunctions that produce the symptoms of the disorder.

Depression by itself can cause weight loss. Conversely, weight loss can lead to depression. As I've indicated, my approach generally is to refeed the patient first and see what happens. If her mood improves, fine; no medication is needed. If not, I will think about using an antidepressant. In certain circumstances I may try these products before the patient regains weight if her mood disturbance is severe, or if she engages in compulsive rituals that interfere with her ability to function.

Even so, antidepressants pose risks, such as lowered blood pressure or problems with the way electric signals travel through the heart. One common side effect may be weight gain. As you might expect, an anorexic who is aware of this may resist taking her medication.

Studies on lithium carbonate haven't shown that it is of much use in treating anorexia. Some reports state that patients gained a little weight and experienced better moods. However, the weight gain may have resulted from salt and water retention, a known side effect of lithium. I wouldn't use this drug on an anorexic unless she also happened to suffer from manic-depressive illness.

Antipsychotic Medications

At one time people thought anorexia might be a form of schizophrenia. We know now, of course, that they are completely different disorders, although in rare cases a person may suffer from both at the same time. An anorexic doesn't usually have the hallucinations commonly seen in schizophrenia. One primary anorexic symptom—feeling fat when actually being very thin—comes close to being a delusion. However, whereas an anorexic can usually see the difference between her body and that of someone who weighs two hundred pounds, a schizophrenic may not be able to make such a distinction.

About thirty years ago, doctors began treating anorexics with chlorpromazine, more commonly known as Thorazine, an antipsychotic drug used in the treatment of schizophrenia. Although these patients did gain a little more weight, their illness didn't improve over the long term. What's more, compared to a control group, a higher percentage of patients on Thorazine developed bulimia. It also took longer for their menstrual periods to return. Although some doctors continue to prescribe Thorazine, its popularity has dropped off substantially.

These medications may perhaps have some particular use for certain very small groups of patients: those who are extremely anxious or who are obsessive-compulsive. Another group may benefit from the drugs' sedating effects, especially very restless patients who, because of their severe medical condition, must be confined to their beds.

Antipsychotics can cause weight gain, a side effect that, in anorexia anyway, is actually desirable. However, antipsychotic medicines have many drawbacks: lowered blood pressure, the risk of seizures, delayed return of menstruation. These drugs are notorious for causing long-term or even permanent neurologic damage, such as the involuntary muscle movements known as tardive dyskinesia.

Antianxiety Medications

When an anorexic is highly anxious, antianxiety medicines can be more helpful than the antipsychotics. Anxiety can take many forms: fear of fatness; concern about living up to "other people's expectations" about thinness; worry about criticism from family and friends. Anorexics have deep fears about body size and shape, and may feel traumatized by bodily changes during puberty.

Anxiety only feeds these fears and makes them worse. For example, a girl may feel that eating anything at all will make her fat. She thus relieves her anxiety by cutting out virtually all foods from her diet. What's more, an anorexic is often perfectionistic by nature. She may grow anxious if something is amiss or out of place in her otherwise tightly structured life.

Antianxiety medications are sometimes used for the small minority of anorexic patients who have such extreme anxiety about eating that they are unable to function even in a supportive environment. Antianxiety medications that are "short acting," such as lorazepam or oxazepam, seem to be tolerated better than the "long-acting" medications such as diazepam (Valium). Side effects can include sedation and dizziness; anorexics are often highly sensitive to such feelings. As we saw earlier, there is also a serious risk of addiction.

I find that anxiety-ridden patients tend to tolerate these medications better and experience fewer side effects than they do with antidepressants. If a patient has extreme anxiety at mealtime, I may consider offering her a short-acting medicine such as lorazepam or oxazepam.

Other Medications

Some physicians have experimented with the use of hormones to treat anorexia. Insulin, for example, stimulates the metabolism of glucose (blood sugar). When the glucose level drops, it causes hypoglycemia (low blood sugar), which in turn triggers the appetite center in the brain to send out "feed me" signals. Thus, administration of insulin can stimulate appetite. This technique has largely fallen out of favor, however; among other things, as we have seen, lack of appetite is not the central problem in anorexia.

Recently there's been increasing interest in the use of cyproheptadine (sold under the brand name Periactin). This antihistamine is used to treat allergies and often causes mild weight gain as a side effect. Cyproheptadine is a serotonin antagonist—that is, it keeps serotonin from linking up with its receptors in the brain. By blocking serotonin, cyproheptadine lets the patient keep eating and thus gain weight. Studies seem to indicate that while cyproheptadine is a little better than a placebo (a "sugar pill") at relieving depression and at helping some hospitalized anorexics gain weight, the difference is generally not significant. Interestingly, this drug seems to produce some weight gain in nonbulimic anorexics, especially those who were born at lower weights than normal, but not in bulimic anorexics.

Because marijuana stimulates appetite, researchers wondered if marijuana's active ingredient, tetrahydrocannabinol, might work in anorexia. As it turned out, it didn't; not only did it produce no effect on weight, it also caused the patients to experience unpleasant moods.

Some medications might have use, not for the anorexia itself, but for some of the other physical problems associated with the disorder. For example, many patients relearning how to eat complain that the presence of food in their stomachs causes them to feel painful bloating. This is normal, even predictable, since their bodies have largely forgotten what it feels like to take in food. As we saw in Chapter Five, anorexia disrupts many of the feedback loops regulating digestion. In some cases, use of medications to speed up emptying might help. Other such medications include bethanechol and metoclopramide. We don't yet have all the facts we need, however, to use these medications regularly as part of the medical treatment plan. Simethicone, a compound used to reduce gas and found in many over-the-counter digestive aids, can also help relieve the discomfort of refeeding.

I've just given you several pages of information on drugs that have been investigated as possible treatments for anorexia. I must state again, however, that medications have not yet proved as helpful for anorexia as they have for bulimia. In my experience, no medication can substitute for a comprehensive program that addresses the many behavioral, cognitive, and family issues contributing to the illness. At best, drugs serve as a means of temporarily relieving a symptom, of taking some of the heat off the patient, so that we can begin to tackle the real problem.

THE FUTURE: WHERE DO WE GO FROM HERE?

There's still a lot we don't know about the use of medications in eating disorders. For instance, we are not yet able to look at the exact patterns and severity of the illness and say, "These patients should have Drug A and these should have Drug B." The presence of depression doesn't necessarily mean that a patient will respond to an antidepressant. Conversely, some patients without depressive symptoms *do* seem to get better after taking these drugs. No formula, no therapeutic "cookbook," exists to tell us how to combine medications with other forms of therapy, or in what quantities. We also lack information on how long patients should continue taking medication or what happens when they stop.

While medication may help control an individual's symptoms or relieve her suffering, it's fair to say that there will never be a perfect eating disorder drug. Eating is not a wholly private affair; it takes place within a larger context. Better to think of eating as an interchange between the body and its environment. No pill or injection is going to change the many outside factors that affect a person's behavior and her attitudes about food and eating.

For that you need other kinds of therapy, as we'll see in the remaining chapters.

8

Breaking the Habit: Learning, Doing, Thinking

In the last chapter, I explained how medical therapy can smooth out the biological "slope" of the eating disorder. But the patient is by no means out of danger. Her metaphorical car has slowed but has not stopped. Remember too that the car is beset with mechanical problems: faulty brakes, a balky steering wheel. What more can be done to help?

Well, imagine that a mechanic, walking along the same road, realizes that the driver is in peril. Somehow he (or she) manages to leap aboard the car as it passes by. Even while the car is in motion, this nimble artisan sizes up the problem, selects the tools needed for the job, and sets to work. With a little bit of luck, he might be able to get the brakes back into some kind of working order, thus restoring even more control.

Translating metaphor into medicine, the mechanic in this story becomes the therapist and the tools are the various treatments. In this chapter we'll look at three of the most important of these therapies: educational, behavioral, and cognitive. *Educational therapy* provides the basic facts the patient needs to know about her condition and how to improve it, *behavioral therapy* helps her act in healthier ways, and *cognitive therapy* shows her where her thinking has gone awry and how to replace distorted thoughts with more realistic ones. Working together, these techniques help to "brake" the bad eating habits that cause so much suffering.

THE ROLE OF THE THERAPIST

Much of any therapy's success depends on the skills and sensitivities of those who administer it. The job description for an eating disorder therapist calls for someone who will take an *active* role in the process, rather than one who adopts the neutral, interpretive stance of classic psychoanalysis. Since sometimes just learning the truth sets the patient on the right road, a therapist must provide accurate information and advice about eating and nutrition. In more severe cases, being therapeutically active means insisting on hospitalization or devising a plan for gaining weight outside the hospital.

The therapist may need to provide reassurance and support at every step. Eating disorder patients can be highly anxious about their situation. Anorexics, for example, often feel a sense of panic when their weight begins to rise or when menstruation returns. The therapist should anticipate this panic and know how to deal with it. Some anxiety arises because the patient has lost her ability to recognize her inner feelings. One of the greatest services a therapist provides is teaching the patient what her true feelings are and showing her that they are valid.

Properly handled, the relationship between the therapist and the patient provides a context of *trust.* The patient is gradually able to discuss "bad" feelings more freely and with less fear or shame. In time she begins to trust *herself.* When she reaches that milestone, she begins to feel she can trust other people as well. Therapy becomes a sort of microcosm of the whole world, and of the patient's process of growth and maturation within that world.

If you are in treatment, or if you are shopping for a therapist, keep the above points in mind. A health-care professional who lacks these basic skills, or who fails to earn your trust, is less likely to be helpful.

There's no hard and fast rule stating which type of therapy should be tried first. The choice depends on many factors. In less extreme cases I might hold off using medication until I've given other forms of therapy a chance. However, in dealing with a patient who has binged and purged every day for fifteen years but who will only be staying in the hospital for a month, I will be inclined to use every means at my disposal—not just medications but intensive individual, group, and family therapy as well. Some might describe this as a shotgun approach—but if you only have one shot, a shotgun can be pretty effective.

EDUCATIONAL THERAPY

Educational therapy, sometimes known as psychoeducational therapy, involves teaching people the facts they need to overcome their disorder. It is not always a substitute for psychotherapy but can be a very helpful adjunct to it. In a sense, this book is in itself a form of psychoeducational therapy.

Some of the best work in this field has come from eating disorder specialists at the University of Toronto. They recently conducted an important piece of research comparing the effectiveness of different treatments in reducing the symptoms of bulimia. Amazingly enough, they found that for the healthiest 40 percent of the bulimia patients, educational therapy—in the form of a short lecture course—was as effective as a much longer treatment involving individual cognitive-behavioral therapy. The lecture course gave information about bulimia as well as self-care strategies to help the patients learn how to return to normal eating habits. The findings of this research suggest that it makes sense to begin treating bulimia patients with educational therapy and reserve costly, time-consuming individual therapy for those who don't get better after learning the facts about their disease.

I can think of few other illnesses in which there can be such a dramatic therapeutic response after taking the simple step of learning the facts. In the next few pages, let's review some of these facts as they might be covered in a course of educational therapy.

Our society keeps turning up the pressure to be thin. As a result many women resort to severe dieting. Our bodies, however, operate under biological rules. Each of us has a certain predetermined weight range—the set point range—that our bodies fight to maintain. For many people, this range is higher than what society says is the "ideal standard" for beauty.

Excessive or constant dieting robs the body of the food it needs to maintain the weight it prefers. The body then turns up the volume on the "hunger" signals. The result: bingeing.

Some people then try to undo the damage by purging, which leads to a vicious cycle. The woman binges with less guilt, since she knows purging will protect her from gaining weight. And she binges because it's easier to vomit with a full stomach. Purging also keeps the body in a constant state of semistarvation and dehydration. The cycle leads to anxiety and depression, which the woman then attempts to relieve through further eating.

After prolonged disruption, a person's body may lose its ability to control eating. A woman must then relearn what it means to feel hungry, how to eat properly, and when to stop eating. She also has to learn to feel comfortable and not feel anxious when her body returns to its natural set point weight range.

But how does she know what that range is? In other words, what should her "goal," or target weight, be? That's something educational therapy can show her. First, the weight should be such that she can maintain it easily. She should be able to stay at that weight without resorting to extreme dieting, which as we have seen promotes bingeing. Secondly, the goal should be an individualized weight, not one derived from statistical charts.

Actually, the best goal is really a "no-goal." By that I mean the woman should stop thinking in terms of weights and numbers and concentrate instead on learning better habits. Through psychoeducation, she learns how to eat reasonably, exercise regularly, and develop ways of coping with stressful feelings without using food as self-medication.

Reaching this no-goal, however, usually occurs at the end of therapy. There are lots of steps in between, some of which involve setting up concrete objectives and working to achieve them. For example, an anorexic needs to know how much weight she has to regain. Her target should be neither too high nor too low, and should be a range rather than a precise number. As a rule, I ask patients to reach roughly 90 percent of the stable highest weight they had prior to the onset of their disorder. Each patient is different, but many find they can reverse starvation and maintain a reasonable weight without subsequently feeling the urge to binge and purge.

MYTHS ABOUT WEIGHT CONTROL

A lot of patients have trouble getting better because they've let certain myths about eating and weight take root in their minds. One aspect of educational therapy is to uproot these myths. Here are some of the most destructive myths, and my responses to them.

"Body weight should be constant." Wrong. Body weight fluctuates daily. Women also experience monthly weight changes because the menstrual cycle affects both calorie intake and the amount of water the body retains. This constant flux is why we urge patients to achieve a weight range, rather than a specific target.

"Laxatives and diuretics will help me lose weight." Diuretics only cause water weight loss (and possible dehydration). They do nothing to reduce the amount of fat stored in the body. A complication arises when a patient stops using diuretics: A "rebound" effect occurs, which may cause her to regain more weight than she had when she started using these products.

Laxatives also affect water weight. You see, laxatives do their work only after the food has reached the large intestine. But by then most of the calories have already been absorbed. Some people use laxatives as a form of self-punishment to "atone" for the guilt they feel after bingeing.

"Bulimia is just a bad habit. It doesn't do any harm." If you've read this far, you know that just isn't true. Denial is a big problem. An eating-disordered person often thinks that if she just ignores the dangers they'll go away. But burying her head in the sand won't stop the rotting teeth, the stomach problems, the seizures, the heart damage. Patients find it easier to cling to this myth than to change their ways. Overturning long-standing habits and jettisoning deeply held values is tough work, especially since our entire thin-loving culture creates and reinforces those values, regardless of their impact on health.

A patient needs to be motivated in her quest to overcome her eating disorder. Psychoeducational therapy can help create this motivation. When she learns the facts, the patient realizes that an eating disorder is a form of Russian roulette, with unhealthy eating as the bullet.

COGNITIVE-BEHAVIORAL TREATMENT FOR BULIMIA

For those patients who require more than simple education to improve, cognitive-behavioral therapy is very useful. One of the leading proponents of this approach is Christopher Fairburn of Oxford University. Some of his insights, which I'll summarize below, provide very useful tools for overcoming bulimia.

Behavioral therapy can be divided into three stages:

Stage One

In the first stage the patient's main goal is to return to a pattern of regular eating. We want to establish a routine whereby she plans to eat three or four meals per day and possibly one or two planned snacks.

The key here is *planning*. A patient should know when she is due to eat next. She shouldn't skip meals, nor should she rely on her appetite to tell her when to eat. If her plan calls for her to eat lunch at one o'clock, then she should do so, eating everything she planned to eat whether she feels hungry or not. She shouldn't snack unless the snack is part of the plan. Of course, the woman should not go for long periods without food. She shouldn't skip breakfast, for example.

Sticking to the plan takes priority over other activities. It's okay to accept dates, for example, but the patient must structure her social life around her meal plan. Her schedule may change on weekends, but she needs to plan those changes carefully.

The *content* of meals is less important than the regular *pattern* of meals during this phase. I urge the patient not to count calories, for instance. Instead she should eat average-size portions. She should wear loose clothing when she eats, since feeling constricted can lead to feelings of fullness. Here are some other helpful hints on controlling eating:

TIPS FOR CONTROLLING EATING

- Don't engage in other activities while eating: Don't watch TV, read, talk on the phone, do homework, and so on
- Restrict eating to one room of the house
- Limit food available when eating. Discard leftovers. Practice leaving some food on the plate. Limit supplies of binge foods in the house; keep "safe" foods around instead
- Plan food-shopping expeditions. Make a shopping list and stick to it. Don't shop when hungry. Carry just a little money when shopping, especially if you feel you aren't in good control
- Buy foods that need a lot of preparation, rather than those that can be eaten immediately
- Get rid of laxatives and diuretics
- Discard clothes that are too small
- Make adequate plans for your time—too much or too little unstructured time increases the possibility of bingeing

---

If a patient eats too rapidly, she needs to slow down. Satiety signals need a little time to take effect. One tip: Put the fork down between mouthfuls and swallow before taking the next bite. It helps to savor food, pausing once in a while to decide whether or not to keep eating. I ask patients not to drink a lot of fluids during the meal, since doing so can exaggerate the feeling of fullness.

At first a patient may feel full after eating very little. Such feelings may trigger the urge to vomit. We work together to create a list of alternative activities so that she can distract herself and counteract these urges. One such list might include the following:

- Make a list of friends' names and telephone numbers and call them when urges strike
- Visit friends
- Exercise (moderately)
- Go to a movie
- Take a bath or shower
- Write a letter
- Garden
- Knit or sew
- Read
- Listen to music

During this first stage the patient needs to keep checking on her progress. She should evaluate her eating daily. If she is successful, she needs to praise herself. On the other hand, she shouldn't overreact to failure. She needs to avoid turning a small slipup into a major catastrophe.

Once regular eating patterns return, her binge frequency should drop. The patient can then begin to examine the causes of her bingeing. Does she eat to relieve anxiety or depression? Is she bored? Does eating bring on sleep? Is she trying to compensate for something (perhaps even a monotonous diet)? Is purging self-punishment, or a way of expressing anger that she should direct at other people?

We also talk about situations that may contribute to the problem. Does she keep too much food in the house? Does her home environment interfere—is there too much stress or chaos?

One way of keeping track of these elements is through the food diary. The patient uses these sheets to record her feelings and actions connected with food. The food diary is a crucial element in therapy, offering a window on the patient's behavior. The vital information on these sheets becomes the raw material for our therapy sessions.

During the first stage of therapy, we work out a plan for keeping track of the patient's weight. Weighing too often can lead to anxiety and obsessions about weight. As I mentioned, everyone has day-to-day fluctuations in weight. For a patient, a slight rise can trigger panic and a sense of failure. These feelings may cause her to give up, leading her back down the path of bingeing and purging. On the other hand, if she never weighs herself, she just continues to feed her phobia about doing so. We have to strike the right balance—usually about once a week is enough.

I encourage the patient to discuss her disorder openly with friends and family. Removing some of the secrecy helps alleviate guilt and shame. It also lets other people take a more active role. Knowing that a family member is having trouble helps others to understand her behavior and offer emotional support.

By the end of this first stage we usually see a lot of improvement. The patient's mood is better, and the frequency of her bingeing drops. If not, though, I will consider adding medication or admitting her to the hospital.

Stage Two

During the second phase, we continue to work on developing regular eating habits. We also begin to change the makeup of her diet.

As we have seen, people with eating disorders often adopt rigid rules about what can and can't be eaten. They create a list of "forbidden foods"—fattening or sweet foods they want but won't allow themselves to have. Avoiding these foods makes them feel in control. However, these are often the very foods they run to when they lose control and binge.

It's a quirk of human nature: Whatever is forbidden becomes the thing we most desire. When a bulimic decides certain foods are "off limits," she creates an overwhelming temptation. In Stage Two, we work to reduce her feeling that she is completely helpless in the presence of forbidden foods. The goal is to take the power away from food and return it to the patient.

One method is to rank these foods in order of "danger level" and then gradually reintroduce them into the diet, starting with the least "dangerous" food. When she learns she can eat a few french fries, for example, and not feel driven to binge, she starts to feel in control. Success breeds success. Regaining a little bit of control reduces fear and gives her encouragement to keep trying. She may need a lot of coaching from her therapist and from others in her family to reach this point.

The best way to handle a phobia is to gradually increase exposure to the thing you fear. When the patient learns how to manage forbidden foods, she conquers some of her fears. Sometimes, for example, a patient tells me she will only eat something if she knows its calorie content. As an exercise, then, we work on eating foods whose calories are unknown. Or she may dread eating in restaurants or at parties. We find ways to expose her to those situations and build up her tolerance. Doing so takes her out of the "danger zone."

One method to help with purging is technically known as *exposure plus response prevention.* We expose the patient to the problem—feeling full after eating—and prevent her usual response to it—vomiting. If the patient is in the hospital, we ask her to sit with a staff member for an hour or so after a meal. Eventually she gets used to the feeling of having food in her stomach. She learns that she needn't respond to the feeling by giving in to her urge to purge. This strategy works especially well when the patient vomits often, or when eating anything at all triggers purging. If needed, we can use the method with outpatients as well.

During the second stage, the patient does better if she reduces her "magical thinking" about food. She also needs to learn new ways of thinking about, and solving, her problems. As I'll explain shortly, cognitive therapy helps her achieve these goals.

In many cases, at the end of the second stage the patient has stopped bingeing completely, or binges only once in a while. Her attitudes about weight, body shape, and herself are much healthier.

Stage Three

During the third phase, we continue to build on successes during the previous stages—continuing regular eating and relaxing the patient's need to control her diet. But now we shift our focus and prepare the patient to leave therapy and strike out on her own.

Many patients notice that their normal feelings of hunger and fullness have returned. This in itself makes it easier to control eating. We still work with the food diary, which will indicate whether there's a problem that we still need to work on.

In fact, slipping back gives us a chance to address a key issue: the risk of relapse. Patients are always in danger of slipping back into old habits. Perfectionism is hard to shake; many patients believe that once they regain control, all will be well forever. Not so. Better to face the reality that relapse is possible, especially during times of stress.

The message is that a little slip does not mean total, crushing defeat. Instead, I urge the patient to remember how far she has come, and that she has learned a lot about how to deal with her illness. Through her diary, she knows how to look at her situation and discover what may have triggered her binge. Eventually she will learn how to avoid these triggers.

BEHAVIORAL TREATMENT FOR ANOREXIA NERVOSA

In anorexia, the first goals are to stop the patient from starving and to reverse her weight loss. Only then can we work on the emotional problems that led to the disorder in the first place.

Another goal is to show her how to reduce anxiety, not just about weight gain, but about food and eating as well. For an anorexic who also binges and purges, an additional goal is to stop her bulimic behavior. Although some of the methods described below are for inpatient treatment, they can also be adapted for use with outpatients.

As in bulimia, there are three phases of behavioral treatment. First is the evaluation. During this time we conduct medical tests and get to know the patient. We draw up the treatment contract, which spells out the goals for weight gain and which both the patient and her parents sign. In this early phase, we tell the patient she must maintain at least the same weight she had when she was admitted. Otherwise she will be confined to her bed to save precious calories.

Once things have settled down we move into the next phase, during which we work toward the goal of bringing her weight back up to a healthier level. The contract specifies this target range, which is not subject to further negotiation because it is based on what we believe will be physically healthy for the patient.

We monitor the patient's progress by weighing her daily. To get the most accurate reading, we weigh her in the morning, before breakfast and after she has gone to the bathroom. She wears only a robe. If knowing her weight will make her anxious, she faces away from the scale. We reward her for actual weight gain, rather than for her eating behavior during meals. The reason for focusing on weight rather than eating behavior is that the patient may give the appearance of eating all she is being served but may be getting rid of the food when no one is looking.

Our usual inpatient contract asks that the patient gain one half-pound a day. Such a goal is both reasonable and safe. Gaining weight too fast can cause edema or cardiac failure. If the patient reaches this goal, and is in no medical danger, she earns full privileges, such as complete recreation and visiting privileges. A gain of between a quarter and half a pound means only partial privileges. No gain—back to bed. This isn't a punishment—bed is simply the safest place for a starving person to be. We also negotiate other incentives for weight gain at various points along the way: new clothes or records, special trips outside the hospital, and so on.

Gaining weight requires more calories than simply maintaining weight. Patients gradually work up to eating perhaps four thousand calories a day. Since the goal is not to teach someone to eat huge quantities of food or become bulimic, I usually add high-calorie liquid supplements such as Sustecal or Ensure to her normal amount of solid food.

Instead of requiring a specific daily weight gain, some doctors use a graph. A curve on the graph represents what the patient should weigh as time progresses. As long as her weight stays above that line, she earns full privileges. This method has one advantage over a daily weight-gain requirement. Especially during the early phases, a patient's weight may fluctuate quite a lot, even if she is eating well, due to changes in water balance. A graph can take such fluctuations into account, which may keep the patient from being unfairly penalized.

Critics of the behavioral contract point out that an anorexic needs to develop a sense of self. She must find an identity that doesn't depend on starvation. The contract, they claim, robs her of the opportunity to grow by imposing on her a mechanistic, prefabricated set of rules.

I disagree. My experience convinces me that many people with eating disorders welcome intervention by others, so long as it is done in a way that genuinely respects their individuality. A contract sets up boundaries and limits. It gives shape and focus to a world that is spinning out of control. The patient knows what to expect and what the consequences of her actions will be. I'm not saying that she necessarily *likes* those limits. Sometimes one benefit of the contract is to give her something to react to—or against. She finally has a focus for her anger. This in turn might help her to express anger rather than turn it inward. For people with an eating disorder, recognizing and dealing with anger is a good step in the right direction.

Having a contract reduces the "arbitrariness" of treatment and makes it easier to accept. The rules are codified, written down, and stored away someplace—somewhat like the Constitution. The patient might argue about how to interpret those rules, or how they should be enforced, but she can't dispute that they exist.

Of course, it's important to work with patients to help them overcome their fears and anxieties. I tell them, "Look, I know this whole situation is pretty scary. But we want to help you. Of course we want you to gain weight, but that's really your responsibility. We're not going to be spies and monitor every mouthful you eat. But if you find you're having trouble, we'll have someone sit with you and help you get through the fear. Yes, we need to give you enough calories so that you begin to gain weight, but we don't want to go too fast. We're not here to just fatten you up and send you on your way. We want to help you gain weight in a healthy and calm manner, so that we can begin to find out what's really troubling you deep down inside."

The food journal provides clues about strategies that might work. Anorexics might not be ready to fill out such sheets, especially at first. They dwell on food constantly anyway; writing it all down might just make them more anxious (that can be true for bulimics, too). If they feel that way, I don't push it. Sometimes keeping a journal focusing just on feelings and events (not food) can be useful.

A journal can provide a vivid record of the patient's thoughts and feelings about her situation. By examining these thoughts, we can often reveal distortions in the way the patient perceives and interprets events in her life. Cognitive therapy, which I will discuss in just a moment, is a good method for correcting such distortions.

In the final phase, we concentrate on helping the patient maintain her weight within the target range. We reinforce normal eating habits and look ahead to her continued recovery as an outpatient.

Before sending her home, we work out a plan to monitor her weight. We agree on who should do the weighing—a doctor, a nurse, her parents. She understands that if her weight drops below a certain limit, she will have to come back to the hospital.

A word about outpatients: It is possible to set up a contract with anorexics treated outside the hospital, even though they are not being monitored twenty-four hours a day. Usually such contracts set lower goals for weight gain—say, between one and two pounds a week. In family therapy sessions we work out the system of rewards and penalties. The parents may agree, for example, that if the patient fails to meet her target, they will suspend her allowance or ground her.

COGNITIVE THERAPY

Cognitive therapy works to change the way the patient thinks, not just about food and eating, but about herself and her world. Of course, thoughts and actions are intertwined. Thus behavioral therapy and cognitive therapy are in a sense two sides of the same coin. Changing distorted ways of thinking can allow healthier behaviors to emerge.

Patients often resist change because they have adopted faulty ideas about food and beauty. Our culture creates and spreads many of these ideas. Over time, patients accept these notions as truth and stop questioning whether they are valid. Cognitive therapy identifies and challenges the characteristic thoughts that reinforce disordered eating.

The food diaries are a good place to start, since they record a woman's thoughts about eating. We can explore these thoughts during therapy sessions.

For example, I recently worked with a patient on the need to eat three regular meals a day. She agreed to try, but at home, alone, she hesitated putting the rule into practice. In her diary she noted that whenever she faced the need to eat on such a schedule, she always thought, "If I eat that much food I will get fat." Another patient reported that every time she stepped on the scale, she automatically thought, "I am so fat that everyone must hate me."

Automatic thoughts may strike when a patient feels angry or suffers rejection. Such thoughts usually center on feeling or looking fat, the fear of losing self-control, or the need to diet. Sometimes the thought takes the form of a mental image. One patient said, "Whenever I eat, I imagine I'm a pig wallowing in a mud-hole. Dozens of people stand at a fence watching me gorging on my slop."

Once we identify these recurring thoughts, we can examine them carefully. The first step is to reduce the thought to its essence. I may ask the patient, "Are you feeling fat because you are afraid that others may see you this way?" Or I may ask, "Do you think that feeling fat is your way of dealing with anger? Does it spring from your belief that you are a worthless person?"

The next step is to gather any evidence that either supports or contradicts the patient's automatic thoughts. For example, if the patient thinks she is fat, we determine whether she has actually gained any weight recently. If she has, then of course her thinking has some basis in reality. If not, her feelings may represent a kind of substitute for her unacceptable feelings of anger.

Once we've identified these characteristic thoughts, the patient and I can begin the search for more valid ways of thinking. For example, we try to turn the false notion "I am fat" into the reality: "My weight is the same, but today I'm wearing a pair of jeans I bought back when I was unhealthily underweight. I'm not fat; my clothes are too small."

Although each patient is different, there are certain typical errors of thinking that they usually fall prey to. Let me describe some of these errors.

Black-and-white thinking: By this I mean the "all or nothing" attitude. For the anorexic, fat is hell, the ultimate nightmare, the horror of horrors. Thinness, however, is heaven, bliss, a goal worth dying for. There is no middle ground. Did she gain a pound this week? Then obesity is just around the corner. "If I can't be one hundred percent perfect," she tells herself, "then I am a total failure."

A bulimic sees certain foods as "good" and others as "bad." Bad foods must be absolutely, totally banished from her diet. Her characteristic thought is, "If I eat a little of this food then I'll lose control. I won't be able to stop until I become extremely fat." But if she gives in to temptation and takes even a single bite of the forbidden food, then all is lost. She goes ahead and stuffs herself until she can hold no more. For her, there is no such thing as eating in moderation. All or nothing. Black or white.

She thinks the same way about other areas of life. She considers a grade of "B" on a school assignment to be a failure, since it is not perfect. Becoming sexually involved with someone means she is a loose woman. One patient saw herself as an "angry monster— if I'm not totally in control, then I'm totally out of control."

One clue to black-and-white thinking is the fact that many of the patient's statements contain such phrases as "I must" or "I should." A patient might remark, "I must eat the same foods every day or I'll swell up like a blimp." Another might say, "I should exercise at least three hours a day." The psychoanalyst Karen Horney coined the phrase "the tyranny of the 'Shoulds'" to describe this state of mind.

When patients divide everything into such extreme categories, they reveal their need for certainty in their lives. Because they mistrust their own feelings, their own ability to judge, they look outside themselves for guidance. The drive to be *perfect* shows their inability to determine when they are *good enough*. In cognitive therapy we spot the "should" and "must" thought-tyrants and challenge their right to rule the patient's life.

Some time ago, researchers devised an ingenious experiment that revealed black-and-white thinking in action. They asked a group of dieters to drink milk shakes and then eat some ice cream. What the dieters didn't know was that the "milk shake" was actually a ringer—it had a relatively low calorie content. Surprisingly, the dieters who were told that the shakes were high-calorie went ahead and ate *more* ice cream than those who were told the truth. Why? Well, the researchers called the dieters' action "counterregulation." The dieters felt that drinking a high-calorie shake had caused them to "blow" their diet. They had already failed, so why bother holding back while eating ice cream?

Magnification: This word describes the patient's tendency to blow things, especially negative things, all out of proportion. Most prominent in their minds, of course, is body size. Many of my patients say they know perfectly well they are thin—they can see it in the mirror, their friends all tell them—but they *feel* fat. That feeling overrides and distorts any logical arguments to the contrary.

Similarly, patients distort their impressions of food itself. A case in point: A twenty-one-year-old, eighty-six-pound woman named Ondine swore up and down that at home she always ate three good-sized, nutritionally balanced meals, plus snacks, a day. I admitted her to the hospital. Yet when the first tray was brought to her, Ondine panicked. "I can't eat all *this*!" she cried. "This is more than I eat in a *week*!" Obviously, her perception of a "good-sized" meal was somewhat skewed.

Magnification occurs in other areas as well. A certain home-work assignment temporarily becomes the be-all and end-all of the girl's life. An interest in sports turns into the compulsion to jog ten miles a day and play tennis to the point of exhaustion. A broken date becomes a billboard announcing the patient's un-desirability to the world.

Personalization: A fifteen-year-old bulimic told me she had been too afraid to go to the beach during the previous summer. "I knew they'd all be staring at me and thinking that a whale had washed up on the beach." This patient was personalizing—assum-ing that everyone's undivided attention was focused on her and her alone.

Patients sometimes personalize an otherwise innocent remark. "You're looking good," an office colleague might say. The patient twists this to mean, "You looked so *bad* before." The idea that people might observe and comment on a patient's appearance can occupy her mind the rest of the day, and trigger a binge when she gets home that night.

Magical thinking: Examples include such statements as, "Bread is poison," or, "With my metabolism, everything I eat after lunch turns into fat." One patient told me, "If I eat one Oreo cookie at ten o'clock at night I'll be all right, but if I give in and eat it earlier I know I'll binge." Magical thinking about eating, exercise, or interpersonal relationships is very common, especially among anorexics.

Sensory distortions: A lot of patients report that their senses become keener during their illness. One patient fought constantly with her brother because he kept his stereo turned up too high. Maybe he did, but there was no doubt that her hearing had become much sharper during starvation. Some patients wear sunglasses, even indoors, because average light has become too bright. Many report that colors are more vivid, smells more potent. Often, these cognitive distortions are direct, physical consequences of starvation itself.

Errors of attribution: These are mistakes in figuring out the relationship between cause and effect. For example, a patient may gain a pound and believe it is because she ate a chocolate-chip cookie the week before. When we look at the facts, however, we may find that her weight gain is actually the result of premenstrual water retention.

CHALLENGING UNDERLYING ATTITUDES

In a sense, automatic thoughts are just the tip of the iceberg. Lurking beneath the surface are some implicit rules by which the patient operates. These rules spring from deeply held assumptions, beliefs, and values.

Dr. Christopher Fairburn has come up with a list of the most common of these attitudes:

—"I must be thin, because to be thin is to be successful, attractive, and happy."
—"I must avoid being fat because to be fat is to be a failure, unattractive, and unhappy."
—"Self-indulgence is bad because it is a sign of weakness."
—"Self-control is good because it is a sign of strength and discipline."
—"Anything less than total success is utter failure."

In therapy we bring these attitudes to the surface, analyze them, and challenge them. We try to discover both the advantages and the disadvantages of holding on to such beliefs. For example, there are reasons why people may base their feelings of self-esteem on their weight. After all, measuring weight, and judging oneself accordingly, is a simple task. Weight is one thing about themselves that people can have some control over. Besides, gaining weight gives a good excuse for failure in other areas of life: "Of course no one asks me out; I'm a fat pig, aren't I?"

The downside of this attitude is that the patient will never be satisfied with her weight—and thus herself—for long. Focusing on weight distracts one from working on real problems in forming and keeping relationships. By concentrating on dieting, a person can avoid having to deal with issues of low self-esteem or other bad feelings.

In therapy we look for insight into how these attitudes arose. What influence did the patient's family, friends, and social forces have on her thinking? When did these beliefs begin? How did they take root and grow? What else was going on in her life at the time the attitude started? One way to shed light on such questions is for the patient to talk to friends of long standing, or look at old family photos or diaries.

The desire to be in control often overwhelms the patient's ability to think clearly. She believes that if she can't control her body functions, such as hunger, menstruation, or sexual drive, then catastrophe will result. Such an attitude is one of the hardest to shake.

FIGHTING BACK

The essence of cognitive therapy is to change these unhealthy beliefs into more flexible and realistic attitudes. Of course, patients may resist changing, since doing so may challenge the basic structure of their lives. One cause of resistance is known as "symptomatic self-reinforcement." In other words, if starving yourself makes you feel good about yourself, then that behavior may be hard to give up. Or the patient may resist because she doesn't want to surrender the "guidelines for living" that she has established for herself. She must confront an onslaught of new feelings and experiences, but she lacks the "rulebook" that in the past told her how to respond.

Naturally, during this time the patient feels confused, frustrated, and frightened. Or she may shut down emotionally. Many patients who reach this phase of therapy tell me, "I just feel empty," or, "I feel nothing at all." Sometimes, as treatment takes effect, she encounters emotions she hasn't felt in ages. She may want to interpret her sadness, anger, or depression as evidence that she is weak. In the past, she knew that such weakness would lead to a dietary catastrophe. In therapy, she learns that such emotions are part of daily life, and that she can learn how to handle them without falling back on her symptoms.

One way to change distorted thinking is through *decentering*. In this strategy, I encourage the patient to think about the problem from another perspective, to remove herself from the center of the issue and try to evaluate things more objectively.

Here's an example. A patient named Liz told me, "Everyone always watches me when I eat." I asked her, "Do you always notice what other people eat?" "Of course not," Liz answered, "why should I?" By exploring this topic further, the patient eventually realized that, just like herself, other people are probably too wrapped up in their own concerns to spend much time noticing her. Liz learned that she was *not* the center of someone else's universe—and found she was much happier with that thought.

Another way to counteract distorted thinking is through *decatastrophizing.* Let me explain. A patient might say, "If I don't get that promotion at work, then my life won't be worth living." I might challenge this by exploring it further, saying, "What's the worst that can happen?" or, "What can you do to make this situation better?" My goal is to help the patient take a more realistic view of the event, and to help her discover some of the alternatives open to her. When you are feeling depressed, it generally helps to be active rather than to sit passively and helplessly.

A similar approach works to counteract the "tyranny of the

'Shoulds.' " If the patient says she "should" do something—study harder, eat less—I will urge her to explore what would happen if she *didn't*. Often, she begins to see that the dire consequences she had predicted would actually fail to materialize.

Through *reattribution,* the patient learns to interpret her experience more accurately. For example, an anorexic might feel that her excess energy is a sign of vitality and health, a vindication of her decision to starve herself. I will work to show her that extreme anxiety may result when the body is threatened with emaciation and that this can result in the need to be constantly active.

Another technique, developed by Christopher Fairburn, focuses on *problem solving.* In this strategy, the patient learns how to tackle problems in new and creative ways without resorting to bingeing.

First she must identify the problem precisely and come up with as many alternative solutions as possible. Say, for example, that her boyfriend breaks their date for Saturday night. Normally such a catastrophe would prompt her to binge. In therapy, though, we look at the other actions she might take: calling another friend, running errands she has been putting off, finishing a project, and so on. She then looks at each of these alternatives and decides which is the most practical and effective. After rehearsing the solution in her head, she carries it out. Later that day or the next, she reviews her decision and decides how well it worked, perhaps giving herself a grade on a scale of one to ten.

I ask patients to use their food-monitoring sheets to note these problems and how they came up with their solution. We can then review the process in therapy sessions. Doing so lessens the impact of problems. What's more, it reduces the frequency with which problems occur.

I've mentioned just a few of the strategies of cognitive therapy. Regardless of the approach, the goal is to help the patient express her thoughts and to examine those thoughts from many different angles. We challenge her overly constricted ways of thinking and feeling. In the process, we help bring about a fundamental change in the way she perceives and interprets the world.

When we reach that goal, the patient finds herself equipped with a magnificent tool for fixing disordered eating: her mind.

9

One-on-One Therapy: Feelings and Problems of Living

Listen to Kelly, a twenty-two-year-old bulimic: "A week before my history final I got so scared I could hardly breathe. It was an oral exam—I was terrified. So naturally, instead of studying, what do I do? Eat. Cramming, yes, but the wrong kind. Weird, but just having food in my mouth gets rid of the anxiety. If I focus on food I don't have to think about anything else."

Here's Joanna, a seventeen-year-old recovering anorexic: "When I feel lonely, it's like my mind plays a trick. I think about food and ways I can cut down on calories even more—like using baking soda instead of toothpaste in case I swallow when I'm brushing my teeth. Or I do more exercise. I'll add repetitions to my weight routine or pedal another couple of miles. I get so distracted that I don't feel lonely any more."

And Tina, who at twenty-four has been bulimic for over five years: "All I ever try to do is please everybody else. Little Miss Wonderful. So when someone criticizes me or seems disappointed, I just smile and apologize and promise to be better. But inside I'm so angry I feel like *exploding*! Instead of telling someone off, I take it out on food. Once my supervisor chewed me out for something I didn't do. Instead of destroying him, I destroyed a quart of ice cream and a whole angel food cake. Of course I threw it up. The next day I was back at work, all meek and humble and smiling. But inside I felt like I'd had my revenge."

THE ROLE OF FEELINGS

Anxiety, loneliness, and anger are common emotions, feelings that are part of being human.

What is a feeling? It's a response that occurs on a nonintellectual level. Feelings are subjective experiences that can't be verified by someone else.

Feelings can spur us into action, usually some form of self-preservation. If we touch something hot, we draw back our hand. Similarly, if something makes us unhappy, we may act by changing the situation or pulling away from it—whatever it takes to save our psychic skins.

Unpleasant feelings can actually serve a healthy purpose: They may prompt action that attacks a problem directly. Yes, an oral final in history can be terrifying, but one way of handling that feeling is to study. Someone who knows everything about the War of 1812 can walk into the exam with confidence. That person conquers anxiety by confronting it. The same with loneliness, or anger, or fear, or any of the dozens of other emotions we experience every day. Emotions can also help guide future actions. A student whose heavy course load causes anxiety may be more careful in planning her schedule the following semester.

Easy to say. But for some people with eating disorders, not so easy to do. Emotions spur them into action, sure, but sometimes in twisted and unhealthy ways.

Kelly coped with her anxiety by turning to food. Bingeing made her feel better for a while, but didn't do a thing to eliminate her real source of trouble. Joanna warded off loneliness by making her exercise bicycle her best friend, but exercise didn't solve her problem; it merely distracted her for a while. Tina took out her aggression on a bowl of ice cream. So long as she was eating she felt in control of her anger, but when the food was gone, she felt ashamed and hopeless.

For years now it seems as if everyone has been running around trying to "get in touch with their feelings." The phrase has been the psychobabble cliché of the last two decades.

Cliché or not, for the person with an eating disorder, getting in touch with her feelings is *exactly what she needs to do.*

That's where individual therapy can help.

WHAT IS INDIVIDUAL THERAPY?

Individual therapy is a one-on-one relationship between the patient and a therapist. The time is devoted to exploring the patient's thoughts and feelings and looking at how she expresses those thoughts and feelings in her actions or her relationships. Individual therapy takes a deeper look at the underlying causes of her behavior, to find out *why she uses food to meet her emotional needs.*

Ideally, individual therapy provides a safe environment, a kind of shelter in which the patient can explore and express emotions. Therapists support this process. They help the patient to look at problems from another point of view and make connections she may be unable to make on her own.

In fact, the very relationship between the patient and the therapist can be an important tool for change. The patient reveals her characteristic ways of feeling, thinking, and relating in her interactions with the therapist. Together they can look at these patterns and see how they may be affecting her life in the "outside world."

One key ingredient in their relationship is the development of *trust.* A person with an eating disorder often mistrusts her basic feelings. She may misinterpret her hunger and suppress her emotional needs. She can be reluctant to reveal her feelings, especially regarding shape and weight, because she feels ashamed or humiliated. Mistrust of other people is also part of the picture.

Through her relationship with a caring therapist whom she

trusts, a woman can reveal her innermost thoughts and feelings. With time, she feels less fear of criticism or judgment. She can then examine those feelings to discover and experiment with other ways of reacting.

In this sense, individual therapy serves as a kind of emotional dress rehearsal for life. A patient can use her therapist as a kind of emotional mirror, by playing out, through the therapist, all of her conflicts with the people in her life. When she sees that the therapist stands by her no matter how ashamed she feels or how disgusting she thinks her behavior is, she feels secure. She trusts herself more and accepts her feelings as valid.

Equipped with a new set of emotional responses, the patient returns to the "real world" relaxed, reinforced, and ready to cope with the pressures that led to her disordered eating. As expressed by Dr. Alan Goodsitt, a psychiatrist from Northwestern University in Chicago and a leading expert in eating disorders: "When one is in touch with inner feelings—what feels good and is enjoyable, what feels bad or is boring, what is satisfying, and what is self-destructive—then one is in a good position to make wise life decisions."

Individual therapy can be handled by a psychiatrist, a psychologist, or a social worker. Depending on the person's skills and training, therapy may draw heavily on the cognitive strategies we discussed in Chapter Eight and may focus on the individual's role within her family, or it may take a psychoanalytical tack. Each professional develops his or her own approach.

In my practice I use all the techniques I feel have a chance of working. Usually this means combining elements of cognitive, behavioral, and educational therapy. A psychodynamic approach—exploring the unconscious motivations that underlie her behavior—can often be quite helpful, especially in the later phases of treatment. Through this approach, the patient gains insight into her situation. She sees how in the past she may have had good reasons for reacting as she did to her problems. But she learns that now, in her present-day reality, those characteristic ways of reacting are misguided.

Individual therapy doesn't replace group or family therapy.

Each strategy supports and contributes to the other, as we'll see in the last chapters of this book.

WHAT HAPPENS IN INDIVIDUAL THERAPY?

"Can I go home now?" Stephanie, a nineteen-year-old college sophomore, spat out the words.

She had been in my office just ten minutes. She had spent the whole time listing reasons why she didn't need help—even though she weighed less than ninety pounds: "I don't need a shrink. I know what I'm doing. I am too fat and I have to lose weight. My diet is no one else's business. It doesn't interfere with my life. I feel fine, I exercise, I get good grades. What I choose to do with my body concerns no one but me."

When she paused for breath, I asked, "What do you think would happen if you tried to stop starving yourself to death?"

Here eyes flashed. "I would lose the one thing that makes me special. That's what you're trying to do—take away the only thing that makes me feel good about myself!"

Stephanie seemed very afraid. "I know you feel that way now," I said. "But working together, we can look at why you don't feel good about yourself, and why you don't think you are special in other ways. I think part of you recognizes the danger you're in. But another part of you is scared to give up your starving identity."

It took many more sessions to complete the process, but in that moment we began work on the most important task of individual therapy: to help the patient find a new identity, free of the suffocating symptoms of an eating disorder.

As Dr. Arnold Andersen puts it, therapy can be a kind of "mourning period." Part of the patient—her starving persona— must pass away. The patient has to let go of her fantasy that being thin will solve all of her problems. That's very hard to do. As her therapist, I try to show that I understand her struggle and realize how difficult and painful it will be for her.

While every patient is different, often there are discernible phases in therapy. In the first phase, the patient and the therapist spend time getting to know one another. However, they also focus on the symptoms themselves. The immediate goal is to break the bulimic cycle of bingeing and purging or to reduce the anorexic's fear of eating and gaining weight.

In the next phase, work to change behavior and thinking patterns continues, but the focus shifts somewhat. Now we begin to explore the patient's characteristic emotional difficulties. During this time the "purpose" of her symptoms—why they developed, what they mean to her—may become clearer. Starving won't solve her problem with self-esteem, for example, but it *does* give her the illusion that she is "in control." I tell her that it's human nature to want to do something we're good at. It helps us forget, or ignore, our other problems, but if our "talent" is self-destructive, then it can get in the way of solving the real problems.

We keep working to identify and change the stresses that trigger her behavior. We explore how eating (or not eating) came to play the central role in her life and why she turns to food (or abstains from it) for emotional support rather than to her parents or a friend. We look at the purpose that starving serves in her life and why weight is so important. If she wants to stop bingeing and purging but can't, we examine the mental roadblocks that thwart her efforts at self-control.

Often we spend time looking at her relationships with her family. I want to know how she sees the interactions between family members. We then talk about what she can do to change the family's style of dealing with each other and to pull back from parental conflicts.

In therapy we try to reduce the symptoms, and ideally eliminate them altogether. For months or even years, though, the patient has defined her personality through the disorder. Without self-starvation, an anorexic may feel she is nothing. For this reason therapy must not only take away, it must offer something in return.

And it does: It offers the chance to develop a mature and rational self. Maturity has many facets. It means the ability to recognize feelings and respond to them in healthy, life-affirming ways. It means breaking free of constricted thought-patterns and solving problems creatively. And it means self-esteem: a belief in one's worth as a human being.

As a therapist I must listen, and listen hard, to what the patient has to say. If she has trouble recognizing feelings or articulating thoughts, I'll do the best I can to help her along. I also encourage her to discover her true values and goals. I take her remarks seriously and accept her feelings as real—a courtesy that perhaps too few people in her life pay her. This doesn't mean I have to agree with everything she says, but I at least acknowledge it as valid *for her.*

In the final phase of therapy, the patient gets ready to strike out on her own. We talk about strategies she can use to cope with problems as they arise. I make sure she knows that temporary relapses may occur in times of great stress. At such times it is important both to reach out to others and to utilize some of the tools that have been helpful in the past.

When it comes time to terminate therapy, the patient usually experiences emotions similar to those she felt during past times of separation or loss. Being aware of these emotions allows us to work through them during therapy sessions and helps the patient grow. Sometimes these feelings are so strong that they trigger a temporary return to poor eating. Helping the patient see the connection between these events works to minimize the damage.

THEMES OF THERAPY

Because each patient is different, I don't believe in starting off with a "shopping list" of goals to be met. However, certain themes usually emerge.

One central theme is *the patient's relationship to food and the significance of eating in her life.* Strangely, some professionals carry on therapy for months without *once* attacking the patient's problem with food. They seem to think that just by exploring underlying issues—problems with parents, for example—her eating will improve.

Nonsense! That's like treating a broken leg with aspirin: It might help the pain a little, but it ignores the bigger problem.

Therapy has to address the *symptoms themselves*, as well as the feelings of guilt and shame that may result from the cycle of bingeing and purging or self-starvation. It must also look at the *reasons* food has become the patient's means of defense, a kind of "anesthetic" against emotional pain.

Another important theme is *autonomy*, by which I mean two things: self-government and independence.

Self-government means having control over impulses and desires, and not being prey to emotional whims. Ironically, people with eating disorders, especially anorexics, feel they are totally in control of themselves. The truth is that their disorder controls them. Bulimics, in contrast, usually realize they are caught in a cycle they can no longer control.

Independence means not relying completely on other people to satisfy one's emotional and physical needs. Many of these patients have tried to please other people all their lives—their parents, their teachers, their friends and lovers. They devote themselves to others' desires and ignore their own. They base their identity on the reactions they stir up in other people.

In therapy, the patient learns to trust her *own* instincts. She recognizes her feelings and accepts them as valid. Through acceptance comes control and self-mastery.

Tina, for example, discovered that she actually had good reason to be angry with her supervisor: "I didn't get mad just because there's some flaw in my character. I got mad because he deliberately pushed me too far." Once this realization dawned, Tina accepted her anger as part of herself. "It's okay to get mad," she said. "I don't have to binge to get rid of tension." She found she could master her anger and express it more directly, in ways that actually did some good.

Similarly, Joanna found that admitting she was lonely was better than trying to push her feelings away through self-starvation. She learned she had alternatives: She could invite a friend over to listen to records or watch a video. "I don't want to rely on anyone but myself to fill any emptiness in my life," she remarked. Through therapy, Joanna made a surprising discovery: Her new independence made her more attractive, since it relieved her friends of the burden of making her happy. "Now my friends come over to have fun, not because they feel they have to baby-sit an emotional basket case."

Another recurring theme in therapy is *learning how to tolerate moods*. Sure, we all have "down times," when depression or feelings of failure creep in. An eating-disordered person seeks relief from these feelings by resorting to her symptoms—bingeing and purging, for example.

As Marti, a twenty-nine-year-old woman, put it: "Some days I just can't drag myself out of bed. I feel so hopeless—nothing is worth doing. I don't care how I look. I don't want to go anywhere or see anyone. Nothing cheers me up. Not the TV, not music, not even the comics in the newspaper. It all just seems so . . . so sad. The only thing I have energy for is eating. Once I start I just keep going. Cookies and leftover Halloween candy and stuff that's been in the freezer probably since the Civil War. Anything. Then I puke. When I was a baby I comforted myself by sucking on my thumb. Now I do it by sucking food off a fork. Throwing up gives me the illusion that I'm in control. It's pretty pathetic."

Marti is describing feelings of depression, a mood she tries to lift by turning to food. Other patients tell how food helps them through periods of anger or jealousy or disappointment. We've seen how Kelly used eating to ease her anxiety. For these people, food acts as a kind of substitute for the emotion itself. Others use food to calm themselves down after exploding in anger, or to soothe their guilt for feeling a "shameful" emotion, such as jealousy.

During therapy we explore these moods. We look at what causes them and how they disrupt the patient's life. I try to help patients see that such moods are part of living. Expressing emotions is normal and nothing to be ashamed of. It's what makes us human! However, in therapy we look for ways to avoid the things that trigger moods in the first place, and look for alternative ways to act when they do occur.

Coping with maturity is another topic that crops up often. As we have seen, anorexia causes the patient to regress to a preadolescent state. Her starving body loses its womanly shape and functions. In therapy I encourage the patient to examine her feelings about growing up, to find out what it is that frightens her so. Does she fear being abandoned by her parents? Is she scared of the responsibilities of adulthood? Is starving a way to avoid dealing with other people and the risk of being rejected? *What is going on inside?*

For the bulimic, too, food and eating substitute for mature relationships. As Enid, a twenty-six-year-old patient, told me, "Friends can say mean things. They're not always around when you need them for support. You can sleep with a man and in the morning the bastard is gone and you never see him again. That's not true with food. Food is always there. And if it isn't, you can just go buy some."

In a way, individual therapy provides a model relationship that the patient can use to explore these issues of maturity. If handled properly, the patient develops trust in her therapist. She learns she can reveal secrets or make mistakes without betrayal or rejection. In the process, she sees how to handle feelings without falling back on the symptoms of her disorder.

Let's take a closer look now at some of those feelings.

FOCUS ON FEELINGS

Imagine you're a telephone operator sitting in front of a huge console of blinking lights. Whenever a red light flashes, you're supposed to plug a cord into a green socket. A blue light means to put the plug into a yellow socket. Orange light—purple socket.

But what if you suddenly became color-blind? Imagine the chaos. Nothing gets connected No one can communicate with anyone else. Everything goes haywire.

In a sense, an eating-disordered person can be emotionally "color-blind." When a bulimic feels angry—when the red light flashes—she plugs into the wrong socket. Instead of dealing directly with her anger, the signal gets diverted and triggers a binge. Similarly, an anorexic may fear intimacy, but her mind reroutes that feeling into a fear of fatness. The feelings are there, but the disorder causes them to short-circuit.

For years these people have denied or suppressed their feelings—"Angry? Me? Impossible." Why does this happen? There are many reasons. Perhaps these people come from families that forbade emotional expression. They thus have no role models to follow when it comes to showing joy or pain. Or perhaps they were punished in some way for being emotional—"Don't cry. Only babies cry. Go to your room." They may think that a feeling such as anger, once it grabs hold, will hurl them out of control, and make them dangerous or bad.

Feelings become strangers, provoking strangely twisted responses. Recently I brought a seventeen-year-old bulimic and her parents into my office. I told them that she had to be hospitalized because, despite intense outpatient treatment, her severe bingeing and purging had put her in medical danger. "No!" she cried, throwing herself down, sobbing and pounding the floor with her fists. "I don't want to go to the hospital! It's not fair!" Despite her protests, the parents agreed to the plan and she was admitted.

The next day, however, she was much calmer. She said, "To be honest, I'm kind of relieved you put me in here. I felt really terrible at home. Yesterday I thought that coming into the hospital meant leaving my mother to cope at home all by herself. I couldn't let her know that I actually *wanted* to come into the hospital. She would think I was deserting her. I realize now that's why I put on that little show in your office."

Even a physical sensation such as hunger gets garbled in transmission. An anorexic says to herself, "Hungry? That's not hunger, that's, uh, nervous energy. I need to exercise more—exercise, yeah, that's the ticket." For a bulimic, the inner monologue might be: "Lonely? Nah. I'm just hungry, that's what I am."

Here are some quick glances at the key emotional issues every patient confronts at some time and to some degree:

Feelings of fear: Like a broadcast from a powerful pirate radio station, fear, especially the fear of fatness, overwhelms and blocks out every other emotional signal. In therapy we work on decreasing these fears so that the patient can pick up other signals—joy, anger, even sorrow.

An important part of the process is talking about inner feelings that may never have seen the light of day. It's natural for people to suppress powerful fears, keeping them buried or vague so as to avoid having to deal with them. Sometimes, though, just articulating fears or "bad" feelings decreases their power. Giving them a name empowers the patient to make a conscious effort at overcoming them.

Strangely enough, a patient may fear not just failure but success as well. She worries that succeeding at something means people will demand more of her—more than she feels she can deliver. At a deeper level, fears of success may come from separation fears connected with fantasies of competing with a parent-figure. The very fact that individual therapy provides an intense relationship with another human being in itself reduces another dominant fear: the fear of intimacy.

Feelings of anger: For a woman in our society, expressing anger and aggression—natural feelings—can be taboo. Thus even when she is genuinely, righteously angry, she often swallows her feelings. But suppressed feelings erupt in other ways, like air in a balloon that's being squeezed. As Tina's story demonstrated, an eating-disordered person takes it out on herself through food. As she learns the art of assertiveness, her fear of her own anger decreases.

Feelings of depression: Depression and eating are closely linked. Bingeing may in fact be a person's misguided attempt to treat her depression, using food as medicine. In many cases, feelings of depression are what drive the patient to seek help in the first place. Therapy can help point out that, although a bout of depression can be draining, there are better ways of coping with it than eating.

Therapy explores where the depression comes from. What's more, it introduces alternative methods for dealing with it. Even simple suggestions can sometimes be helpful. I ask my patients to remember the "Three N's": Say NO to unreasonable demands. Do something NEW. Do something to NURTURE yourself. Of course, it's important that we distinguish between the *feeling* of depression and the clinical *syndrome* of depression. The former is a response to temporary situations; the latter is a psychiatric illness, for which effective medical treatment is available.

Feelings of being fat: Feeling fat though actually being emaciated is so common among anorexics that, as we've seen, it's one of the diagnostic criteria for the disorder. Patients need to learn that feeling fat is a genuine part of their illness—the feeling is really there, no doubt about it. It's just distorted. It's another example of a crossed wire in the emotional circuit. However, simply confronting the patient—"Look in the mirror! You're not fat!"—doesn't work. Better to find out what being fat *means* to her, and how she interprets this distorted feeling. As patients learn to recognize and trust their feelings, they see a clearer image of their body shape and size. As one recovering patient told me, "I feel like I got a new prescription for my emotional contact lenses."

Feelings about control: Because her life is chaotic, the anorexic focuses all her energy on controlling what she eats. Often this means controlling everyone else around her too. In time the disorder controls her. A bulimic "controls" eating by skipping meals; when she binges, she tries to reassert control by purging. In therapy we work to restore a sense of healthy control over eating.

Distorted thinking: The need to be in control often leads to certain limited ways of thinking—everything becomes "black or white," "all or nothing." Individual therapy offers the patient a chance to explore other ways of thinking. If she says, "I know that if I gain an ounce I'll go on and gain thirty pounds," we'll talk about why she feels her only alternatives are extremes. The goal is to help her rediscover balance and moderation in thought as well as behavior.

Poor self-image: Susie Orbach, a well-known eating disorder therapist, believes that "low self-esteem" is much too mild a description of this symptom; *self-hatred* is more accurate. She has a point. Patients are often so perfectionist that one mistake, one little slip, can shatter them. They feel like failures because they can't meet their own impossibly high standards. Therapy allows a patient to experiment with feelings, to take risks. In scaling back her standards to a more realistic level, she discovers that a mistake needn't destroy her, that she isn't a horrible, rotten person after all. A therapist helps by praising the patient for her success rather than being overly critical of her failures.

Social failure: Patients often have difficulty making friends or feeling comfortable around other people. These feelings may contribute to the development of an eating disorder. What's more, once the disorder has taken hold, these feelings can help maintain and reinforce the anorexia or bulimia. Fear can make a patient avoid situations that pose the slightest risk of rejection. Making and keeping friends is a skill, and like other skills people need to learn it and practice it. Therapy can help patients do so. After all, no one rides a bicycle very well the first time she tries.

STRUCTURE OF THERAPY

There is no single "recipe" for a course of individual therapy. It works for inpatients as well as outpatients. Treatment may begin while the patient is hospitalized and continue after discharge.

Outpatient therapy usually takes place once or twice a week. In the early stages, more frequent sessions may offer the additional support a severely symptomatic patient needs. Sessions generally last forty-five to fifty minutes, but more frequent, shorter sessions are sometimes a practical option.

Successful therapy may require anywhere from several months to several years. Shorter programs focus more intently on reducing immediate symptoms and on changing ways of thinking and behaving. Longer programs may transform a patient's personality in profound and healthy ways.

Throughout the process, I try to provide a sense of constancy by keeping all appointments, meeting in the same place, and so on. Doing so helps supply some of the stability the patient's life lacks.

THE ROLE OF THE THERAPIST

Dr. Alan Goodsitt of Northwestern University describes the job beautifully:

> Therapists are many things. They are parents, guides, teachers, and coaches. They make themselves available as committed, caring professionals. They are involved. They relate. They encourage, cajole, and exhort. They provide their expert knowledge and experience to relate to another person, to use sound judgment, and help the patient integrate her thoughts, feelings, and actions. They empathically anticipate and care about the patient's experience. They patiently explain and clarify her thinking about significant issues. Because they know there are good reasons for her behavior and feelings, they do not criticize or belittle her defensive adaptation but at the same time they truthfully acknowledge her present shortcomings. Most important, they are the carriers of hope for the future of the patient.*

My first words to the patient—"How may I help?"—tell her that I am on her side. We'll work together to learn how she sees the world and what we can do to make her life better.

I use my intuition to figure out what the patient's "inner voice" is saying to her. If I can help her articulate those thoughts, I will open a window into her mind, a window through which we both can look. I know, too, that she may come into therapy frightened and suspicious. I try to communicate that I understand her fears. I show her I will listen to what she has to say—listen in a way perhaps no one else ever has.

Sometimes patients are afraid that their feelings are so "bad" that no one would like them if they revealed their innermost self.

*Adapted from "Self Psychology and the Treatment of Anorexia Nervosa." In Garner, D.M., Garfinkel, P.E., eds.: *Handbook of Psychotherapy for Anorexia Nervosa and Bulimia.* New York: The Guilford Press, 1985.

Exploring this "dark side" freely, guided by a supportive and nonjudgmental therapist, can be a powerful new experience for the patient, an experience that in itself helps the patient change and grow.

As a teacher, I try to supply the patient with the information she needs to plan healthy meals and to eat properly. As coach, I help her set goals for herself, encourage her to meet those goals, and support her when she fails. As her "parent," I help her deal with the feelings that she originally developed toward her own mother and father and that are now "transferred" onto me. We may work on her wishes for someone to take care of her, her fears about growing up, her anger and shame about events from her childhood.

How do we know when therapy has done its job? One way is that the patient shows she can maintain normal weight and eating habits. She reports feeling more comfortable in relationships with others, especially her peers, and can solve problems in inventive new ways, without falling back on her old habits. She gains an enhanced sense of personal freedom and the ability to take responsibility for her choices in life.

Of equal importance is that she feels strongly rooted in her new personality—an identity that is no longer defined by her symptoms or by her enmeshment with other people. The work she began in therapy proceeds after therapy ends, as she continues to evolve and to meet life's new challenges.

10

Safety in Numbers: Group Therapy and Self-Help Groups

Excerpts from the food diary of a bulimic named Corinna:

> Monday: I feel so ashamed of myself.
> Tuesday: I am such a disgrace. I can't control myself!
> Wednesday: Shame on me! Bingeing again. That's the last time, I swear.
> Thursday: I blew it! If I weren't so weak I know I could get back in control.
> Friday: I can't do it. I'm such a disgusting pig.

I had been treating Corinna for about a month. I knew this twenty-seven-year-old woman, a cable TV sales rep, was trying as hard as she could, but she wasn't making any progress. She continued to binge and purge.

What's more, she seemed unable to address the emotional difficulties that triggered her binges. She made a great effort to use her food diary to write down what she ate as well as her feelings connected with eating. Yet, as her journal showed, she kept dwelling only on her feelings of shame and the notion that, if she would just work harder, she could regain control.

In our individual therapy sessions, we focused on her need to be overly critical of herself and on how, by continuing to regard herself as a failure, she was promoting rather than decreasing her bingeing. Corinna was able to see that, despite my support, she expected harsh criticism from me and that she was replaying a lifelong pattern of expecting criticism from her parents. I knew that, given enough time, Corinna and I would be able to work through this problem, but I also sensed that she might benefit from additional help. Such help could come in the form of group therapy, in which she could talk about her illness with other patients.

When I first mentioned the idea of group therapy, Corinna immediately responded, "No way. I'm not going to pour out my heart in front of a bunch of strangers. It's hard enough talking about it with just you!"

I let the subject drop for a while, but a week later, after I felt we had reached a higher level of trust, I brought it up again. We talked about her initial negative reaction and discussed her objections to the idea. With some hesitation, she eventually agreed to join a group.

At the next group meeting, I spoke with the members about having a new person participate. They agreed, and the following week Corinna joined. During her first session she barely said a word, but I could tell she listened intently to everything the others said. The following week, while the others told their stories and described how their illness affected them, Corinna nodded or flashed smiles of understanding and agreement. Toward the end of that session, she opened up and began talking about her own experience.

Afterward she came up to me and said, "I thought I was battling this thing alone. I see now there's a bunch of us and we're all in this together."

For Corinna, as for many other patients, the experience of group therapy marked a turning point in her struggle.

Group therapy shares the same goals as individual therapy—

improvement in symptoms, and changes in thinking and behavior. Group therapy isn't just an assembly line for treating a lot of patients quickly. Something valuable happens in a group that happens in no other forum: *interaction among people in the same predicament.*

The human urge to seek out others with similar problems is as ancient as society itself. While group therapy is a proven way of handling emotional and other problems, its use in managing eating disorders is a recent phenomenon. Few scientific studies exist to show which methods work best and which patients will benefit. However, speaking purely from clinical experience, I have seen group therapy do a lot of good for a lot of patients.

THE ROLE OF GROUP THERAPY

Group therapy is tailor-made to address some of the problems eating disorders cause—loneliness, isolation, hopelessness. As Corinna found, just *seeing* other patients in the room shows a patient she is not alone and bolsters her confidence that therapy will be worthwhile. Patients gain hope by meeting others who have gotten better. Hearing another patient express feelings gives her the strength to speak out for herself. If two heads are better than one, imagine having half a dozen heads all working on the same problem!

After group sessions, patients lose the attitude that "nobody understands me," because they've just encountered a lot of people who *do* understand. Another benefit is a rise in self-esteem. Patients begin to feel useful to other people. Their experience is respected, their advice is welcome. They sense they are helping one another, and thus begin to feel more effective and worthwhile as human beings.

In group therapy, a patient sees that others who are concerned about her health and who challenge her self-destructive behavior aren't enemies. What a discovery! Ideally, she comes to realize that friends, loved ones, and other patients can be her allies in the struggle to get better.

TYPES OF GROUP THERAPY

Asked to imagine group therapy, most people probably picture the "Bob Newhart" variety, in which a handful of colorful characters sit in a room and interact with each other. That's called interpersonal group therapy, and is one valid method. But group therapy comes in many forms, and groups operate in different ways. Some, for example, don't focus on eating behavior at all; others focus on eating exclusively. Let's take a look at some of the different types of group therapy.

Psychodynamic Group Therapy

Psychodynamic therapy helps the patient gain insight into her situation and works to bring about changes in her personality. This type of group offers patients the chance to express themselves and interact with others in a safe, supportive environment. Therapists in eating disorder groups often take a more active role than they do in other types of group therapy.

One goal of treatment is usually to help the patient identify and trust her feelings. Another goal is to improve her close relationships with other people. Conversation often focuses on family issues, such as problems with parents or siblings, responsibilities at home, and so on. Other common themes include:

- The sense of ineffectiveness
- Low self-esteem
- Anxiety
- Misperception of feelings
- Mistrust of others and of oneself
- Disturbances in body image
- Avoiding maturity
- Behavior that reinforces symptoms of the illness

Dr. Irving Yalom, a psychiatrist at Stanford University and a noted group-therapy expert, has shown that group therapy works partly because the issues that concern patients aren't just talked about as abstract theories, as may happen in individual therapy. Instead the issues are *experienced* firsthand, in the "here and now" of the therapeutic process itself.

Let me give an example. A seventeen-year-old anorexic named Terri had trouble keeping friends because, as a certified perfectionist, she couldn't tolerate the slightest personal shortcoming. She was always correcting other people's grammar or brushing lint off their clothes. Once, in a group session, she told a patient named Gail, "You can't say 'irregardless.' There's no such word."

"What's it to you?" Gail fired back. "Why does it bother you if I make a mistake?" Picking up on this exchange, we were then able to examine Terri's perfectionist attitude and how it affected her relationships—not in the outside world, but *in that very room at that very moment.*

One drawback to the psychodynamic method is that discussions may not give enough focus to symptomatic behavior. Poor eating habits that contribute to the illness may go unaddressed.

Psychoeducational and Cognitive-Behavioral Group Therapy

We talked about many cognitive-behavioral techniques in Chapter Eight. The same principles can work in a group setting as well.

Groups provide a natural forum for patients to learn the facts about eating disorders. Food diaries can be looked at in groups. Another advantage of groups is that they give patients an opportunity to share strategies for improving unhealthy eating and reworking outmoded patterns of thinking and feeling.

Family Support Groups

Family groups, often led by a social worker, involve members of anywhere from five to ten families of eating disorder patients. Families learn how to be more supportive of their child, how to set limits, and how to handle problems that crop up. In sessions, people share experiences and trade advice, giving each other much-needed emotional support in the process. Many participants report feeling much less shame and guilt following a course of therapy.

Other Types of Groups

These include *creative therapy,* such as movement or dance therapy, to help patients get in touch with their bodies, and *art therapy,* where patients draw or sculpt to express their feelings about their bodies, their relationships with others in their family, and so on. In *psychodrama groups,* patients act out scenes, playing different roles to carry on conversations or demonstrate feelings. This strategy helps a patient uncover her feelings and bring them into the room, where they then take on a life of their own. *Women's issues groups* focus on concerns relating to sexuality and the role of women in society. Finally, there are *self-help groups* that offer emotional support, socialization, and hope. More on this later.

STRUCTURE OF THERAPY GROUPS

How many patients should there be in a therapy group? Between four and eight patients seems ideal—small enough so each can relate to the others, large enough to bring together people with a range of experiences. Many groups are made up entirely of women because there are relatively few males with eating disorders.

Most outpatient groups meet once a week, with sessions lasting from one and a quarter to two hours. Some shorter-term programs meet twice a week. Meeting more frequently provides additional support to very symptomatic patients.

Inpatient groups are more varied. I have found it helpful to combine daily group psychotherapy with other groups, such as psychodrama, art, movement, nutrition, relaxation, women's issues, and body image groups.

Outpatient groups can meet for a limited number of weeks or they may be open-ended. Short-term groups are generally more structured. They may have a preset agenda with different specific topics each week. In addition, members continue to monitor their symptomatic behavior and work to change it.

Group leaders should make sure all members know when and where meetings will be and how to get there. An eating-disordered patient has enough trouble dealing with her insecurities. She doesn't need to wander the halls of some huge building, anxious and alone, looking for the meeting room. Lack of clear instructions can cause a patient to quit the group before she has even started.

Groups are usually more effective if they are made up of patients with similar problems. Like oil and water, anorexics and bulimics in the same group may not easily mix. An anorexic may feel "bullied" by a bulimic, while the bulimic may feel frustrated that the anorexic won't open up and share what's going on inside. Higher-weight patients may feel angry or envious in the presence of emaciated ones.

GROUP THERAPY FOR ANOREXIA NERVOSA

Anorexic patients often have trouble with the idea of group therapy. They resist relationships because they fear rejection. They use their thinness as a shield to protect them from having to deal with other people. If they feel anxious, they tend to respond by losing more weight or running way. Because their social skills aren't as developed, they may need more support than other members.

However, group therapy can help some anorexics precisely *because* it shows them how to express their feelings and interact with others. Recently Pam, a former patient, called to tell me how happy she was in her new job as a receptionist. We shared a laugh, because before treatment, Pam was notoriously shy and refused to speak to anyone. Her experience in group gave her the emotional strength to reach out to others. Now here she was, greeting visitors and talking on the phone—tasks that, just a year before, would have driven her to starvation.

When the members of a group are more compatible—similar in age, level of education, length of illness, and so on—there is usually greater group cohesion. Group therapy also stands a better chance of helping if the anorexic is not severely ill, is highly motivated, and has responded to other treatments.

It sometimes works to have at least one patient in the group who has returned to a normal body weight and maintained that weight for a period of time. Such people serve as role models. Similarly, including a patient who is on her way to recovery, who can express her feelings more easily, helps shift focus away from body weight and onto other issues.

Inpatient programs: Because they are more severely ill and their treatment is more intense, inpatients are generally willing to take part in groups. The size of the group varies. Sometimes inpatient groups are larger than outpatient groups, but because each patient may take part in several group sessions a day, she has more chances to contribute.

Of course, the goal of hospitalization is to get the patient better and send her home as soon as possible. Thus inpatient groups, by definition, are short-term groups.

A challenge comes when the patient must make the transition from the hospital to the outside world. We encourage patients who respond to the group approach to continue with therapy as outpatients.

Outpatient programs: Outpatient anorexic groups work better if their numbers are small—groups of four to six patients may better address interpersonal problems than groups of seven or eight, the size of most other outpatient therapy groups.

Programs vary, but most groups meet once a week. It's probably best if the group plans to run for at least six months, and if it is an "open" group—that is, it allows members to come and go. This policy helps replenish the membership and keep the group operating when patients drop out, as some inevitably will.

THE STAGES OF THERAPY

Preparation: Preparing patients for the group experience is absolutely crucial. Half an hour spent explaining what to expect and how the group operates can mean the difference between success and failure. I tell patients that group therapy will give them a chance to see others express all kinds of feelings—positive and negative—and will provide feedback and encouragement. Therapy helps fight the feeling of isolation, that the patient is battling alone.

Group therapy is a challenge. Patients may feel bewildered at times. Change takes time—longer, perhaps, than they may think. They may feel discouraged. The rewards, though, can be great. They will enjoy a rare opportunity to have their thoughts and feelings recognized and accepted by others. This in turn will lead to new feelings: trust, closeness, and the sense of emotional support.

Early sessions: Patients introduce themselves and describe their experiences. Soon they find things in common—friends, feelings, even symptoms. I encourage these links between people, but at the same time work to draw in other members who may feel different or left out. All patients should have a chance to speak during the session, and there should be time at the end to discuss their reactions to the group experience.

Usually a patient is surprised to hear that other people share her thoughts or feelings. She may be surprised to hear girls (who even she can see are emaciated) stating that they feel fat.

Hearing someone express self-hatred or disappointment can stir up similar feelings in another patient, making her painfully aware of emotions she didn't know she had. That's the downside of "getting in touch with your feelings"—you may not like what you find. Patients may want to run away from this experience—and thus the group—to avoid dealing with it. But recognizing and talking about these feelings reduces their impact. I encourage patients to keep attending even if they are not yet able to express their feelings to the group.

A therapist in an eating disorder group, unlike the leaders of other types of groups, will usually encourage contact between members outside of the session. At the first meeting, patients exchange phone numbers; we encourage them to call each other as an alternative way of coping with their urge to binge or starve.

Later meetings: At first, patients may tend to direct their thoughts and feelings to the group leader. Eventually, though, patients speak more freely to each other. When that happens, the impact can be enormous. As one patient told me, "I couldn't believe it—I gave someone in the group some advice and she actually took it! I really felt worthwhile for a change!" For many patients, such an experience may be the first time that something she says is listened to and treated as being of value.

Though each group is different, common themes emerge. At first, talk of eating behavior may dominate the scene: "I've forgotten how to eat," "I don't know what to eat or how much," "I'm afraid that if I start to eat again I won't know when to stop." As time passes, other themes appear: assertiveness, the fear of displeasing others, anger, isolation, emptiness, and hopelessness.

Eventually patients explore broader issues, such as family relationships or the role of women in society. The issues vary depending on the age and background of the patients. While younger patients generally deal with problems of sexual maturity and the frightening path to adulthood, older patients may be wrestling with unstable marriages, child-rearing problems, or career choices.

As group therapy progresses, so do other forms of treatment. For example, patients often use their individual sessions to discuss feelings that emerge during group.

Progress in group therapy means symptoms grow less severe. Patients report that they have gained weight, their physical strength has increased, and they feel less bothered by cold. Success reinforces their commitment to therapy and gives others hope and encouragement.

Termination: Bringing group therapy to an end can be tricky. Groups stop meeting for many reasons: They reach the cutoff point agreed to earlier; the therapist leaves; members drop out. Leaving the group can be a sad and difficult time for some patients.

For each patient, leaving the group is a mixed blessing. On the positive side, it means stepping into the future armed with self-awareness. On the downside, some patients leave before they're really ready, or they leave to avoid digging any deeper into their disorder.

Terminating therapy is easier if the group has been open—that is, without a fixed time frame or membership roster. In an open group, patients leave only when they feel ready. Leaving is a decision they make for themselves, a step toward autonomy. An open structure might mean a member can return to the group if she finds she needs further support.

Problems: The biggest problem with group therapy is the high dropout rate. The same factors that cause patients to drop out of any therapy group also affect eating disorder patients. These factors, as identified by Dr. Irving Yalom, include denial, low motivation, feelings of inadequacy, social insecurity, and fear of other people.

There may be *external factors* as well. The patient may be afraid to ask permission to leave work to attend a session, or her school activities may conflict. Sometimes her reluctance relates to difficulties with assertiveness or excessive rigidity.

Competition is often a problem: Patients may vie with one another to see who can be thinnest in the group. Members need to confront such rivalry directly and work through the problem during group discussions. Also, in individual therapy the patient has the therapist all to herself. Not so in a group. Sometimes patients feel they must compete for the therapist's time and attention. If they fail, they feel inadequate or worthless.

GROUP THERAPY FOR BULIMIA

Bulimics are generally better suited to the group approach than anorexics. They tend to be older, more socially involved, and thus less afraid of other people. But for many bulimics, dealing with others produces feelings of inadequacy, rejection, and worthlessness, feelings that drive them to seek solace in a heaping plate of food. Groups can provide a setting to improve social interactions.

Groups work better if, as in anorexia, members are selected carefully. Some groups are comprised of members who have never been anorexic or who are all married, for example. Having patients of similar age reduces the risk that older patients will ignore younger patients who may have different concerns. However, groups are never "perfectly" compatible. It helps to have patients explore their differences in order to lower resistance and increase their willingness to engage in therapy. The goal should be to achieve a "good enough" fit among members.

One way of selecting a group is by severity of the illness. Patients who binge and purge frequently (at least once a day for several years) but who aren't in immediate medical danger may need an intensive program with several sessions a week. Twice-a-week bingers might do better in a more relaxed program.

In any case, group therapy should focus on symptomatic eating behavior. When patients regain healthy control over their eating, they can work more productively on other issues.

One such issue is assertiveness. We spend a lot of time discussing ways of handling apologies, compliments, and criticism. One patient complained, "I always do exactly what my husband tells me to do. If I don't he'll sulk and pout and make me feel guilty. Maybe we bulimics need a 'Just Say No' campaign of our very own!"

Problems: As in anorexia, some common features of bulimia can interfere with group therapy. One writer, Janice M. Cauwels, put it this way: "Bulimics tend to distrust people, especially other women, and most of all bulimic women."

Bulimics can be perfectionists. If other members of the group don't quite live up to their expectations, they may feel frustrated or angry.

Some patients place too much emphasis on food. They may use a "verbal binge" as they would a food binge to escape from their feelings. Group should address this issue. For example, during one session a patient said, "Hilary talks so much about food that I feel like I'm stuck in quicksand. I think she's just doing that so she won't have to talk about her problems with her boyfriend."

Some patients expect a "magic cure," believing that if they just show up at group meetings their symptoms will disappear. The group can help them confront and deal with this misconception.

Gradually, members realize that getting better takes time and work.

As with any group, feelings of competition and rivalry may emerge among patients. In groups that have a more psychodynamic orientation, members—guided by the therapist—can explore such conflicts. Doing so usually results in a deeper understanding of how the patients' feelings influence their past and present relationships.

Group therapy should offer patients positive role models. Sometimes, however, newer members may feel jealous or inadequate when they see how other people have succeeded at reducing their symptoms. Conversation should focus on such feelings, especially if the patient's pattern is to binge immediately before or after the group session.

One final note: Eating-disordered patients with drug or alcohol problems need additional help, because such problems can both substitute for bulimic symptoms and trigger them. Abstinence from substance abuse is usually a prerequisite for successful eating disorder treatment.

SELF-HELP GROUPS

In self-help groups, people bond together to solve their common problems. Members know they can learn from others who are further along in recovery while helping those who still have a way to go. A self-help group offers members the chance to share experiences, fellowship, and advice.

The notion of self-help is an ancient one. Some American Indian tribes had healing cults in which people who survived a disease became tribal healers. They acquired their knowledge through suffering as they struggled to overcome a particular illness.

Modern self-help groups follow this ancient principle, that people who have emerged from a "trial by fire" can offer guidance to those struggling with similar problems. Self-help groups reflect traditions of self-reliance and voluntarism.

A thread that ties most self-help groups together is support through empathy and mutual affirmation. The groups reinforce change by offering role models for behavior and a forum for sharing successful strategies and attitudes. Self-help groups emphasize personal responsibility and effectiveness—valuable lessons for anyone with an eating disorder. They communicate the message that members are not helpless or hopeless, even though they may feel that way at times.

For some, a self-help group is the first step toward recovery; for others, it may be the only step they take. Ideally, such groups reinforce other kinds of treatment and offer ongoing support through a network of concerned, like-minded people.

Some self-help groups arise because patients feel that professionals have failed to understand their condition or treat it properly. Sometimes groups form because facilities don't exist in their areas of the country. People may turn to such groups when they can't afford other treatment.

Let me state my bias clearly: I strongly believe that self-help groups can do tremendous good. Ideally, self-help is a *complement* to professional treatment, not an alternative. Patients usually do better when they combine self-help with other forms of treatment. Using self-help exclusively can lead to problems if the patient is actively suicidal or psychotic. In these cases, a sensitive self-help group leader can steer the patient to find the professional help she needs.

The chief advantages of self-help treatment include its low cost, its availability (in areas where programs exist), and the limited degree of commitment required. Other benefits include anonymity, confidentiality, education about the illness, positive feelings of effectiveness and self-esteem, an increased sense of control, and the feeling that one is valuable to oneself and others.

How they work: The concept of self-help for eating disorders is about thirty years old. Goals, formats, and principles are still evolving.

Most eating disorder self-help groups welcome both anorexics and bulimics. Some groups start off with a lecture, then open the floor for discussion. Other groups prefer to let members bring up the subjects they want to discuss. The most helpful part of the meeting may come during the informal interaction afterward, as members chat freely, exchange phone numbers, and share advice.

SELF-HELP VERSUS THERAPY

One major difference between self-help groups and therapy is cost. Professional therapy, by definition, involves people who are reimbursed for their time. Self-help groups are usually free, though they welcome donations. While therapy groups usually meet in clinics or professional offices, self-help meetings take place wherever adequate (and, one hopes, free) space can be found.

A self-help group usually does not screen members; anyone may join. In contrast, a support group or a professionally led group may ask that prospective members meet with leaders before attending to make sure that there is a "fit." Attendance at self-help groups is voluntary; therapy group members are expected to show up.

A handful of self-help groups require their members to participate in some kind of professional therapy. Most make no such demand, although they sometimes encourage their members to get other help. This can be especially important in dealing with eating disorders, since these are sometimes life-threatening illnesses that require a doctor's attention.

Having a professional involved with a self-help group is both a blessing and a curse. In the "plus" column, professionals are usually up to date on the latest information. They can teach useful skills relating to self-esteem, assertiveness, and better communication. Professional leaders can often help by developing meeting guidelines and then stepping back from the group while remaining available for consultations as needed.

In the "minus" column, a group may feel it must surrender its autonomy to the professional. Members may thus forget the original goal, which was to look to themselves for support. Professionals may confuse self-help with group therapy, and lose sight of the needs of group members.

OVEREATERS ANONYMOUS (OA)

Founded in 1960, Overeaters Anonymous is the oldest self-help group devoted to eating disorders. At first OA focused exclusively on compulsive eaters. Now some OA groups include anorexics and bulimics, sometimes forming separate groups to help support these individuals.

Following the Alcoholics Anonymous (AA) model, OA treats overeating as a disease and food as an addictive substance. Eating disorders are seen as affecting their victims on many levels: spiritual, physical, and emotional. Like alcoholics, members of OA believe that their disorder is an illness, a lifelong addiction. Members see themselves as powerless over food, believing that they can't control their behavior through willpower alone.

One goal of OA is to help members regain self-respect. During meetings, members offer each other unqualified love and support. They share stories of struggle, revealing deep feelings not just of shame and humiliation but of triumph as well.

An OA meeting may take place wherever there are people in need. A typical meeting begins with members holding hands and reciting the Serenity Prayer: "Lord, grant me the serenity to accept what cannot be changed, the strength to change what can be changed, and the wisdom to know the difference. Amen."

Next they may recite a version of the Twelve Steps of Alcoholics Anonymous (see page 189), changing only the words "alcohol" and "alcoholic" to "food" and "compulsive overeater." These steps reflect the idea that eating disorders are diseases to be managed, not conquered. They stress the need to recognize and admit the problem—to themselves and others—since only then can members overcome denial, eliminate rationalization, and set about the task of recovery.

THE TWELVE STEPS OF ALCOHOLICS ANONYMOUS*

1. We admitted we were powerless over alcohol—that our lives had become unmanageable.
2. Came to believe that a Power greater than ourselves could restore us to sanity.
3. Made a decision to turn our will and our lives over to the care of God *as we understood Him.*
4. Made a searching and fearless moral inventory of ourselves.
5. Admitted to God, to ourselves, and to another human being, the exact nature of our wrongs.
6. Were entirely ready to have God remove all these defects of character.
7. Humbly asked Him to remove our shortcomings.
8. Made a list of all persons we had harmed, and became willing to make amends to them all.
9. Made direct amends to such people wherever possible, except when to do so would injure them or others.
10. Continued to take personal inventory and when we were wrong promptly admitted it.
11. Sought through prayer and meditation to improve our conscious contact with God *as we understood Him,* praying only for knowledge of His will for us and the power to carry that out.
12. Having had a spiritual awakening as the result of these Steps, we tried to carry this message to others, and to practice these principles in all our affairs.

During meetings, members share their experiences and feelings. At one meeting, Helene, a twenty-eight-year-old anorexic,

*The Twelve Steps reprinted with permission of Alcoholics Anonymous World Services, Inc.

told how having food inside her stomach made her feel "filthy": "I feel like I need to take a shower twenty-four hours a day." Another woman told of her anguish in losing her boyfriend: "Why," she asked, "do I feel I'm nothing unless I'm in a relationship with a man? I'm a good and worthwhile person, but when I have a date and he doesn't call back I feel so . . . so utterly disappointed."

Another, a compulsive runner, said, "This morning my husband reached out to touch me. I said, 'Not now, honey.' Why? Because I felt I needed to get up and run or I would feel fat all day. I hate the way this disease has taken over my life." Each confession, each revelation, brings nods of recognition and agreement from others in the room.

As a rule, members don't judge or comment on another's remarks. This keeps meetings from turning into emotional free-for-alls. Ideally, members use the time following a structured meeting to speak to each other and provide another, and sometimes critical, level of personal support.

One key principle is sponsorship. A sponsor is a member who is further along in recovery and who makes herself available for counseling and support. A member can call on her sponsor at any time to help her when the urge to binge strikes, or for any other reason.

OA has some distinct advantages. For a woman suffering from loss of self-esteem, it offers unconditional acceptance: No one is a failure at OA. Meetings provide a chance to socialize and an opportunity for a woman to better understand herself and her condition. Meetings are like classes in feelings; they provide a profound education in "living and learning." Members hear others speak about pain, anger, disappointment, and frustration, and they begin to recognize their own troubled feelings—possibly for the first time.

For some people, there may be disadvantages to the OA approach. One problem, for example, might be exposure to food myths, such as portraying "white" sugar to be as addictive as cocaine. Also, as we'll see in a moment, the concept of abstinence doesn't work as well for eating disorders as it does for substance abuse. Misunderstanding what abstinence is can increase some people's rigid attitudes and their sense of perfectionism. This in turns poses a risk of a heightened sense of guilt and shame if a person should "slip" and experience a binge.

Let's look carefully at the original first step of the twelve-step approach: "We admitted we were powerless over alcohol—that our lives had become unmanageable." The first part of the statement contains a marvelous therapeutic paradox: To succeed in overcoming alcohol, one must first admit total defeat. No longer is the struggle seen as "me versus booze"—the patient versus a problem that is attacking from the outside. Instead, the problem is identified as being *within* oneself: "I am an alcoholic." With this admission of surrender, one can pull back from an obsessional struggle that depends solely on individual will power to succeed. One can then ask for help, from other people as well as from one's own "higher power."

Once one has admitted the limits of willpower, it follows that the only successful strategy is to abstain completely from alcohol. This means avoiding the people, places, and things that will lead one back to alcohol abuse.

In eating disorders, however, abstinence takes on a different meaning. We have a biological need for food; we don't have a biological need for alcohol. Therefore people must develop sound judgments about eating, rather than to practice total avoidance. "Keep it simple" is a famous AA slogan. Alcohol is a simple substance that can be dealt with on reasonably simple terms. In contrast, deciding when eating becomes "compulsive overeating" can require a complex set of judgments.

Another important difference between alcohol and food is that the strength of your urge to binge may be greater if your weight is much less than your natural set point range. Use of alcohol is not necessarily connected to fluctuations in body weight or one's perception of body image.

Some eating-disordered patients, taking their cue from the AA philosophy, feel that their disease can be arrested but not cured. It's possible the reason they feel this way is that they are significantly underweight or that they eat so erratically that strong

binge urges constantly arise. I have worked with too many patients who have indeed been cured to accept that eating disorders
are just chronic conditions that one must adjust to for the rest of
one's life.

Dr. Walter Vandereyken, a Belgian psychiatrist, has recently
proposed an interesting modification of the OA approach that
takes into account the latest findings from medical research. He
feels that merely teaching patients to abstain from binge eating
and purging is dangerous, and is like training someone to acquire
the skills of anorexia. A better target, he suggests, would be to
reduce the "addiction" to excessive thinness and starvation that
causes much of the physical desire to binge.

Keeping these concerns in mind, let me state my belief that for
some patients OA can be valuable, as long as the program keeps
in mind two goals: maintaining healthy weight and striving for
nutritional balance. On the other hand, if you base your diet on
myths about sugar or other foods, rather than on sound medical
information, then you may be limiting your chances for recovery.

11

Family Therapy

Whitney Dwyer, a twenty-three-year-old anorexic, sat in a chair between her mother and her father. Weighing just eighty-four pounds, she barely made a dent in the cushion. With the ghost of a smile on her lips, she sat calmly—all except for her right foot, which quivered like an aspen leaf in a breeze.

Her mother, Lenore—petite, impeccably dressed—moved her chair next to Whitney's, so close that they touched. Often during the session I saw her lightly stroke her daughter's arm.

Behind them, Whitney's seventeen-year-old sister, Annette, perched on the window sill, glancing at the street below. She tried to ignore us, but her ears caught every word.

Her father, a gray bear of a man, leaned away from his wife and daughter, his chin drilling into the knuckles of his clenched fist. A noted investment banker—I'll call him Ken—he seemed alternately annoyed and embarrassed.

"Let's get one thing straight," Ken was saying. "If you try to tell us we're responsible for what Whitney is doing to herself, we'll be out that door in a shot. That's what the last two doctors said, and I won't have it. We have given that girl everything. I never struck her, I never raised my voice, I never even cut off her allowance, for God's sake. Why she is torturing us like this I don't know. But that's what we're paying you to tell us, I guess."

"Easy, Ken," the mother said. She and Whitney exchanged an amused and knowing look.

"You sound frustrated," I said.

"Damn right," he replied.

I turned to Whitney. "Let me ask you—when did you start to lose weight?"

Her mother jumped in. "About two years ago, Ken and I had a trial separation. Well, we've patched things up, but Whitney was terribly hurt by it all, weren't you, dear?"

Whitney was silent.

Annette let out an exasperated sigh: "Can I go?"

Ken turned. "You'll stay here until I say so," he said in a tight, even voice. "I'm paying for family therapy, and you're part of the family."

"Lucky me," she muttered.

Do families "cause" eating disorders? The short answer, as you realize by now, is no.

But when you consider the way that families like the Dwyers function—and malfunction—it's tempting to conclude otherwise.

In their first few minutes in my office, the Dwyers presented a kind of living family portrait—or perhaps a "family X-ray." Their body language—how they placed themselves, how they sat in their chairs, their closeness or separation—spoke volumes. Lenore showed how tightly bound up she was with her daughter. Not only did she stay in physical contact, she also spoke for Whitney by answering questions and articulating emotions. The father tried to exert control over himself, his family, even me. The conspiratorial glances between Whitney and her mother revealed mocking amusement. Annette felt shut out, resentful of the time and attention her sister's illness consumed.

Aha, some would say, a textbook example of a typical anorexic family: overprotective mother, cold and distant father, marital discord, an unhealthy alliance between mother and daughter against the father. No wonder poor Whitney won't eat. Your honor, only one verdict is possible: The family is guilty. Case closed.

A "typical" anorexic family? *There is no such thing.* True, some families with a self-starving daughter share these traits. But many other families feel the same tensions, the same clash of personalities, and never see a disturbed eating pattern emerge. What's more, families can be warm, loving, supportive, intact—and still struggle with an eating disorder.

No, the family is not at fault. Families don't *cause* the disorder, but they may *contribute* to its development or its severity.

In fact, the family traits that some people cite as causes may actually be effects. A child suffering from any severe illness brings out the natural protective instincts of her parents. A father who never learned to deal with his emotions may withdraw, putting more strain on the marriage. The mother and the daughter grow closer in what appears to be a conspiracy against the father.

When a family seeks help, often the first question on family members' minds, if not on their lips, is, "Are we to blame?" The parents pore over their past in search of clues: "Were we too lenient? Too strict? Too involved? Not involved enough? Overprotective? Underprotective?*Where did we go wrong?*"

Because dwelling on guilt keeps the family focused on the past, family therapy works to "unask" such questions. Instead, therapy focuses on the here and now so that we can get on with the *real* work: helping the patient get better.

A FAMILY PORTRAIT

To paraphrase the poet John Donne, no human is an island. We are all connected.

Our most basic connection is to family. Family ties link us to a genetic, as well as a cultural, past. Through marriage, work, and play, one family interacts with others, forming the network of society. Each thread in this fabric affects, and is in turn affected by, the others.

How, exactly, do families contribute to eating disorders? Researchers use different criteria. Some look at how members communicate. Do they use facts or emotions? Do they express emotions openly or in a disguised way? What about problem-solving: Does the family take a creative approach, or is it stuck with rigid, unworkable solutions? And leadership: Who's in charge?

Alas, no formula can capture the complex interactions of any family, let alone a family coping with an eating disorder.

Is an eating disorder hereditary? Studies of identical twins, who share the same genetic traits, found that when one of a pair of twins has anorexia, her sister has a better than 50 percent chance of developing the disorder. The correlation is pretty high, but is it proof? Not really—remember that both twins are reared in the same family environment and experience the same social and psychological pressures. What we need are studies of identical twins who have been brought up in *different* homes. If both twins develop a disorder, then the evidence for a genetic predisposition would be strong.

Michael Strober, a psychologist at UCLA, recently found that anorexia nervosa was eight times as common among close relatives of anorexic patients as in the general population. He writes: "At least some cases of the illness arise from a familiarly transmitted liability, although the manner in which genetic and environmental factors combine to produce illness remains uncertain."

The stereotype holds that eating-disordered people are white and come from upper-middle-class backgrounds, but patients actually come from many different races and all levels of society. The parents of eating-disordered children tend to be older, but the same holds true of many psychiatric illnesses. Nor is birth order significant—being born first, second, or twelfth doesn't make any difference. And proportionally, as many eating-disordered individuals come from broken homes as they do from intact ones.

Do families with an eating-disordered member have more physical and psychiatric disease? Studies produce different—and conflicting—answers. There does appear to be a higher incidence of weight problems, especially among families with a bulimic child. And the rate of depression is higher, again particularly among bulimics, than in the population as a whole.

What about personality? Is there a "typical" eating disorder family? Are there certain traits that would lead a bystander to say, "If the Joneses aren't careful, they're going to turn their daughter into an anorexic one day"?

No, although a lot of studies *claim* to identify such traits. One researcher, Dr. Joel Yager of UCLA Medical School, took a close look at these studies. He found they contained more different "family portraits" than you'd find on the walls of a photographer's waiting room.

One such study declared that an anorexic family was characterized by a fussy, nervous mother and a father who alternated between being quick-tempered and laid-back. No, said another, an anorexic's mother is robust and nagging, her father passive. Wrong, said a third; fathers are domineering and aggressive. Close, another chimed in; fathers are domineering but *non*aggressive. Or sometimes domineering or sometimes not. Depending on your source, mothers are either attached or ambivalent toward their daughters; they are too strict or too lenient. Fathers are lenient, kind, and affectionate. No, they are cool, antagonistic, and hostile.

Remember the blind men and the elephant?

As Dr. Yager concluded, "If common personality patterns are to be found in these families, they will have to be at more subtle levels."

Does this mean that therapists must start from scratch every time a family walks into their office? Is there any pattern among eating-disordered families that provides *some* basis for therapy?

Yes—sort of. Recent research has found a number of different patterns among anorexic families, but certain anorexic families do fit to some extent the "model" of functioning I'll describe in a minute. While these traits are by no means universal, they may provide a good place to begin working with an anorexic family.

Perhaps the most important trait is the *lack of joint parental authority.* The parents disagree about basic issues in child rearing. As a result, the child gets mixed signals; she doesn't know what's expected of her.

Another common theme is that the mother tends to be the center of the family. Fathers tend to be absent because of work, death, or divorce. The children understandably develop closer relationships with the mothers.

The stereotype of an anorexic family is that the members all think and act as one unit—they are, to use the technical term, highly cohesive. Conversely, bulimic families are often thought to be highly disorganized. The reality is much more complex. Some anorexic families are so chaotic they can't plan a trip to the mall without arguing, while some bulimic families stick together like Velcro. Interestingly, as the patient gets older and is ready to leave home, some families grow more cohesive. It's as if they realize that the illness has served as a stabilizing force, and they are reluctant to face the changes that will befall once the patient leaves.

One last point. Families can sometimes delude themselves that the eating disorder is the only problem they must confront. One father said, "If only Gwen weren't starving herself, we'd be the all-American family." Such families are sometimes in for a rude shock: When the eating disorder abates, they must confront the presence of other issues in their lives.

FAMILY THERAPY

Family therapy—the treatment of more than one member of a family in the same session—is based on the idea that an emotional disorder in one person may be just the tip of the iceberg, hinting at problems with the way the family operates as a whole. The eating disorder will only get better if the whole family system can change.

(In family therapy, the "patient" is really the family itself; the girl with the poor eating habits is sometimes known as the "symptom-bearer." In this chapter, however, "patient" refers to the girl herself.)

The family approach looks at the disorder as a kind of nonverbal message from the patient. The symptoms are her reaction to problems in her family relationships.

In therapy we ask, "What *function* does the behavior serve in the family context?" That seems like an odd question, but it's really not. Consider Whitney. Her parents separated but had "patched things up." In therapy, however, we found that the parents continued to have very mixed feelings toward each other, which they ignored by focusing on Whitney's illness. For Whitney, starving became her way of holding the family together. And it worked! The crisis forced her parents to strive toward a common goal. Here's the downside, though: By spending all their emotional energy on Whitney, they had none left to deal with another important issue—their marital problems. The anorexia provided a distraction.

You see the trap. Sometimes, as dangerous as it is, an eating disorder can actually stabilize a family. When that happens, the disorder can become even more entrenched. The longer the illness persists, the worse it gets, and the more focus it gets from the family.

GOALS OF FAMILY THERAPY

As with any treatment, the first task is to help the patient break her abnormal eating pattern. Family members can support her better if they learn the facts. Part of therapy, then, involves educating other members about what's going on. Once that's done, the family can shift its focus away from the symptoms and onto the deeper issues.

We then work to change the harmful ways the family interacts. We help parents to pull back, to disentangle themselves. In doing so, they help their daughter develop her sense of autonomy. They also help themselves by shifting responsibility for the illness to where it needs to be—on the patient.

In therapy, we try to shore up the good things the family does and curb the bad things. With the Dwyers, we used the fact that they hadn't given up in their search for help as a basis for moving forward. But we also worked to encourage Whitney to speak for herself, and not let her mother do it for her.

Often, family members find that they suppress huge chunks of their personalities when dealing with one another. Ken Dwyer, for example, thought he had to appear before his daughters as "Father Fantastic": the capable provider, the man in control, the king of his realm. Anything less than that, and no one would respect him. But then he mentioned that he loved to relax by reading detective stories. "So do I," said Whitney with surprise. In therapy, family members shed their masks—their "partial selves"—and get to know each other more fully.

Sometimes, getting rid of these masks is hard because families have become so rigid. In this sense, the patient is a "victim of tradition." Therapy helps families loosen their grip on the past and concentrate on the here and now.

The exact goals of therapy depend somewhat on the patient's age. When the patient is under eighteen, we usually focus on the parents. We want them to work together to combat the illness. With an older patient, we concentrate more on her need for autonomy. Our aim is to help her separate from her family and live life on her own.

Through therapy, a patient takes control by changing her relationships with others in the family. Like Whitney, she learns she can't "protect" her family through her illness; she also learns how to get others to stop being so protective of her. She sees new sides of her family members' personalities. If the patient is married, we need to work on marital issues as well as her eating problems.

THE ROLE OF FAMILY THERAPY
IN THE TREATMENT PLAN

The more doctors learn about eating disorders, the more we see the need to tackle family issues. As the number of people with the disorders has risen, so has the use of the family approach. Although we're still learning which strategies work best, the success of family therapy has led to its increasing use for a range of other problems. Family therapy offers many benefits: It identifies the problem as solvable, it provides practical solutions, it creates a relationship with a caring professional, and, perhaps best of all, it offers hope.

Of course, family therapy often needs to be integrated into a more comprehensive treatment approach. Hilde Bruch, a pioneer in the treatment of eating disorders, stated: "Regardless of what the family contribution to the illness has been in the past, the patient has integrated these abnormal concepts about herself and others into her own personality." Bruch felt that individual therapy is needed to correct the patient's faulty assumption that starving will resolve her emotional conflicts.

Ken and Lenore Dwyer found that once their daughter got control of the eating disorder, they had to face their own deep-seated problems. They did so through a course of marital therapy.

INDICATIONS FOR FAMILY THERAPY

Careful assessment reveals whether family therapy will be appropriate in a given case. If so, we then work out when and how often sessions will be held, and who will attend.

I usually suggest family therapy in virtually every case where the patient is young—under eighteen—and living at home. If the family gets help early on, it may have a shorter and easier course of therapy.

Sometimes, though, the family comes for help only after it has struggled with the problem for years on its own. In some cases, the family gets treatment only when something occurs to upset the stability of the "sick" family system, such as another sibling going off to college.

Patients who are married or live away from home can still benefit. Despite their independence, these women are often still strongly tied to their families. Even if we can't meet with other family members, we set up at least some sessions with as many as can attend.

Though valuable, family therapy is not required in all cases. A crisis doesn't necessarily mean the family is sick or can't function. Sure, parents might be angry or frightened—that's a normal, even healthy response. One study by Dr. Arnold Andersen found that 12 percent of eating disorder families were enviably healthy, providing all the love, nurturance, and autonomy a child should have. These marriages were strong and loving, and the relationships among family members stayed within proper boundaries.

Thus, while family therapy isn't always necessary, a family-*oriented* approach is.

ROLE OF THE FAMILY

What if they gave a family session and nobody came? A therapist might be the most learned and caring person in the world, but if the family won't exert honest effort, if members can't support each other in their struggle, then things will be very difficult indeed.

Parents and siblings, and sometimes the extended family as well, need to learn about the illness and understand what the patient is experiencing so that they can better support her treatment. While it may help to learn from the family how the patient arrived at the faulty assumptions that underlie her illness, the focus also should be on her *current* beliefs and how they affect her *immediate* behavior.

There are lots of reasons family members refuse to get involved. Of course, they must wrestle with their own feelings of shame or guilt or pain. They may feel they can handle things just fine "in-house," not realizing that "in-house" is where the problem sprang up. Sometimes siblings resist because they gain from the illness by earning special favors or freedoms because they don't cause their parents any grief.

The therapist's attitude toward the family has a lot to do with its willingness to take part in treatment. Some caregivers think of parents as meddlers or adversaries and cut them out of the treatment loop. Others see them as "disturbed" and shuttle them off to a course of couples therapy.

No go. Families have to be actively involved as *co-therapists.*

ROLE OF THE THERAPIST

Therapists sometimes seem to become "temporary parents" of the families they treat. As in a corporate takeover, they step in and shake up the old organization, pointing out problems and suggesting new solutions.

They encourage families to temporarily set aside differences and unite to solve problems. They shore up the parents' authority to make rules to control their child's behavior, but insist that they treat the child with respect and give her as much autonomy as her age and maturity warrant.

Often therapists work with parents to hammer out a plan specifying how much weight their daughter must gain or how they will react to bingeing and purging. The therapist then supports the family in working through the difficulties that arise when the plan is put into practice.

I find it effective to be directly involved in all aspects of the patient's therapy—individual, group, and family. If this is impossible, I work closely with the other caregivers to make sure we're all rowing in the same direction.

FAMILY STRUCTURE

Therapy fixes problems in the way a family operates, but how do we define those problems? That depends on how the therapist thinks about families and their interactions. Experts from different schools have explored the key issues of family functioning and how they contribute to eating disorders.

Two of the most prominent pioneers in the family therapy of eating disorders have been Dr. Mara Selvini-Palazzoli from Milan, Italy, and Dr. Salvador Minuchin, originally from the Philadelphia Child Guidance Clinic. Although their techniques and language differ, they share certain goals in family treatment. One of these goals is to achieve more effective leadership by parents in the family system, with less involvement of the anorexic child in the running of the family.

Dr. Selvini-Palazzoli has speculated that there are hidden rules by which anorexic families operate. One such rule: "No family member has the right to assume leadership." Shifting blame to another family member is a common practice in anorexic families, as is forming secret coalitions.

Dr. Selvini-Palazzoli also believes that the onset of symptoms occurs when the patient perceives that she no longer occupies a privileged position in the nuclear and extended family. For example, the patient sees it as a betrayal when her mother turns her affection toward a younger sibling and the father stands by, powerless to help. The patient then decides she needs to regain her lost status, and does so by adopting anorexic behavior, which forces the others to pay attention to her. The "perfect" child becomes a source of trouble when she realizes the power that her symptoms give her to control others.

In the past decade or so, Selvini-Palazzoli has shifted her approach to treatment from "paradox" to "prescription." By paradox I mean a treatment strategy that appears—on the surface at least—to be headed in an opposite direction from the presumed goals of therapy. An example of a paradoxical strategy would be to praise the starving girl for her sacrifice and to warn her not to change too quickly, since doing so would upset the stability of her family. Although this technique sometimes shocked the family into making positive changes, Dr. Selvini-Palazzoli was troubled by some of the "side effects," including among other things a high rate of relapse.

Her current strategy uses what she calls the prescription. Here's how it works. In the first session, the entire nuclear family, plus some representative from the extended family—say an influential grandmother—is invited. Only the nuclear family (father, mother, siblings) is invited to the second session. For the third session, only the parents come in. This approach underscores the importance of the parents, first by removing the elder generation (the grandparents) and then the younger generation (the children).

During the third session, the parents are informed of a "secret plan" by the therapist: On prearranged evenings they will disappear from the home, leaving only a note that reads, "We shall not be in tonight." (If there are younger children, the parents arrange for a baby-sitter and leave food in the refrigerator.) The parents are told not to reveal any details concerning their whereabouts or their activities to the rest of the family.

Dr. Selvini-Palazzoli reports that this "prescription" binds the parental couple more closely together and helps establish their role as family leaders. It also helps to draw the anorexic child closer to her siblings as they all struggle to cope with this bewildering turn of events in their family.

Comparing the styles of Dr. Selvini-Palazzoli and Salvador Minuchin is like comparing the musical *Oklahoma!* with the opera *La Traviata*. In Minuchin's view, a person's social context—including the family—lets her express some parts of her personality but suppresses others. Therapy restructures the context so that the more poorly developed part of the self can grow and emerge. For this reason Minuchin calls his approach "structural therapy."

Minuchin sees the sick child as the force that maintains the family balance; in his term, she is the homeostatic regulator—the emotional "thermostat"—of the family. Her job is to protect the family from change. The more successful she is, the more persistent her illness becomes.

THEMES IN FAMILY THERAPY

As a child develops, she passes through stages. At each stage the tasks that confront her increase in complexity. The challenges of one stage prepare her to tackle the next. The tasks of adolescence are to form an identity, to separate from the family, to develop more mature relationships outside the family, and to accept one's growing and changing body.

Sometimes, however, family interactions combine with the fears of an eating disorder patient in a way that makes it difficult for her to face and overcome these developmental challenges. For example, when parents are overly critical of friendships outside the home, a child may limit the depth of her involvement with her friends. Later, as her friends grow and mature, she is left behind. To cope with abandonment, the girl retreats to a world focused on the things she *can* control—food and eating.

Family therapy identifies family problems that contribute to the child's symptoms. Once they are identified, work begins to correct those problems and to help everyone, not just the patient, find other ways of interacting.

The key elements in any family structure, according to Minuchin, are hierarchy, subsystems, and boundaries. *Hierarchy* is the way tasks are assigned based on ability and maturity. In a normal hierarchy, leadership is shared jointly by the parents. Children take on roles that fit their age and development—helping around the house, caring for siblings, earning money. *Subsystems* are smaller units based on roles within the family: parents, spouses (not the same thing!), and siblings. *Boundaries* are the invisible, but very real, lines between subsystems, and between the family and the outside world. Proper boundaries allow each member the highest degree of freedom while providing safety and security.

In some families, not only are boundaries between subsystems inadequate, but the boundaries between the family and the outside world are too rigid. Children can't play with neighbors: "Not our kind, dear." Dating is discouraged; a teenager may be told not to take a job: "We'll give you more money, if that's what you want."

Minuchin's approach to family therapy, which I have found helpful in my practice, changes these pathological interactions by firming up the boundaries between parents and child. We urge parents to take on their natural roles as family leaders and to collaborate with and support each other. We also work with all members to help the patient become more autonomous. The family members learn new ways to communicate, and pick up pointers on solving problems in more creative, effective ways. In the process, they lose the feeling of helplessness that drove them to seek help in the first place.

Minuchin and his co-workers list five characteristics that describe the interactions of families with an anorexic member. These characteristics are:

- Enmeshment
- Overprotectiveness
- Rigidity
- Lack of conflict resolution
- Involvement of the sick child in unresolved parental conflict.

Enmeshment: One patient described her family as a "monster with six heads but only two feet—we each have an opinion, but we can't get anywhere until we all agree on the direction." She was describing enmeshment, the restricting web that binds family members to each other. Members are overly attuned to each other, and seldom offer any overt criticism. They infer one another's feelings or opinions, and act accordingly. This gets to be such a habit that members *expect* others to know what they are thinking.

There may be little privacy, physical or emotional, in an enmeshed family. Such closeness blurs the normal family boundaries. Often, in a family therapy session, a conversation with one member is interrupted by another: "What she means is . . ." or, "No, let me tell you what really happened." Such interruptions can reveal the enmeshment of family members with each other.

Overprotectiveness: By overprotectiveness, we mean an attempt to save someone from pain or suffering that prevents the person from developing a normal sense of autonomy. Overprotectiveness arises when members of a family feel highly vulnerable to the terrors of the outside world.

Let me give you an example. One anorexic patient, fourteen-year-old Neva, told her mother she was afraid no one would ask her to dance at an upcoming school party. The next day her mother called the other parents, begging them to "be sure and tell your son to ask Neva to dance. It'll make her *so* happy." When

Neva found out all of her dances at the party were setups, she felt worse than if she hadn't danced at all.

Rigidity: Rigidity means that the family can't adapt to new circumstances. Parents continue to treat their teenagers by the same rules as when they were much younger. In a rigid family, a child's natural independence threatens to disrupt the balance. Sometimes rigidity shows up as an attitude about the roles each person must play. "My father says I shouldn't get a job," one seventeen-year-old girl told me. "He says my mother never worked, *his* mother never worked. I told him things change. He said, 'Not in this family they don't.' "

Lack of conflict resolution: Sometimes families bury their problems rather than confront them and resolve them. In an eating-disordered family, this is one of the most ingrained characteristics and one of the hardest to change. Through therapy, the family learns that an emotional disagreement is a normal part of living, not something that has to be avoided. On the contrary, it should be confronted and resolved. Therapy gives family members a safe forum in which they can express their disagreements— and not just those related to food. Then, under the guidance of the therapist, they learn and practice ways of resolving them.

Involvement of the child in parental conflict: In some families, a child allies herself with one parent against the other. Such alliances are unhealthy. They undermine the parents' ability to exert authority jointly. They create factions that sap the family's ability to function. Therapy helps the family recognize these patterns.

Some recent work has extended these observations to make them more useful to a family with a bulimic member. Dr. Richard Schwartz, a psychologist at the University of Illinois, has found that in addition to the characteristics identified by Minuchin, there are several other features typical of bulimic families: family isolation, excessive consciousness of physical appearance, and "special" meanings placed on food and eating. He has also outlined a number of possible ways that a bulimic's symptoms function within a family. These include an excuse for not performing well enough, a passive form of rebellion, a way of getting nurturing attention, and a way to protect the parents' marriage.

Although each family is different, here are some helpful "do's and don'ts" for parents in bulimic families.

Do:

- Allow family members to decide what they eat
- Hold the patient responsible for the effects of her behaviors—for example, she should replace food after a binge or clean the bathroom after a purge
- Hold the patient responsible for her chores; however, it's okay to substitute other household chores for kitchen chores

Don't:

- Excessively monitor behavior
- Comment on her weight or appearance
- Fight at meals
- "Mind-read"—it's better to ask

THE PROCESS OF FAMILY THERAPY

It's hard enough for an individual to enter therapy. How does a whole family manage it?

Families' needs, and thus their motivations, are different. Many families come because they have reached a point where therapy simply seems like "the thing to do." They have struggled with the disorder for a long time, have handled it on their own, but now feel something more is needed. Sometimes, however, such families spend much of the session denying anything is wrong. They want to convince the therapist they are perfectly normal, and receive his or her blessing to go on living their lives as before. As Selvini-Palazzoli observes, such families go through the "ritual" of seeking help but have no real intention of changing.

Other families come because a crisis occurs that tips the balance. Often an older child is about to leave the family, perhaps because of an impending marriage or the start of school. The patient—the symptom-bearer—experiences a worsening of her illness in a desperate attempt to hold the family together and maintain the status quo.

Sometimes the family has grown so used to the patient's ways that her starving or her bingeing fails to produce any emotional effect. She no longer gets the attention she once drew. As a result her symptoms may worsen, or she may become depressed. Sometimes it is this depression that brings the patient into treatment.

Another main reason for getting help is relentless pressure from other people. Oddly, many parents blind themselves to their daughter's condition. Only when an outsider notices—"My God, Tricia has gotten so thin!"—does the ball start rolling.

How does the family select a therapist? The usual method is through a referral by a psychiatrist, pediatrician, or family doctor, or a recommendation from the local mental-health association. A few families let their fingers do the walking and look in the phone book.

It helps if the parents and the patient all attend the first session. Doing so provides a snapshot of how the family operates in each other's presence, clues that will affect the course of therapy. It also prevents "splitting"—giving the patient the feeling that her parents have ganged up with the therapist against her, or that the patient and one parent have conspired against the other. It also gets all the therapeutic cards on the table: No one can accuse the others of telling tales behind his or her back.

STAGES OF FAMILY THERAPY

Dr. John Sargent and Dr. Ronald Leibman, who worked with Salvador Minuchin at the Philadelphia Child Guidance Clinic, have divided family therapy into three phases. In the *initial phase*, we evaluate the patient and the family and establish the therapeutic relationship. For low-weight anorexic patients, we devise a contract that identifies the problem, then spells out in specific terms the treatment's goals and the methods for achieving them. The contract usually focuses on the patient's weight; we hold off dealing with other problems, such as marital difficulties, until a later time. The first thing is help the anorexic gain weight, or the bulimic to break her binge-purge cycle, and improve her psychosocial skills.

During the assessment, we get the facts: ages, educational level, and the nature of the family's social interactions. We also want to know how each member perceives and defines the problem. What factors affect the situation: physical illness, social issues, religion? What was the family like before the illness? What stressors triggered the problem? Who is closest to whom? Is there an extended family—grandparents, for example? Who outside the family plays important roles in their lives? Teachers? Friends? Employers?

We then probe a little deeper. What are the patterns of interaction: Who communicates with whom? Are some family members "friends" and others "enemies"? How strong is the marriage? Is the couple satisfied? Do they agree on parenting strategies? How flexible is the family—are roles rigidly laid out? Are members oversensitive to each other, or detached and distant? How strong are their social networks? Are there financial or other medical problems? Do the children have family responsibilities that fit their stage of development? To what extent is the family aware of the illness? What are its fears, beliefs, and attitudes about it?

The *middle phase* of treatment begins once the symptoms are more under control. We now shift our focus to the patient's problems with her emotional and physical development, especially as they relate to unresolved family conflict. We identify the stresses that might have led to the weight loss or bulimia, and find other ways of dealing with them. It helps if we can relate symptoms to family processes—for example, seeing that a binge might occur if the patient feels unloved or pressured in some way.

It often happens that as the patient gains control she experiences a flood of new feelings. A little success might bring up fears about handling new tasks. We caution family members to expect that their daughter or sibling might have feelings of depression, or of ineffectiveness and rejection. If we're not careful, the family might focus on these new problems and become even more enmeshed than before.

During this second phase, we help the family learn how to tolerate open conflict, and show them new ways of resolving problems. We stress that the patient's separation from the family is an inevitable and healthy process—but perhaps a painful one for everyone involved. It helps if the parents learn to deal with each other directly. Once they do, the patient will feel less protective and can work on her relationships with her friends. As Richard Schwartz puts it, she can "grow up" without having to "grow away."

This second stage is critical, since it marks the transition from focusing on the disorder itself to focusing on the broader issues. When therapy is working, everyone wins. The parents learn new ways of helping their daughter grow; the patient shows she can take responsibility for herself and that she has earned the right to "declare independence" from her family.

In the *final phase,* we work to "wean" the family from therapy. If we have identified problems that still need work—the parents' marriage, for example—we steer people toward therapy designed to address those issues. At this point, the patient's individual therapy might focus on how she can change the way others in her family treat her, to keep harmful interactions to a minimum. Just as important, we identify those things that might *not* change. Forewarned, as they say, is forearmed.

PROBLEMS IN FAMILY THERAPY

Lack of progress frustrates everyone, including a therapist. Patients also come from many different family situations—divorced, single-parent families, married patients. Such circumstances call for modifications in the course of family therapy.

In family therapy we encounter resistance on two fronts: from the patient and from her relatives. While an anorexic might want to be rid of her illness, she nonetheless relishes the special feeling of power her starved state gives her. Parents might sense the need to "give up" their child, but if they believe their children are holding the marriage together, they will be reluctant to make any changes in their family structure. "Giving up" their child means they will have to confront—and correct—the problems in their own relationship. During therapy we show the family that sometimes the changes they see—more open discussion of feelings, and thus more emotional conflict—are actually signs of *progress* and should be welcomed rather than avoided.

With younger patients especially, parents may not admit the seriousness of the problem. They delude themselves into believing that their daughter's self-control, her physical activity, or her devotion to schoolwork are all signs of superiority. They delay therapy, or see the doctor hoping to be told that everything is all right, that their daughter is truly a noble, self-disciplined individual.

Sometimes parents recognize the problem but believe they can handle it on their own. They feel that asking for help is a sign of weakness, or that therapy might expose their own defects that they'd rather not have to confront.

SPECIAL PROBLEMS IN FAMILY THERAPY

Divorce: Families with only one parent may be more vulnerable to problems such as eating disorders if there is inadequate parental control. There may also be more stress due to financial pressure or other such factors. Sometimes the symptom-bearer becomes a kind of substitute parent: taking care of siblings, holding down a job, or acting as a liaison between the separated parents. Sometimes a single parent depends more on his or her family of origin—calling on the grandparents to baby-sit, for example. Such intergenerational households might find themselves embroiled in many different types of conflicts, as different cultural traditions or ways of disciplining children clash.

It's not uncommon for a divorced young mother, especially one who previously had an eating disorder herself, to revert to her old ways; she might find it easier to become an "ill child" than face up to her new life as a divorced woman. In such cases therapists need to offer extra support. A single mother may need individual therapy to cope with grief or anger over separation from her husband.

Married couples: An anorexic woman who marries may be looking for a husband who will accept her self-starving unconditionally. Similarly, a man who marries an anorexic may imagine himself as the knight in shining armor who will rescue the fair maiden from peril. This type of marriage can be pretty shaky. A woman who develops anorexia after marriage may be wrestling with serious conflicts about maturity. Pregnancy—or the fear of the changes it imposes on the body—may complicate things. Other issues include the emotions stirred as children become independent, or when the marriage starts to fall apart due to incompatibility or an extramarital affair.

Marital therapy improves the couple's skills at communicating with one another. They may need to explore their attitudes about sex, or learn how to cope with disappointment when marriage fails to live up to their fantasies. Marital therapy may be needed after other forms of treatment have begun to work. A husband may be surprised, for example, when his compliant wife suddenly becomes more assertive or when she discovers deep currents of untapped anger. Counseling can help these people maintain the loving balance that drew them into marriage in the first place.

The multigenerational family: Never overlook the power and influence of the extended family. Many times, a patient's grandparents, aunts, or uncles exert a tremendous influence on family functioning. Such families are often highly bound by tradition. Loyalty to family is the highest value. Members are expected to sacrifice themselves to "preserve the family honor." One risk of a large, close-knit family is that members may feel no need to find emotionally satisfying relationships outside the home. Children may be pressured not to marry so that they can stay home and take care of the older generation. As the Belgian psychologist Johan Vanderlinden notes, these families may be starved for the stimulation that comes from contact with the outside world. "The whole family," he writes, "is emotionally hungry and the anorectic child translates [this] hunger into starvation."

Family therapy must address the deep and knotty issues related to the extended family. This may mean involving the grandparents in at least some sessions. It's important for patients in such families to develop autonomy and discover how to balance family loyalties with the need to explore life outside the home. As Vanderlinden puts it, the patient must discover her roots as she develops her wings.

In this book we have looked at the nature and characteristics of anorexia nervosa and bulimia nervosa—what these disorders are and what they are not. We have discussed, too, how changing social ideals of beauty and thinness have collided with a population that—due in part to an abundance of highly palatable foods—is increasing in weight. The result: a rising incidence of these serious, sometimes life-threatening "illnesses of an affluent age."

In order to understand how eating disorders emerge, we've examined the biological forces at work and taken a look at some of the new biopsychiatric treatments. We've seen the therapeutic tools that may help reduce emotional difficulties, change distorted thoughts, and improve misguided behavior. We've seen, too, how those tools work in the context of individual, group, self-help, and family therapy.

As helpful as these methods are, however, there's something that I feel would help even more: a revolution in our cultural attitudes about thinness. As a physician who deals daily with the tragic consequences of those attitudes, I keep looking for signs of change. Sometimes I sense the pendulum is indeed swinging away from the ideal of the days of "Twiggy" and toward a healthier concept of the human body. At other times, however, I'm not so sure.

Meanwhile, until the revolution comes, people at risk—and their families—need to prepare themselves in every way they can. Perhaps you have found the information in this book helpful.

My goal has been to show you the path that leads to recovery from an eating disorder. I hope that the end of this book marks the beginning of your journey along that path.

Go in good health!

National Resources

The American Anorexia/Bulimia Association
418 East 76th Street
New York, NY 10021
(212) 734-1114

ANAD-National Association of Anorexia Nervosa and
Associated Disorders
P.O. Box 7
Highland Park, IL 60035
(708) 831-3438

ANRED-Anorexia Nervosa and Related Disorders, Inc.
P.O. Box 5102
Eugene, OR 97405
(503) 344-1144

The National Anorexia Aid Society
1925 East Dublin-Granville Road
Columbus, OH 43229
(614) 436-1112

Overeaters Anonymous
World Service Office
P.O. Box 92870
Los Angeles, CA 90009
(213) 542-8363

Sources

Agras, W.S.: *Eating Disorders*. New York: Pergamon Press, 1987.

———, H.C. Kraemer: "The Treatment of Anorexia Nervosa: Do Different Treatments Have Different Outcomes?" In: Stunkard, A.J., and E. Stellar, eds.: *Eating and Its Disorders*. New York: Raven Press, 1984:183–208.

American Psychiatric Association: *Diagnostic and Statistical Manual of Mental Disorders, Third Edition*. Washington, D.C.: American Psychiatric Association, 1980.

———: *Diagnostic and Statistical Manual of Mental Disorders, Third Edition Revised*. Washington, D.C.: American Psychiatric Association, 1987.

Andersen, A.E.: *Practical Comprehensive Treatment of Anorexia Nervosa and Bulimia*. Baltimore: The Johns Hopkins University Press, 1985.

———: "Anorexia Nervosa and Bulimia Nervosa in Males." In: Garner, D.M., P.E. Garfinkel, eds.: *Diagnostic Issues in Anorexia Nervosa and Bulimia Nervosa*. New York: Brunner/Mazel, 1988:166–208.

———, ed.: *Males with Eating Disorders*. New York: Brunner/Mazel, 1990.

———, C. Morse, K. Santmyer: "Inpatient Treatment for Anorexia Nervosa." In: Garner, D.M., P.E. Garfinkel, eds.: *Handbook of Psychotherapy for Anorexia Nervosa and Bulimia*. New York: The Guilford Press, 1985: 311–343.

Bell, R.M.: *Holy Anorexia*. Chicago: University of Chicago Press, 1985.

Bennet, W.I.: "Dieting: Ideology Versus Physiology." *Psych Clin North Am,* June 1984; 7(2):321–334.

Blinder, B.J., B.F. Chaitin, R.S. Goldstein: *The Eating Disorders.* New York: PMA Publishing Corporation, 1988.

Bliss, E.L.: "History of Anorexia Nervosa." In: Gross, M., ed.: *Anorexia Nervosa: A Comprehensive Approach.* Lexington, Massachusetts: The Collamore Press, 1982:5–8.

———: "The Psychology of Anorexia Nervosa." In: Gross, M., ed.: *Anorexia Nervosa: A Comprehensive Approach.* Lexington, Massachusetts: The Collamore Press, 1982:163–176.

Blovin, A.G., *et al.:* "Treatment of Bulimia with Fenfluramine and Desipramine." *Journal of Clinical Psychopharmacology,* 1988; 8:261–269.

Blundell, J.E.: "Systems and Interactions: An Approach to the Pharmacology of Eating and Hunger." In: Stunkard, A.J., E. Stellar, eds.: *Eating and Its Disorders.* New York: Raven Press, 1984:39–66.

Brinch, M., T. Isager, K. Tolstrup: "Anorexia Nervosa and Motherhood: Reproduction Pattern and Mother Behavior of 50 Women." *Acta Psychiatr Scand,* 1988; 77:611–617.

Brody, J.E.: "Personal Health: In Quest of a Healthy Body Self-image that Can Liberate Women from Societal Obsessions." *The New York Times,* October 20, 1988:B14.

Brownell, K.D.: "New Developments in the Treatment of Obese Children and Adolescents." In: Stunkard: A.J., E. Stellar, eds.: *Eating and Its Disorders.* New York: Raven Press, 1984:175–184.

———, J.P. Foreyt, eds.: *Handbook of Eating Disorders: Physiology, Psychology, and Treatment of Obesity, Anorexia and Bulimia.* New York: Basic Books, 1986.

Bruch, H.: *Eating Disorders.* New York: Basic Books, 1973.

———: *The Golden Cage: The Enigma of Anorexia Nervosa.* New York: Vintage Books, 1978.

———: "Four Decades of Eating Disorders." In: Garner, D.M., P.E. Garfinkel, eds.: *Handbook of Psychotherapy for Anorexia Nervosa and Bulimia.* New York: The Guilford Press, 1985:7–18.

———: *Conversations with Anorexics.* New York: Basic Books, 1988.

Byrne, K.: *A Parent's Guide to Anorexia and Bulimia.* New York: Schocken Books, 1987.

Carey, W.D.: "Anorexia and Gastrointestinal Disorders." In: Gross, M., ed.: *Anorexia Nervosa: A Comprehensive Approach.* Lexington, Massachusetts: The Collamore Press, 1982:31–40.

Sources

Casper, R.C.: "Hypothalamic Dysfunction and Symptoms of Anorexia Nervosa." *Psych Clin North Am,* June 1984; 7(2):201–214.

Cauwels, J.M.: *Bulimia: The Binge-Purge Compulsion.* Garden City, New York: Doubleday and Company, 1983.

Chernin, K.: *The Obsession: Reflections on the Tyranny of Slenderness.* New York: Harper Colophon Books, 1982.

Chiulli, R., M. Grover, E. Steiger: "Total Parenteral Nutrition in Anorexia Nervosa." In: Gross, M., ed.: *Anorexia Nervosa: A Comprehensive Approach.* Lexington, Massachusetts: The Collamore Press, 1982:141–152.

Craigen, G., S. Kennedy, P.E. Garfinkel *et al.:* "Drugs That Facilitate Gastric Emptying." In: Garfinkel, P.E., D.M. Garner: *The Role of Drug Treatments for Eating Disorders.* New York: Brunner/Mazel, 1987:161–180.

Crisp, A.H.: *Anorexia Nervosa: Let Me Be.* Orlando, Florida: Grune and Stratton, 1980.

———: "The Psychopathology of Anorexia Nervosa: Getting the 'Heat' Out of the System." In: Stunkard, A.J., E. Stellar, eds.: *Eating and Its Disorders.* New York: Raven Press, 1984:209–234.

Daniels, J.S.: "The Pathogenesis of Obesity." *Psych Clin North Am,* June 1984; 7(2):334–348.

Demitrack, M.A., *et al.:* "CSF Oxytocin in Anorexia Nervosa and Bulimia Nervosa: Clinical and Pathophysiologic Considerations." *American Journal of Psychiatry,* 1990; 147:882–886.

Devlin, M.J., *et al.:* "Metabolic Abnormalities in Bulimia Nervosa." *Archives of General Psychiatry,* 1990; 47:144–149.

Doering, E.J.: "The Role of the Primary-Care Physician in the Diagnosis and Management of Anorexia Nervosa." In: Gross, M., ed.: *Anorexia Nervosa: A Comprehensive Approach.* Lexington, Massachusetts: The Collamore Press, 1982:15–26.

Dorman, L.M.: "Theoretical Perspectives on Anorexia Nervosa." In: Gross, M., ed.: *Anorexia Nervosa: A Comprehensive Approach.* Lexington, Massachusetts: The Collamore Press, 1982:9–14.

"Drugs Win Support as a Bulimia Treatment." *The New York Times,* March 22, 1988:C7.

Dyment, P.G.: "Hematological Changes Induced by Anorexia Nervosa." In: Gross, M., ed.: *Anorexia Nervosa: A Comprehensive Approach.* Lexington, Massachusetts: The Collamore Press, 1982:27–30.

Eckert, E.D.: "Characteristics of Anorexia Nervosa." In: Mitchell, J.E., ed.: *Anorexia Nervosa and Bulimia: Diagnosis and Treatment.* Minneapolis, Minnesota: University of Minnesota Press, 1985:3–28.

Sources

———, L. Labeck: "Integrated Treatment Program for Anorexia Nervosa." In: Mitchell, J.E., ed.: *Anorexia Nervosa and Bulimia: Diagnosis and Treatment.* Minneapolis, Minnesota: University of Minnesota Press, 1985:152–170.

"Elizabeth L.": *Twelve Steps for Overeaters.* New York: Harper & Row, 1988.

Enright, A.B., P. Butterfield, B. Berkowitz: "Self-help and Support Groups in the Management of Eating Disorders." In: Garner, D.M., P.E. Garfinkel, eds.: *Handbook of Psychotherapy for Anorexia Nervosa and Bulimia.* New York: The Guilford Press, 1985:491–512.

Fairburn, C.G.: "Bulimia: Its Epidemiology and Management." In Stunkard, A.J., E. Stellar, eds.: *Eating and Its Disorders.* New York: Raven Press, 1984:235–258.

———: "Cognitive-Behavioral Treatment for Bulimia." In: Garner, D.M., P.E. Garfinkel, eds.: *Handbook of Psychotherapy for Anorexia Nervosa and Bulimia.* New York: The Guilford Press, 1985:160–192.

———, S.J. Beglin: "Studies of the Epidemiology of Bulimia Nervosa." *American Journal of Psychiatry,* 1990; 147:401–409.

Fairburn, C.G., D.M. Garner: "Diagnostic Criteria for Anorexia Nervosa and Bulimia Nervosa: The Importance of Attitudes to Shape and Weight." In: Garner, D.M., P.E. Garfinkel, eds.: *Diagnostic Issues in Anorexia Nervosa and Bulimia Nervosa.* New York: Brunner/Mazel, 1988.

Faust, I.M.: "Role of the Fat Cell in Energy Balance Physiology." In: Stunkard, A.J., E. Stellar, eds.: *Eating and Its Disorders.* New York: Raven Press, 1984:97–108.

Fichter, M.M., R. Noege: "Concordance for Bulimia Nervosa in Twins." *International Journal of Eating Disorders,* 1990; 9:255–265.

"Finding the Name for What Ails You." *USA Today,* December 2, 1987:5D.

Frawley, T.F.: "Obesity and the Endocrine System." *Psych Clin North Am,* June 1984; 7(2):299–306.

Frisch, R.E., J. McArthur: "Menstrual Cycles: Fatness as a Determinant of Minimum Weight for Height Necessary for Their Maintenance or Onset." *Science,* 1974; 185:949–951.

Frisch, R.E., G. Wyshak, L. Vincent: "Delayed Menarche and Amenorrhea in Ballet Dancers." *New England Journal of Medicine,* 1980; 303:17–19.

Garfield, G.: "The 1983 Articles Most Cited in the SSCI, 1983–1985. Part 1. Fifty-three Papers Highlight Studies of Law, Nuclear Winter, and Eating Disorders." *Current Comments,* October 26, 1987; 43:3–11.

Garfinkel, P.E., D.M. Garner: *The Role of Drug Treatments for Eating Disorders.* New York: Brunner/Mazel, 1987.

Sources

————, S. Kennedy: "Special Problems for Inpatient Management." In: Garner, D.M., P.E. Garfinkel, eds.: *Handbook of Psychotherapy for Anorexia Nervosa and Bulimia*. New York: The Guilford Press, 1985:344–362.

Garner, D.M., K.M. Bemis: "Cognitive Therapy for Anorexia Nervosa." In: Garner, D.M., P.E. Garfinkel, eds.: *Handbook of Psychotherapy for Anorexia Nervosa and Bulimia*. New York: The Guilford Press, 1985:107–146.

Garner, D.M., G. Fairburn: "Relationship Between Anorexia Nervosa and Bulimia: Diagnosis Implications." In: Garner, D.M., P.E. Garfinkel, eds.: *Diagnostic Issues in Anorexia Nervosa and Bulimia Nervosa*. New York: Brunner/Mazel, 1988:56–79.

Garner, D.M., P.E. Garfinkel, eds.: *Diagnostic Issues in Anorexia Nervosa and Bulimia Nervosa*. New York: Brunner/Mazel, 1988.

————, eds.: *Handbook of Psychotherapy for Anorexia Nervosa and Bulimia*. New York: The Guilford Press, 1985.

Garner, D.M., M.P. Olmsted, R. Davis, *et al.:* "The Effect of Bulimic Symptoms on State and Trait Measures" (unpublished).

Garner, D.M., W. Rockert, M.P. Olmsted *et al.:* "Psychoeducational Principles in the Treatment of Bulimia and Anorexia Nervosa." In: Garner, D.M., P.E. Garfinkel, eds.: *Handbook of Psychotherapy for Anorexia Nervosa and Bulimia*. New York: The Guilford Press, 1985:513–572.

Geracioti, T.D., R.A. Liddle: "Impaired Cholecystokinin Secretion in Bulimia Nervosa." *New England Journal of Medicine*, 1988; 319:683–688.

Gidwani, G.P.: "Gynecological Signs and Symptoms in Anorexia Nervosa." In: Gross, M., ed.: *Anorexia Nervosa: A Comprehensive Approach*. Lexington, Massachusetts: The Collamore Press, 1982:41–44.

Giesey, G., F.H. Trieder: "Attending to Family Issues in Anorexia Nervosa." In Gross, M., ed.: *Anorexia Nervosa: A Comprehensive Approach*. Lexington, Massachusetts: The Collamore Press, 1982:81–90.

Gilligan, C.: *In a Different Voice*. Cambridge, Massachusetts: Harvard University Press, 1982.

"Girls, at 7, Think Thin, Study Finds." *The New York Times*, February 11, 1988:B9.

Golding, R.: "Eating Disorders—An Internist's Perspective." *American Anorexia/Bulimia Association Newsletter*, March–May 1988; 11(1):1.

Goodsitt, A.: "Self Psychology and the Treatment of Anorexia Nervosa." In: Garner, D.M., P.E. Garfinkel, eds.: *Handbook of Psychotherapy for Anorexia Nervosa and Bulimia*. New York: The Guilford Press, 1985:55–82.

Sources

Gross, M., ed.: *Anorexia Nervosa: A Comprehensive Approach.* Lexington, Massachusetts: The Collamore Press, 1982.

Gross, M.: "An In-Hospital Therapy Program." In: Gross, M., ed.: *Anorexia Nervosa: A Comprehensive Approach.* Lexington, Massachusetts: The Collamore Press, 1982:91–102.

————: "Bulimia." In: Gross, M., ed.: *Anorexia Nervosa: A Comprehensive Approach.* Lexington, Massachusetts: The Collamore Press, 1982: 153–162.

————: "Hypnotherapy in Anorexia Nervosa." In: Gross, M, ed.: *Anorexia Nervosa: A Comprehensive Approach.* Lexington, Massachusetts: The Collamore Press, 1982:119–128.

Grossman, S.P.: "Contemporary Problems Concerning Our Understanding of Brain Mechanisms That Regulate Food Intake and Body Weight." In: Stunkard, A.J., E. Stellar, eds.: *Eating and its Disorders.* New York: Raven Press, 1984:5–14.

Hall, A.: "Group Psychotherapy for Anorexia Nervosa." In: Garner, D.M., P.E. Garfinkel, eds.: *Handbook of Psychotherapy for Anorexia Nervosa and Bulimia.* New York: The Guilford Press, 1985:213–239.

Hall, R.C.W., R.S. Hoffman, T.P. Beresford: "Hypomagnesemia in Patients with Eating Disorders" (unpublished).

Halmi, K.A.: "Behavioral Management for Anorexia Nervosa." In: Garner, D.M., P.E. Garfinkel, eds.: *Handbook of Psychotherapy for Anorexia Nervosa and Bulimia.* New York: The Guilford Press, 1985:147–159.

————, E. Eckert, T.J. LaDu, J. Cohen: "Anorexia Nervosa: Treatment Efficacy of Cyproheptadine and Amitriptyline." *Archives of General Psychiatry,* 1986; 43:177–181.

Hardy, G.E.: "Body Image Disturbance in Dysmorphophobia." *Br J Psychiat* 1982; 141:181–185.

Harkaway, J.E., ed.: *Eating Disorders.* Rockville, Maryland: Aspen Publishers, 1987.

Hatsukami, D.: "Behavioral Treatment of Anorexia Nervosa and Bulimia." In: Mitchell, J.E., ed.: *Anorexia Nervosa and Bulimia: Diagnosis and Treatment.* Minneapolis, Minnesota: University of Minnesota Press, 1985:105–133.

————, J.E. Mitchell, E.D. Eckert: "Eating Disorders: A Variant of Mood Disorders?" *Psych Clin North Am,* June 1984; 7(2):349–366.

Herman, C.P., J. Polivy: "A Boundary Model for the Regulation of Eating." In: Stunkard, A.J., E. Stellar, eds.: *Eating and Its Disorders.* New York: Raven Press, 1984:141–156.

Herzog, D.B.: "Are Anorexic and Bulimic Patients Depressed?" *American Journal of Psychiatry,* 1984; 141:1594–1597.

————, A.W. Brotman: "Use of Tricyclic Antidepressants in Anorexia Nervosa and Bulimia Nervosa." In: Garfinkel, P.E., D.M. Garner: *The Role of Drug Treatments for Eating Disorders.* New York: Brunner/Mazel, 1987:36–58.

Herzog, D.B., P.M. Copeland: "Bulimia Nervosa—Psyche and Satiety." *New England Journal of Medicine,* 1988; 319:716–718.

Hillard, J.R., P.J.A. Hillard: "Bulimia, Anorexia Nervosa, and Diabetes: Deadly Combinations." *Psych Clin North Am,* June 1984; 7(2):367–380.

Hirsch, J., R.L. Leibel: "What Constitutes a Sufficient Psychobiologic Explanation for Obesity?" In: Stunkard, A.J., E. Stellar, eds.: *Eating and Its Disorders.* New York: Raven Press, 1984:121–130.

Hoebel, B.G.: "Neurotransmitters in the Control of Feeding and Its Rewards: Monoamines, Opiates, and Brain-Gut Peptides." In: Stunkard, A.J., E. Stellar, eds.: *Eating and Its Disorders.* New York: Raven Press, 1984:15–38.

"Hooked on Food: The CoA Connection. *Changes,* March–April 1986; 1(2):5.

Horne, R.L., S. Emerson, J.C. Van Vactor, J.L. Jaeger: Disturbed Body Image in Eating Disorders." September 5, 1987 (unpublished).

Horne, R.L., J.M. Ferguson, H.G. Pope Jr., *et al.:* "Treatment of Bulimia with Bupropion: A Multicenter Controlled Trial." *J Clin Psychiatry,* July 1988; 49(7):262–266.

Hornyak, L.M., E.K. Baker: *Experimental Therapies for Eating Disorders.* New York: The Guilford Press, 1989.

Hsu, L.G.: "Lithium in the Treatment of Eating Disorders." In: Garfinkel, P.E., D.M. Garner: *The Role of Drug Treatments for Eating Disorders.* New York: Brunner/Mazel, 1987:90–95.

————: *Eating Disorders.* New York: The Guilford Press, 1990.

Hudson, J.I., H.G. Pope, Jr., eds.: *The Psychobiology of Bulimia.* Washington, D.C.: American Psychiatric Press, 1987.

————, J.M. Jonas: "Treatment of Bulimia with Antidepressants: Theoretical Considerations and Clinical Findings." In: Stunkard, A.J., E. Stellar, eds.: *Eating and Its Disorders.* New York: Raven Press, 1984:259–274.

Huerta, E.: "Group Therapy for Anorexia Nervosa Patients." In: Gross, M., ed.: *Anorexia Nervosa: A Comprehensive Approach.* Lexington, Massachusetts: The Collamore Press, 1982:111–118.

Humphrey, L.L.: "Comparison of Bulimic-Anorexic and Nondistressed Families Using Structural Analysis of Social Behavior." *American Academy of Child and Adolescent Psychiatry,* 1987; 26:248–255.

Johnson, C.: "Initial Consultation for Patients with Bulimia and Anorexia Nervosa." In: Garner, D.M., P.E. Garfinkel, eds.: *Handbook of Psychotherapy for Anorexia Nervosa and Bulimia.* New York: The Guilford Press, 1985:19–54.

———, M.E. Connors: *The Etiology and Treatment of Bulimia Nervosa: A Biopsychosocial Perspective.* New York: Basic Books, 1987.

Johnson, C., C. Lewis, J. Hagman: "The Syndrome of Bulimia." *Psych Clin North Am,* June 1984; 7(2):247–274.

Johnson, C., M. Stuckey, J.E. Mitchell: "Psychopharmacology of Anorexia Nervosa and Bulimia." In: Mitchell, J.E., ed.: *Anorexia Nervosa and Bulimia: Diagnosis and Treatment.* Minneapolis, Minnesota: University of Minnesota Press, 1985:134–151.

Jonas, J.M., M.S. Gold: "Naltrexone Treatment of Bulimia: Clinical and Theoretical Findings Linking Eating Disorders and Substance Abuse." In: *Advances in Alcohol and Substance Abuse.* 1988, Vol. VII:29–37.

———: "Opiate Antagonists as Clinical Probes in Bulimia." In: Hudson, J.I., H.G. Opoe, Jr., eds. *The Psychobiology of Bulimia.* American Psychiatric Press, 1987:117–127.

———: "The Use of Opiate Antagonists in Treating Bulimia: A Study of Low-Dose Versus High-Dose Naltrexone." *Psych Res.* 1988, Vol. 24: 195–199.

Josephson, A.M.: "Psychodynamics of Anorexia Nervosa and Bulimia." In: Mitchell, J.E., ed.: *Anorexia Nervosa and Bulimia: Diagnosis and Treatment.* Minneapolis, Minnesota: University of Minnesota Press, 1985:18–104.

Kalucy, R.S., P.N. Gilchrist, C.M. McFarlane *et al.:* "The Evolution of a Multitherapy Orientation." In: Garner, D.M., P.E. Garfinkel, eds.: *Handbook of Psychotherapy for Anorexia Nervosa and Bulimia.* New York: The Guilford Press, 1985:458–490.

Kaplan, A.S.: "Anticonvulsant Treatment of Eating Disorders." In: Garfinkel, P.E., D.M. Garner, eds.: *The Role of Drug Treatments for Eating Disorders.* New York: Brunner/Mazel, 1987:96–123.

Kapoor, S.: "Treatment for Significant Others of Bulimic Patients May Be Beneficial." *J Am Dietetic Assn,* 1988; 88:349–350.

Katz, J.L., *et al.:* "Is There a Relationship Between Eating Disorder and Affective Disorder? New Evidence from Sleep Recordings." *American Journal of Psychiatry,* 1984; 141:753–759.

Katzman, M.A., S.A. Wolchik: "Bulimia and Binge Eating in College Women: A Comparison of Personality and Behavioral Characteristics." *J Consult Clin Psychol,* 1984; 52(3):423–428.

————, S.L. Braver: "The Prevalence of Frequent Binge Eating and Bulimia in a Nonclinical College Sample." *Int J Eat Disorders,* Spring 1984; 3(3):53–62.

Kaufman, M.: "Hers" column. *The New York Times,* February 4, 1988:C2.

Kaye, W.H.: "Opioid Antagonist Drugs in the Treatment of Anorexia Nervosa." In: Garfinkel, P.E., D.M. Garner: *The Role of Drug Treatments for Eating Disorders.* New York: Brunner/Mazel, 1987:150–160.

————, W. Berrettini, H. Gwirtsman, D.T. George: "Altered Cerebrospinal Fluid Neeuropeptide y and Peptide yy Immunoreactivity in Anorexia and Bulimia Nervosa." *Archives of General Psychiatry,* 1990; 47: 548–558.

Kaye, W.H., H.E. Gwirtsman, eds.: *A Comprehensive Approach to the Treatment of Normal Weight Bulimia.* Washington, D.C.: American Psychiatric Press, 1985.

Kaye, W.H., *et al.:* "CSF Monoamine Levels in Normal-Weight Bulimia: Evidence for Abnormal Noradrenergic Activity." *The American Journal of Psychiatry,* 1990; 147:225–230.

Keesey, R.E., S.W. Corbett: "Metabolic Defense of the Body Weight Setpoint." In: Stunkard, A.J., E. Stellar, eds.: *Eating and Its Disorders.* New York: Raven Press, 1984:87–98.

Kelly, J.T., S.E. Patten: "Adolescent Behaviors and Attitudes Toward Weight and Eating." In: Mitchell, J.E., ed.: *Anorexia Nervosa and Bulimia: Diagnosis and Treatment.* Minneapolis, Minnesota: University of Minnesota Press, 1985:191–204.

Kennedy, S., B.T. Walsh: "Drug Therapists for Eating Disorders: Monoamine Oxidase Inhibitors." In: Garfinkel, P.E., D.M. Garner: *The Role of Drug Treatments for Eating Disorders.* New York: Brunner/Mazel, 1987:3–35.

Keys, A., T. Brozek, A. Henschel, O. Michelson, H.L. Taylor: *The Biology of Human Starvation: Volume 1.* Minneapolis, Minnesota: University of Minnesota Press, 1950.

Kovach, K.M.: "The Assessment of Nutritional Status in Anorexia Nervosa." In: Gross, M., ed.: *Anorexia Nervosa: A Comprehensive Approach.* Lexington, Massachusetts: The Collamore Press, 1982:69–80.

Lacey, J.H.: "Time-Limited Individual and Group Treatment for Bulimia." In: Garner, D.M., P.E. Garfinkel, eds.: *Handbook of Psychotherapy for Anorexia Nervosa and Bulimia.* New York: The Guilford Press, 1985: 431–457.

Lachenmeyer, J.R., P. Muni-Brander: "Eating Disorders in a Nonclinical Adolescent Population: Implications for Treatment." *Adolescence,* Summer 1988; 23(90):303–312.

Larocca, F.E.F.: "An Inpatient Model for the Treatment of Eating Disorders." *Psych Clin North Am,* June 1984; 7(2):287–298.

Leary, W.E.: "Young Women Are Getting Fatter, Study Finds." *The New York Times,* February 23, 1989:B10.

Levy, A.B., K.N. Dixon, H. Schmidt: "Sleep Architecture in Anorexia Nervosa and Bulimia." *Biol Psychiatry,* 1988; 23:99–101.

McCann, V.D., W.S. Agras: "Successful Treatment of Nonpurging Bulimia Nervosa with Desipramine: A Double Blind, Placebo-Controlled Study." *The American Journal of Psychiatry,* 1990; 147:1509–1514.

McGrew, R.E.: *Encyclopedia of Medical History.* New York: Macmillan, 1985.

McKee, M.G., J.F. Kiffer: "Clinical Biofeedback Therapy in the Treatment of Anorexia Nervosa." In: Gross, M., ed.: *Anorexia Nervosa: A Comprehensive Approach.* Lexington, Massachusetts: The Collamore Press, 1982:129–140.

Maloney, M.J., J. McGuire: "Eating Attitudes and Dieting Behavior in Young Children" (unpublished).

Minuchin, S.: *Family Kaleidoscope.* Cambridge, Massachusetts: Harvard University Press, 1984.

———, C.S. Fishman: *Family Therapy Techniques.* Cambridge, Massachusetts: Harvard University Press, 1981.

Minuchin, S., B.L. Rosman, L. Batier: *Psychosomatic Families.* Cambridge, Massachusetts: Harvard University Press, 1978.

Mitchell, J.E.: "Medical Complications of Anorexia Nervosa and Bulimia." In: Mitchell, J.E., ed.: *Anorexia Nervosa and Bulimia: Diagnosis and Treatment.* Minneapolis, Minnesota: University of Minnesota Press, 1985:48–77.

———, ed.: *Anorexia Nervosa and Bulimia: Diagnosis and Treatment.* Minneapolis, Minnesota: University of Minnesota Press, 1985.

———, D. Hatsukami, G. Goff *et al.:* "Intensive Outpatient Group Treatment for Bulimia." In: Garner, D.M., P.E. Garfinkel, eds.: *Handbook of Psychotherapy for Anorexia Nervosa and Bulimia.* New York: The Guilford Press, 1985:240–256.

Mitchell, J.E., R.L Pyle: "Characteristics of Bulimia." In: Mitchell, J.E., ed.: *Anorexia Nervosa and Bulimia: Diagnosis and Treatment.* Minneapolis, Minnesota: University of Minnesota Press, 1985:29–47.

Mitchell, J.E., *et al.:* "A Comparison Study of Antidepressants and Structured Group Psychotherapy in the Treatment of Bulimia Nervosa." *Archives of General Psychiatry,* 1990; 47:149–161.

Sources

Moodie, D.S.: "Cardiac Function in Anorexia Nervosa." In: Gross, M., ed.: *Anorexia Nervosa: A Comprehensive Approach.* Lexington, Massachusetts: The Collamore Press, 1982:45–48.

Morin, L.: "Eating Disorders: A Study of the Quebec Francophone Families." May 1988 (unpublished).

Morley, J.E., J.E. Blundell: "The Neurobiological Basis of Eating Disorders: Some Formulations." *Biological Psychiatry,* 1988; 23:53–78.

Munoz, R.A.: "The Basis for the Diagnosis of Anorexia Nervosa." *Psych Clin North Am,* June 1984; 7(2):215–222.

Orbach, S.: *Fat Is a Feminist Issue.* New York: Berkley Books, 1978.

———: "Accepting the Symptom: A Feminist Psychoanalytic Treatment of Anorexia Nervosa." In: Garner, D.M., P.E. Garfinkel, eds.: *Handbook of Psychotherapy for Anorexia Nervosa and Bulimia.* New York: The Guilford Press, 1985:83–106.

Palla, B., I.F. Litt: "Medical Complications of Eating Disorders in Adolescents." *Pediatrics,* 1988; 81:613–623.

Perez, E.L., J. Blouin, A. Blouin: "The Dexamethasone Suppression Test in Bulimia: Nonsuppression Associated with Depression and Suboptimal Weight." *J Clin Psychiatry,* March 1988; 49(3):94–96.

Pillay, M., A.H. Crisp: "The Impact of Social Skills Training for Anorexia Nervosa." *British Journal of Psychiatry,* 1981; 139:533–539.

Piran, N., A. Kaplan, eds.: *A Day Hospital Group Treatment Program for Anorexia Nervosa and Bulimia Nervosa.* New York: Brunner/Mazel, 1990.

Pirke, K.M., J. Pahl, V. Schweiger, M. Warnhoff: "Metabolic and Endocrine Indices of Starvation in Bulimia: A Comparison with Anorexia Nervosa." *Psychiatry Research,* 1985; 15:33–39.

Pope, H.G., Jr., J.I. Hudson: *New Hope for Binge Eaters.* New York: Harper Colophon Books, 1984.

———, R.L. Spitzer *et al:* "Revisions in the DSM-III Criteria for Bulimia Nervosa." In: Garner, D.M., P.E. Garfinkel, eds.: *Diagnostic Issues in Anorexia Nervosa and Bulimia Nervosa.* New York: Brunner/Mazel, 1988:26–35.

Powers, P.S., D.L. Coovert, D.R. Brightwell: "Sexual Abuse History in Three Eating Disorders" (unpublished).

Pyle, R.L., E.D. Eckert, D. Hatsukami: "The Interruption of Bulimic Behaviors." *Psych Clin North Am,* June 1984; 7(2):275–286.

Pyle, R., T. Perse, J.E. Mitchell, D. Saunders, K. Skoog: "Abuse in Women with Bulimia Nervosa." March 7, 1988 (unpublished).

Raeburn, P.: "Eater's High." *American Health,* December 1987:42–43.

Reece, B.A., M. Gross: "A Comprehensive Milieu Program for Treatment of Anorexia Nervosa." In: Gross, M., ed.: *Anorexia Nervosa: A Comprehensive Approach.* Lexington, Massachusetts: The Collamore Press, 1982: 103–110.

Reinhart, J.B.: "Failure to Thrive." In Gross, M., ed.: *Anorexia Nervosa: A Comprehensive Approach.* Lexington, Massachusetts: The Collamore Press, 1982:59–68.

Rockwell, W.K.J., J.K. Nishita, E.H. Ellinwood, Jr.: "Anorexia Nervosa: Current Perspectives in Research." *Psych Clin North Am,* June 1984; 7(2):223–234.

Root, M.P.P., P. Fallon, W.N. Freidrich: *Bulimia: A Systems Approach to Treatment.* New York: W.W. Norton, 1986.

Rosen, J.C., H. Leitenberg: "Exposure Plus Response Prevention Treatment of Bulimia." In: Garner, D.M., P.E. Garfinkel, eds.: *Handbook of Psychotherapy for Anorexia Nervosa and Bulimia.* New York: The Guilford Press, 1985:193–212.

Rubel, J.A.: "The Function of Self-help Groups in Recovery from Anorexia Nervosa and Bulimia." *Psych Clin North Am,* June 1984; 7(2):381–394.

Russell, G.F.M.: "The Diagnostic Formulation in Bulimia Nervosa." In: Garner, D.M., P.E. Garfinkel, eds.: *Diagnostic Issues in Anorexia Nervosa and Bulimia Nervosa.* New York: Brunner/Mazel, 1988:3–25.

———, S.A. Checkley, J. Feldman, I. Eisler: "A Controlled Trial of d-Fenfluramine in Bulimia Nervosa." *Clinical Neuropharmacology,* 1988; 11:-146–159.

Sacker I.M., M.A. Zimmer: *Dying to Be Thin: Understanding and Defeating Anorexia Nervosa and Bulimia—A Practical, Lifesaving Guide.* New York: Warner Books, 1987.

Sandbek, T.J.: *The Deadly Diet: Recovering from Anorexia and Bulimia.* Oakland, California: New Harbinger Publications, 1986.

Sargent, J., R. Liebman: "Outpatient Treatment of Anorexia Nervosa." *Psych Clin North Am,* June 1984; 7(2):235–246.

———, M. Silver: "Family Therapy for Anorexia Nervosa." In: Garner, D.M., P.E. Garfinkel, eds.: *Handbook of Psychotherapy for Anorexia Nervosa and Bulimia.* New York: The Guilford Press, 1985:257–279.

Schwartz, J.D.: "A Matter of Degree: Body Temperature Linked to Weight Gain." *Health,* January 1988:16.

Schwartz, R.C., M.J. Barrett, G. Saba: "Family Therapy for Bulimia." In: Garner, D.M., P.E. Garfinkel, eds.: *Handbook of Psychotherapy for*

Anorexia Nervosa and Bulimia. New York: The Guilford Press, 1985: 280–310.

Selvini-Palazzoli, M.: *Self-Starvation.* New York: Jason Aranson, 1978.

———: *The Work of Mara Selvini-Palazzoli.* Northvale, New Jersey: Jason Aranson, 1988.

———, M. Viaro: "The Anorectic Process in the Family: A Six-Stage Model as a Guide for Individual Therapy." *Family Process,* June 1988; 27: 129–148.

Selvini-Palazzoli, M., et al.: *Family Games: General Models of Psychotic Process in the Family.* New York: W.W. Norton, 1989.

Siegal, M., J. Brusman, M. Weinshel: *Surviving an Eating Disorder.* New York: Harper & Row, 1988.

Smith G.P.: "Gut Hormone Hypothesis of Postprandial Satiety." In: Stunkard, A.J., E. Stellar, eds.: *Eating and Its Disorders.* New York: Raven Press, 1984:67–76.

Sours, J.A.: *Starving to Death in a Sea of Objects.* New York: Jason Aranson, 1980.

Steiger, H., J. Van der Feen, C. Goldstein, P. Leichner: "Defense Styles and Parental Bonding in Eating-disordered Women" (unpublished).

Stein, P.M., B.C. Unell: *Anorexia Nervosa: Finding the Life Line.* Minneapolis, Minnesota: CompCare Publications, 1986.

Steiner, H.: "Defense Styles in Eating Disorders." *Int J of Eating Disorders,* 1990; 9:141–153.

Stellar, E.: "Neural Basis: Introduction." In: Stunkard, A.J., E. Stellar, eds.: *Eating and Its Disorders.* New York: Raven Press, 1984:1–4.

Stern, J.S.: "Is Obesity a Disease of Inactivity?" In: Stunkard, A.J., E. Stellar, eds.: *Eating and Its Disorders.* New York: Raven Press, 1984:131–140.

Stierlin, H., G. Weber: *Unlocking the Family Door: A Systemic Approach to the Understanding and Treatment of Anorexia Nervosa.* New York: Brunner/Mazel, 1989.

Striegel-Moore R.H., L.R. Silberstein, J. Rodin: "Toward an Understanding of Risk Factors for Bulimia." *American Psychologist,* March 1986; 41(3):246–263.

Strober, M., J.L. Katz: "Depression in the Eating Disorders: A Review and Analysis of Descriptive, Family, and Biological Findings." In: Garner, D.M., P.E. Garfinkel, eds.: *Diagnostic Issues in Anorexia Nervosa and Bulimia Nervosa.* New York: Brunner/Mazel, 1988:80–111.

Strober, M., C. Lampert, W. Morrell, J. Burroughs, C. Jacobs: "A Controlled Family Study of Anorexia Nervosa: Evidence of Familial Aggregation and Lack of Shared Transmission with Affective Disorders." *Int J of Eating Disorders,* 1990; 9:239–155.

Strober, M., J. Yager: "A Developmental Perspective on the Treatment of Anorexia Nervosa in Adolescents." In: Garner, D.M., P.E. Garfinkel, eds.: *Handbook of Psychotherapy for Anorexia Nervosa and Bulimia.* New York: The Guilford Press, 1985:363–390.

Stunkard, A.J.: "The Current Status of Treatment for Obesity in Adults." In: Stunkard, A.J., E. Stellar, eds.: *Eating and Its Disorders.* New York: Raven Press, 1984:157–174.

——, E. Stellar, eds.: *Eating and Its Disorders.* New York: Raven Press, 1984.

Swift, W.J., S.A. Wonderlich: "Personality Factors and Diagnosis in Eating Disorders: Traits, Disorders, and Structures." In: Garner, D.M., P.E. Garfinkel, eds.: *Diagnostic Issues in Anorexia Nervosa and Bulimia Nervosa.* New York: Brunner/Mazel, 1988:112–165.

Theander, S.: "Outcome and Prognosis in Anorexia Nervosa and Bulimia: Some Results of Previous Investigations, Compared with Those of a Swedish Long-term Study." *Journal of Psychiatric Research,* 1985; 19: 493–508.

Treasure, J.L., G.F.M. Russell, I. Fogelman, B. Murphy: "Reversible Bone Loss in Anorexia Nervosa." *British Medical Journal,* 1987; 295:474–475.

Vandereycken, W.: "The Use of Neuroleptics in the Treatment of Anorexia Nervosa Patients." In: Garfinkel, P.E., D.M. Garner: *The Role of Drug Treatments for Eating Disorders.* New York: Brunner/Mazel, 1987: 74–91.

——: "The Addiction Model in Eating Disorders: Some Critical Remarks and a Selected Bibliography." *Int J of Eating Disorders,* 1990; 9:95–103.

——, E. Rog, J. Vanderlinden, eds.: *The Family Approach to Eating Disorders.* New York: PMA Publishing Corporation, 1989.

Van Itallie, T.B.: "The Enduring Storage Capacity for Fat: Implications for the Treatment of Obesity." In Stunkard, A.J., E. Stellar, eds.: *Eating and Its Disorders.* New York: Raven Press, 1984:109–120.

Walsh, B.T.: "Pharmacotherapy of Eating Disorders." In Blunder, B.J., B.F. Chaitin, R.S. Goldstein, eds.: *The Eating Disorders.* New York: PMA Publishing Corporation, 1988.

——, H.R. Kissileff, S.M. Cassidy, S. Dantzic: "Eating Behavior in Women with Bulimia." *Archives of General Psychiatry,* 1989; 46:54–58.

Weiss, L., M.A. Katzman, S.A. Wolchik: *Treating Bulimia: A Psychoeducational Approach.* New York: Pergamon International Library, 1985.

Sources

————: *You Can't Have Your Cake and Eat It Too: A Program for Controlling Bulimia.* Saratoga, California: R&E Publishers, 1985.

Weiss, S.R.: "Obesity." *Psych Clin North Am,* June 1984; 7(2):307–320.

Wempner, M.P.: "The Role of Social Work in a Model Self-help Organization." *Psych Clin North Am,* June 1984; 7(2):395–404.

Wilson, C.P.: "The Fear of Being Fat and Anorexia Nervosa." *Int J Psychoanal Psychother,* 1982; 83(9):233–255.

Wolchik, S.A., L. Weiss, M.A. Katzman: "An Empirically Validated, Short-Term Psychoeducational Group Treatment Program for Bulimia." *Int J Eat Disorders,* 1986; 5(1):21–34.

Wonderlich, S.A., W.J. Swift: "Personality Factors and Diagnosis in Eating Disorders: Traits, Disorders, and Structures." In: Garner, D.M., P.E. Garfinkel, eds.: *Diagnostic Issues in Anorexia Nervosa and Bulimia Nervosa.* New York: Brunner/Mazel, 1988:112–165.

Wooley, S.C., C.A. Kearney: "Intensive Treatment of Bulimia and Body Image Disturbance. In Brownwell, K.D., J.P. Foreyt, eds.: *Handbook of Eating Disorders.* New York: Basic Books, 1986

Wooley, S.C., O.W. Wooley: "Should Obesity Be Treated at All?" In: Stunkard, A.J., E. Stellar, eds.: *Eating and Its Disorders.* New York: Raven Press, 1984:185–192.

————: "Intensive Outpatient and Residential Treatment for Bulimia." In: Garner, D.M., P.E. Garfinkel, eds.: *Handbook of Psychotherapy for Anorexia Nervosa and Bulimia.* New York: The Guilford Press, 1985: 391–430.

Worthington-Roberts, B.: "Eating Disorders in Women." *Focus on Critical Care,* August 1985; 12(4):32–41.

Wu, J.C., *et al.:* Greater Left Cerebral Hemispheric Metabolism in Bulimia Assessed by Positron Emission Tomography." *American Journal of Psychiatry,* 1990; 147:309–311.

Wurtman, J., *et al.:* "Effect of Nutrient Intake on Premenstrual Depression." *American Journal of Obstetrics and Gynecology,* 1989; 162: 1228–1234.

Wurtman, R.J., J.J. Wurtman: "Nutrients, Neurotransmitters Synthesis, and the Control of Food Intake." In: Stunkard, A.J., E. Stellar, eds.: *Eating and Its Disorders.* New York: Raven Press, 1984:77–86.

————: "Carbohydrates and Depression." *Scientific American,* 1989; 260: 68–76.

Yager, J.: "Family Issues in the Pathogenesis of Anorexia Nervosa." *Psychosomatic Medicine,* 1982; 44:43–60.

Sources

————, J. Landsvente, C.K. Edlestein: "A 20-Month Follow-up Study of 682 Women with Eating Disorders I: Course and Severity." *American Journal of Psychiatry*, 1987; 199:1172–1177.

Yalom, I.: *Theory and Practice of Group Psychotherapy* (2nd edition). New York: Basic Books, 1975.

Yates, A., K. Leehey, C.M. Shisslate: "Running—An Analogue of Anorexia." *The New England Journal of Medicine*, 1983; 308:252–255.

Yellowlees, P.M., M. Roe, M.K. Walker *et al.:* "Abnormal Perception of Food Size in Anorexia Nervosa." *Br Med J.* June 18, 1988; 296:1689–1690.

Index

PLUME (0452)

ISSUES IN HEALTH AND MEDICINE

☐ **THE LOSS OF SELF:** *A Family Resource for the Care of Alzheimer's Disease and Related Disorders* **by Donna Cohen, Ph.D., M.D.** This acclaimed sourcebook offers sound strategies and in-depth advice for maintaining the fullness of life while sustaining the Alzheimer's patient. "Outstanding . . . an outpouring of help and understanding."—*The American Journal of Alzheimer Care* (259460—$9.95)

☐ **WHEN SOMEONE YOU LOVE HAS AIDS by BettyClare Moffatt.** An unforgettable account of how a mother and son's love for each other helped them tap their inner strength in the face of unspeakable tragedy. A supportive and medically helpful guide for anyone touched by the reality of this mysterious, unforgiving disease. "Deeply moving . . . can be helpbul and give hope to all who read this book."—Gerald Jampolsky, M.D., Founder, *Center for Attitudinal Healing* (259452—$8.95)

☐ **FASTING GIRLS** *The History of Anorexia Nervosa* **by Joan Jacobs Brumberg.** This groundbreaking book explores the private world of sufferers in the past, and shows why America's young women are so vulnerable to anorexia, and what treatments have proven effective. "Fascinating!"—*Kirkus Reviews* (263271—$10.95)

Prices slightly higher in Canada.